AF531733

CONSUMER RIGHTS AND AWARENESS

Edited by

Dr. M. Nazer

M.Com., M.Phil., PGDCA., Ph.D., MBA
Associate Professor
Deptt. of Commerce
Khadir Mohideen College
Adirampattinam
Tamil Nadu
(India)

DISCOVERY PUBLISHING HOUSE PVT. LTD.
NEW DELHI-110 002

Published by:
Tilak Wasan

DISCOVERY PUBLISHING HOUSE PVT. LTD.
4383/4B, Ansari Road, Darya Ganj
New Delhi-110 002 (India)
Phone : +91-11-23279245, 43596064-65
Fax : +91-11-23253475
E-mail : parul.wasan@gmail.com
discoverypublishinghouse@gmail.com
web : www.discoverypublishinggroup.com

***First Edition:* 2012**

ISBN: 978-93-5056-069-3

Consumer Rights and Awareness

Printed at:
Shree Balaji Art Press
Delhi

Foreword

This is a nice collection of research articles on the topics of Consumerism and Consumer Awareness. From the origin to the development and the current trends on the Consumers' Behaviour and the Consumer Protection Acts, the articles presented in this book are well set in a fine manner. As most of the papers are research oriented, the end result is suggestive and educative. I am congratulating the authors for their fine editing and presenting and also I am wondering about the various contributors for their keen interest in presenting the papers.

Certainly this will be helpful to the future researchers, academicians, social workers, consumer activists and the students in a rich manner.

I am quite confident that this work done by Dr. M. Nazer will help the academics, research scholars, Executives, Managers, 'Social Workers, Consumers activities' and the students of reap rich rewards.

Dr. S. Nakkiran
Professor of Cooperation
Ambo College of Agriculture
Ambo, Western Shoa
Ethiopia

Preface

In a developing country like India, measures for consumer protection are very much required. The illiteracy and ignorance of the majority of consumers both in the rural and urban areas provide opportunities for business communities to follow unfair trade practices. These have to be curtailed through various measures of the Government and other non-Governmental organisations. Of the various legal remedies available, the principle legal protection is the Consumer Protection Act, 1986. Under this Act, the consumer gets opportunities to entrust his grievances through the consumer forums organised at the District, State and National levels and other voluntary consumer organisations. The Consumer awareness, protection and preservation of consumer rights are well analyzed in this book.

If anything has to be denoted a special one about the book, it is about the consumers—from the children to the aged, student to the teacher, buyer to the seller and the workers to the managers—all were dealt by various contributors in depth.

We hope this book will help not only to the academicians but also to all the public who are interested in the affairs of the consumers.

Dr. M. Nazer

Acknowledgement

I would like to express my deep gratitude to Dr. A. Mohamed Abdul Khader, Principal, Khadir Mohideen College, Adirampattinam for his unfailing encouragement in all my research oriented activities. Without him this work would not be a complete one. I sincerely thank him for his continuous suggestions in this work.

I am thankful to Dr. S. Mohamed Aslam, Secretary of Khadir Mohideen Institutions, Adirampattinam for his guidance in completing this book.

I take this golden opportunity to express my sincere thanks to Indian Institute of Public Adminstration, New Delhi for financial assistance that supported me to conduct the seminar in a grand manner.

I wish to convey my special thanks to Dr. O.M. Haja Mohideen, HOD, and the faculty members of the Department of Business Administration for the advice and encouragement during the seminar and the bookwork.

I couldn't forget to thank to all the faculty members of Khadir Mohideen College, Adirampattinam, who rendered an invaluable help in the completion of this work, which couldnot be compensated.

I am thankful to the Publisher Discovery Publishing House Pvt. Ltd., New Delhi and their staff for enthusiastically bringing out the publication in a neat form.

Last, but not least I thank one and all who have directly or indirectly helped me in conducting the seminar as well as bringing up of this book.

Above all, I thank the Almighty Lord for showing me the right path.

Dr. M. Nazer

Contents

List of Contributors

1. *Dr. A. Mohamed Abdul Khader,* Principal and Associate Professor of Economics, Khadir Mohideen College, Adirampattinam-614701
2. *Dr. S. Nazeerdeen,* Vice-Principal and HOD of History, K.M. College, Adirampattinam-614701
3. *Dr. O.M. Haja Mohideen,* Head, Department of Business Administration, K.M. College, Adirampattinam-614701
4. *Dr. S. Shahul Hameed,* Associate Professor, Department of Business Administration, K.M. College, Adirampattinam-614701
5. *Ms. P. Seethalakshmi,* Research Scholar, Department of Business Administration, K.M. College, Adirampattinam-614701
6. *Dr. M. Nazer,* Associate Professor, K.M. College, Adirampattinam-614701
7. *Ms. Mariam Jenofer,* Research Scholar in Commerce, K. M College, Adirampattinam-614701
8. *Dr. N. Abdul Jaleel,* Associate Professor, Department of Business Administration, K.M. College, Adirampattinam-614701
9. *J. Manivannan,* Research Scholar, Department of Business Administration, K.M. College, Adirampattinam-614701
10. *Dr. A. Jalal,* Associate Professor, Department of Commerce, K.M. College, Adirampattinam-614701
11. *Dr. K. Murali Selvam,* Lecturer in Commerce, Selvam Arts and Science College, Namakkal
12. *Dr. A. Peer Mohideen,* Associate Professor in Commerce, K.M. College, Adirampattinam-614701
13. *P. Kumaravel,* Lecturer in Commerce, Enathi Rajappaa College, Pattukkottai-614615

14. *Dr. A. Mohamed Siddique & Dr. A. Mohamed Nazar,* Associate Professors, Department of Business Administration, K.M. College, Adirampattinam-614701
15. *A. Raja Mohamed,* Head Department of Economics, K.M. College, Adirampattinam-614701
16. *Dr. P. Ganapathy,* Associate Professor, Department of Business Administration, K.M. College Adirampattinam-614701
17. *Dr. A. Babu Hussain Sherriff,* Department of Social Science, Laurel Higher Secondary School, Pattukkottai-614 602
18. *Mrs. A. Ayesha Mariam,* Head, Department of Physics, K.M. College, Adirampattinam-614701
19. *Dr. N. Chithra & S. Abudhahir,* Faculty Members, Department of Economics, K.M. College, Adirampattinam-614701
20. *Mrs. M. Paritha Begam,* Assistant Professor, Department of History, K.M. College, Adirampattinam-614701
21. *Dr. V. Balasubramanian,* Associate Professor of Commerce, Alagappa Government Arts College, Karaikudi-630003
22. *Dr. P. Mohamed Sirajudeen,* Associate Professor, Department of Chemistry, K.M. College, Adirampattinam-614701
23. *S. Chandrasekaran,* Head, Department of Mathematics, K.M. College, Adirampattinam-614701
24. *Dr. M. Gomatheeswaran,* Lecturer (SS) in Commerce, CMS College of Science and Commerce, Coimbatore-641006
25. *Dr. T. Sivagnanasithi,* Lecturer in Commerce, Hindustan College of Arts and Science, Coimbatore
26. *Dr. S. Sivasankaran,* Assistant Professor of Commerce, S.T. Hindu College, Nagercoil-629002
27. *Dr. Mrs. K. Mahuthammal,* Head, Department of Commerce, Government Arts College for Women, Pudukkottai
28. *Srinivasa Rao Boyine,* Lecturer in Accounting and Finance, International School of Business and Tech, Kampala-Uganda
29. *Mr. K. Neelamegam,* Asst. Professor and Head, Department of BBA, Thanthai Hans Rover College, Perambalur
30. *Dr. G. Ganesan,* Head Department of Commerce, Bharathiar University, Coimbatore
31. *Ms. S. Vijayalakshmi,* Research Scholar, Department of Commerce, Bharathiar University, Coimbatore

32. *Mrs. S.P. Manickavasugi,* Assistant Professor, Department of MBA, ARJ College of Engineering and Technology, Mannargudi

33. *J. Arul Mani & N. Manickavasagam,* Lecturers in Commerce, Enathi Rajappa College, Pattukkottai-614 615

34. *Mrs. Malathi,* Assistant Professor, Nadar Saraswathi College of Arts and Science, Theni

35. *Mr. Al-Ameen,* Ph.D Research Scholar, Department of Commerce, K.M. College, Adirampattinam-614701

36. *Dr. A. Ganesan,* Head, Department of Corp. Secretaryship, Sri Vasavi College, Erode

37. *Dr. S. Bhuvaneswari,* Lecturer in Commerce, GVG Visalakshi College (Women), Udumalpet

38. *Dr. S. Chitra,* Principal-in-charge, N. S. College of Arts and Science, Theni

39. *Mrs. B. Sumathi,* Lecturer, Nadar Saraswathi College of Arts and Science, Theni

40. *M. Ganesh,* Assistant Professor and Head, Department of MBA, Thanthai Hans Roever College, Perambalur

41. *K. Soundarapandiyan,* Faculty, Sri Sai Ram Institute of Management Studies, Chennai

42. *Ms. Deepa Viswam,* Lecturer, Mother Terasa Women's University, Kodaikanal

43. *Dr. K.M. Murugesan and Mr. K. Alagar,* Lecturers in Business Administration, Alagappa Government Arts College, Karaikkudi-630003

44. *Mrs. M. Fowzia Sultana,* Faculty in Commerce, Mother Teresa Women's University, Kodaikanal

45. *Ms. S. Sowdeeswari,* Faculty in Commerce, Mother Teresa Women's University, Kodaikanal

46. *N. Jayaveeran,* Head, K.M. College, Adirampattinam-614701

47. *A. Shaik Abdul Khadir,* Associate Professor in Computer Science, K.M. College, Adirampattinam-614701

48. *Ms. S. Srimathi,* Lecturer in Commerce, TUK Arts College, Karanthai, Thanjavur

49. *Ms. P. Jayanthi,* Lecturer in Commerce, TUK Arts College, Karanthai, Thanjavur

50. *V. Maheswaran,* Assistant Professor, Devanga Arts College (Autonomous), Aruppukkottai-626101
51. *S. Aravind Krishnan,* Research Scholar, Jamal Mohamed College, Tiruchirappalli-620020
52. *P. Chilar Mohamed & N. Mohamed Mohideen,* Associate Professors, Department of Commerce, K.M. College, Adirampattinam-614701
53. *N. Veerapandian and S. Abbas,* Assistant Professors of Mathematics, K.M. College, Adirampattinam-614701
54. *M. Mathialagan,* Head of Department of Commerce and Business Administration, Enathi Rajappa College, Pattukkottai-614615
55. *Dr. P.K. Venkatachalam,* Director in Management Studies, PA College of Engineering and Technology Pollachi-642002
56. *Mr. A. Rathinam,* ONGC, Cauvery Asset, Karaikkal
57. *M. Natharshah,* ARJ College of Engineering and Technology, Edayarnatham
58. *R. Bhuvaneswari and K. Sudha,* Lecturers, Department of Business Administration, STET Women's College, Mannargudi-614001
59. *V.S. Rajakrishnan,* Head of Department Commerce, EGS Pillay Arts and Science College, Nagapattinam-611002
60. *R. Natarajan,* Head of Department, Business Administration, EGS Pillay Arts and Science College, Nagapattinam-611002
61. *R. Senthil Kumar, P. Arivalagan and E. Prabhu,* Research Scholars in Commerce (FT), KSR College of Arts and Science, Tiruchengode-637215
62. *S. Pradesh Kumar,* Lecturer in Commerce, Sree Narayana Guru College, Coimbatore-641105
63. *Dr. M. Mohamed Mohideen,* Associate Professor of Commerce, K.M. College, Adirampattinam-614701
64. *R. Prushothaman,* Faculty of Commerce, Sree Narayana Guru College Coimbatore-641105
65. *P. Radhakrishnan,* Head, Sree Narayana Guru College, Coimbatore-641105
66. *K. Parimala Kanthi,* Sr. Lecturer, Department of Commerce (CA), Sree Narayana Guru College, Coimbatore-641105

67. *S. Anthony Raj,* Lecturer in International. Business, Department of Commerce and International. Business CMS College of Science and Commerce, Coimbatore-641006

68. *V. Pothigaimalai & S. Meenakshi,* Lecturers, S.T.E.T. Women's College, Mannargudi-614001

69. *Dr. A. Ziaudeen,* Associate Professors of Commerce Khadir Mohideen College, Adirampattinam

70. *G. Jivek,* Department of Business Administration, Khadir Mohideen College, Adirampattinam

71. *By G. Balamurugan,* Assistant Professor of Management Studies, Anna University and Technology, Tiruchirappali

72. *Dr. U. Nazarudeen,* Reader in Commerce, Iqbal College, Perinngamala, Trivandrum, Kerala State

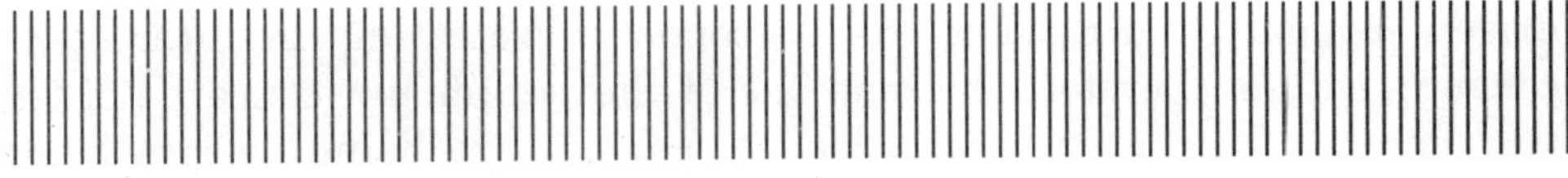

CHAPTER

1
Consumer Movement in India

—Dr. A. Mohamed Abdul Khader

Introduction

The consumer movement in India is as old as trade and commerce itself. Even in Kautilya's *Arthashastra*, there are references to the concept of protection of consumers against the exploitation by trade and industry, short weighment and measurements, adulteration along with the punishment for these offences. There was, however, no organized and systematic movement actually safeguarding the interests of the consumers. Prior to Independence, consumer interests were considered mainly under laws like the Indian Penal Code, Agricultural Production Grading and Marketing Act 1937, and Drugs and Cosmetics Act, 1940. Even though different parts of India had varying degrees of awareness, in general the level of awareness was low.

It is generally believed that the consumer movement in India as of today is quite strong when it is compared with other developing countries in Asia, Africa and Latin America. India is a vast country with a very large population of which a sizeable percentage lives below the poverty line. Because of economic inequality, low level of literacy and ignorance, particularly amongst women, the level of consumer awareness is not too high and, therefore, the consumers are not able to assert and protect themselves. They easily get exploited by trade and industry and service providers. With the liberalisation process which started in 1991 the entire economic scenario is undergoing a complete change from a government-driven economy to a market-driven economy. Protecting the interests of consumers has, therefore, become one of the paramount concerns of the Government than ever before. Hence, policies are being designed and legislations enacted to protect the consumers' interest and grant them the right to choice, safety, information and redressal.

Status of Consumer Organisations in the Current Scenario

The Consumer Protection Act 1986 in India would encourage consumers to stand up for their rights and lead to an overwhelming number of disputes in consumer courts. Although a consumer movement has yet to get going in India, existence of the act has stimulated the creation of many consumer organizations across the country. The movement has not blossomed because not all of the organizations are active enough to make an impact, there has hardly been any unified action which would demonstrate their strength, and there has been no active consumer participation in the movements. Consumers claim that the lack of consumer education makes them passive and apathetic, and blame consumer organizations. The majority of consumers in the country are even unaware of the existence of consumer courts to which they may take their grievances. Consumer rights organizations, however, counter that they lack sufficient funds and blame the government for their inaction.

Consumer Behaviour and Consumer Protection in India

The process of development coupled with increasing liberalization and globalization across the country has enabled consumers to realize their increasingly important role in society and governance. In a developing country like high and the level of literacy is very low, the people face a volume of problems, particularly in the context of consumer related issues. Consumer welfare is the responsibility of the state. Accepting this, policies have been framed and the Consumer Protection Act, 1986 was introduced. A separate Department of Consumer Affairs was also created in the Central and State Governments to exclusively focus on ensuring the rights of consumers as enshrined in the Act. This Act has been regarded as the most progressive, comprehensive and unique piece of legislation. Although in Kautilya's Arthashastra, strict rules were set for the trade and industry and punishments for exploitation were prescribed. But, there was no organised and systematic movement safeguarding the interests of the consumers in India.

Rampant food shortages, hoarding, black marketing, adulteration of food and edible oil gave birth to the consumer movement in an organised form in the sixties. Consumers started voicing their concerns and demanding better products and services. Till mid seventies, consumer organisations were largely engaged in writing articles and holding exhibitions. They formed consumer groups to work on the malpractices in ration shops and overcrowding in the road passenger transport. The eighties witnessed an upsurge in the number of consumer groups.

Strengthening the Consumer Movement

Consumer Protection Act, 1986

One of the most important milestones in the consumer movement in the country has been the enactment of the Consumer Protection Act, 1986 to better protect the interest of the consumers. This has revolutionised consumer rights. It is one of the most progressive and comprehensive pieces of socio-benevolent legislation covering all goods and services. The Act provides for a separate three-tier quasi-judicial consumer dispute redressal machinery, popularly known as consumer courts, at the national, state and district levels to provide simple, speedy and free redressal against consumers' complaints. Filing of a simple complaint on plain paper with the details of the case with supporting documents seeking relief or compensation is enough and it is not obligatory to engage a lawyer. According to the objects and purposes of the Consumer Protection Act, these quasi-judicial bodies observe the principles of natural justice while adjudicating consumer complaints against defective goods, deficient services and restrictive and unfair trade practices through summary trials. The Act applies to all goods and services and covers all sectors, whether private, public or cooperative.

In India, 24 December is celebrated as National Consumer Rights Day as the Consumer Protection Act, 1986 was enacted on that day. 15 March is observed as World Consumer Rights Day since 1983, when International Organization of Consumer Unions declared it so.

Consumer Rights

The Consumer Protection Act, which has been defined as "*the Magna Carta of Consumers*", spells out six consumer rights: Right to Safety; Right to Information; Right to Choice; Right to Representation; Right to Redress; and Right to Consumer Education. India has the biggest consumer movement today due to the efforts of consumer organisations and the establishment of consumer courts. India is the only country in the world which has exclusive courts for consumer redressal. This has been internationally praised including the developed countries. The Consumer Protection Act (COPRA) has succeeded in bringing about fair play in the supply of goods and services to a large extent. The Act applies to almost all goods and services.

Amendments

The Act was amended in 1991 mainly to incorporate provisions for the quorum of District Forum, appointing persons to preside over State Commission/District Forum in case of absence of the President to enable the court function uninterruptedly. In 1993 the Act was again amended exhaustively to make it more effective and purposeful.

The Government has formulated comprehensive proposals for amending the Consumer Protection Act mainly based on the recommendations of the Working Group and Expert Group set up for the purpose and the wide-ranging consultations its had with the representatives of consumer interests, presidents of the national and state commissions and Central Government Ministries and Departments. These amendments are mainly aimed at facilitating quicker disposal of complaints, enhancing the capability of redressal agencies, strengthening them with more powers, streamlining the procedures and widening the scope of the Act to make it more effective to protect the consumers' interest.

Government's Role

A separate Department of Consumer Affairs was created in 1997 to act as the nodal outfit in the Central Government for promoting and protecting the welfare of consumers. It seeks to do this in various ways such as ensuring availability of essential commodities at reasonable prices including monitoring of prices, formulating standards of goods and services, regulation of weighing and measuring instruments and prepacked commodities and providing a legislative framework for safeguarding consumers' interests and establishment of machinery for redressal of consumer complaints.

To meet these objectives the Department has been undertaking various measures involving all concerned to strengthen the consumer movement in the country. Some of the important measures being taken to strengthen the consumer movement include initiating multimedia publicity programmes to educate the consumers, providing financial assistance through consumer welfare fund to the NGOs and State Governments to generate consumer awareness, setting up of district information centres to guide the public, national awards on consumer protection to encourage outstanding work by women and youth, observing national and World Consumer Rights Day to remind the consumers to be vigilant, interactions with various interests through Central and State Consumer Protection Council to promote and protect the rights of the consumers, formulation of citizens' charters containing their entitlements to public services, standards of performance and redressal of grievances for providing an efficient and responsive administration.

The success of the consumer movement mainly depends upon the level of consumer awareness around the country. The Government can only be playing the role of a facilitator or catalyst. The growth of consumer movement is a voluntary effort involving the participation of one and all. Only alert consumers can protect themselves and the society.

Issues of Consumer Exploitation

- Liberalization is paving way for a market-driven economy, where the manufacturers seek to maximize profits.
- Manufacturers are not often concerned about the quality of goods and services and their impact on the health of people and the environment.
- Instead of the consumer guiding the producer about what should be produced, it is the producer who decides what the consumer should want.
- The plight of a consumer is further worsened by the use of advertising techniques.
- Consumers are saddled with the problem of choosing between too many products with too less information. With the concentration of market in the hands of a few large corporations, it becomes important that the consumers are aware of their rights in order to ensure proper standards for the goods and services for which they make payment.
- There are many goods which are sold in the market without much information about their quality, quantity and purity.
- In case of goods meant for mass consumption like, food, milk products, edible oil etc. the ingredients are not known.
- Manufacturers or producers seldom follow the safety regulations in the products like, lamps, batteries, footwear, electrical equipments, wires, cement, LPG cylinders, stoves, switches, plugs, sockets etc. leading to many fatal accidents.
- Adulteration of food is another major problem. Milk can contain detergent, refined oil, caustic soda or urea. Mustard oil can be adulterated with argemone oil and arhar dal with yellow colour. Vegetables and fruits are artificially coloured.
- Indiscriminate use of pesticides by farmers and untreated effluents by industries, have led to the problem of food contamination by pesticide residues and toxic heavy metals.

Consumer Protection and Competition Policy

Promotion of consumer welfare is the common goal of consumer protection and competition policy. At the root of both consumer protection and competition policy is the recognition of an unequal relationship between consumers and producers. Protection of consumers is accomplished by setting minimum quality specifications and safety standards for both goods and services and establishing mechanisms to redress their grievances. The objective of competition is met by ensuring that there are sufficient numbers of producers so that no producer can attain a position of dominance. If the nature of the industry is such that dominance in terms of market share cannot be avoided, it seeks to ensure that there is no abuse on account of this dominance. Competition policy also seeks to forestall other forms of market failure, such as formation of cartels, leading to collusive pricing, division of markets and joint decisions to reduce supply. Mergers and acquisitions also need to be regulated as they reduce competition.

Conclusion

Still, the present scenario is not very encouraging. Unfortunately the consumer courts have become replica of legal courts, as the procedure is no longer simple and quick. The consumer redressal process is relatively cumbersome and more expensive and time-consuming than desired. The process involves engaging a professional personnel, requires time for filing the case and attending the court proceeding and certain other formalities like producing the bill, warranty cards etc. These procedures need to be made simpler and quicker for making the process more meaningful and realistic.

Consumers have the social responsibility of exposing the manufacture/ supplier or the service provider for resorting to illegal trade practices. Unethical notings like "Goods once sold will never be taken back" are in sharp contrast to the practice in some of the developed countries, where the sellers declare, and "In case you are not fully satisfied with our product, you can bring the same to us within a month for either replacement or return of your money." This is the result of consumer consciousness. Consumers have to realize their role and importance. The consumer movements can be winner movements only with our active involvement by knowing our rights and enforcing them. It requires a voluntary effort involving the participation of one and all. If the consumers remain passive, they will continue to be exploited. It is necessary that consumers take action with solidarity to get a fair deal and timely redressal.

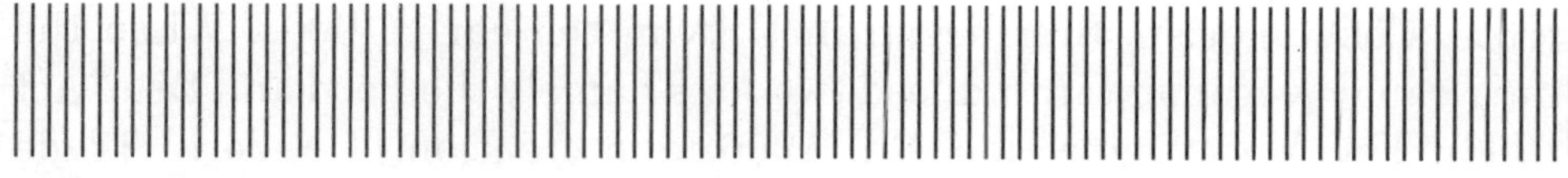

CHAPTER

2

Consumerism

Modern Changes

— Dr. S. Nazeerdeen

Introduction

Consumerism is a national problem affiliating every section of the society, men and women whether old, youth or child, rich or poor, rural or urban, literate or illiterate. Consumer protection is a form of Social Action which is designed to attain the well being of one group within a society namely the Consumers.

In India, Consumerism encompasses the evolving set of activities of Government, business enterprises and Independent Consumer Organizations that are resigned to protect the rights and the Interest of consumers.

Peter F Trucker pointed out that, "*Consumerism is the shame of the total marketing concept*". Consumerism should succeed in marketing the business and the Government more responsive to the right of the consumer.

Consumerism according to Gulshan "refers to the widening range of activities of government, business and independent organisation that are designed to protect individuals from policies that infringe upon their rights as Consumers"

Origin of Consumerism

Consumerism is the discovery of the twentieth century. Two nations namely U.S.A. and U.K., have made pioneering efforts for protection of consumer rights. Consumerism first began in USA in the early 1900s. When the American Government introduced two Acts namely the Food and Drug Act (1906). The Meat Inspection Act (1906) and creation of Federal Trade Commission (1940) for protection of Consumer interest.

Every since then more and more Consumer Acts and Laws have been passed in USA, UK, and many other countries. The movement received further impacts when the American President John F Kennedy (1962) sent an exclusive message on the Protection of Consumer Interest to the Congress, in his address.

The Presidential concern highlighted the primary rights-right to safety, right to be informed, right to choose, and the right to be heard. The term was not put the wider use until 1963 or 1964 when a variety of commendations identified it with the very visible concerns triggered indirectly by *Rachel Carson*, and directly by Ralphnader's all to safety investigations and President Kennedy's efforts.

Consumerism

Consumerism is an organised effort of Consumers seeking redresses restitution and remedy for dissatisfaction. They have accumulated in the accusation of their standard of living. Consumerism is a policy or programme of protecting the rights and interests of the Consumers.

The Philosophy of marketing is based on consumer. The Consumer is not only a heart of marketing but also the controller of marketing function.

Need for Consumerism

- The need for consumerism has been primarily due to the indifference of the business community. The main aim of all business is to maximize profit.
- Consumers have not only been called upon to pay higher prices but also have to settle at lower quality, spurious, duplicate and adulterated products that are being sold through misleading and powerful advertisement Media. Hence, consumerism is required to protect consumer interest.

Scope of Consumerism

- Consumerism today includes three broad areas of consumer dissatisfaction and its remedial efforts. Consumerism involves discontent with direct buyer-seller exchange relationships, and between the consumer and the business firm

- The second area of consumer discontent extends to all organisations with which there is an exchange relationship. Consumerism therefore involves such diverse organisations as hospitals, schools, and government agencies.
- The third area of consumer discontent involves the Indirect impact that an exchange relationship has between two social units. In other words, an exchange between two people or groups can create a problem for the third group.

Uses of Consumerism

Well-organised and dynamic Consumerism may be expected to produce the following results:

- Producers and sellers will not take the consumer for granted. When consumers strive to protect their rights, business will be compelled to shun its unfair trade practices.
- Consumerism will provide feedback for the business. It will enable the producers to understand the consumer's needs and wants. This will assist in the more effective implementation of the marketing concept or societal marketing concept, depending upon the nature of consumerism.
- Consumerism will make the government more responsive to consumer interests, prompt it to take necessary statutory measures and make the required institutional arrangements to safeguard consumer rights.

Causes of Consumerism

All of us are consumers, wherever we live and whatever we do, irrespective of age, sex, colour, or creed, makes as a consumer. Being a consumer we purchase and use goods produced by other members of the society. And certainly each of us (as a consumer) has experienced the cumulative frustration associated with products that do not conform to expectations.

In free market economy, it is said that consumer is the king. It is his rupee choice in the market, which decides success or failure of producers.

Consumerism is also one of the many form of social movements. It also passes through a few development stages, as does social movement. In the beginning (of civilization) man would get things of his need by exchange of commodities (barter system) but as be become aware of his surroundings he also started his own production.

The introduction of machineries brought about low production cost and also specialization of commodities. In this industrialization race, producers almost forget the consumer and went on multiplying the production.

In the 19th Century producers became more concerned with introduction new commodities and paid no need to providing information to consumers, which resulted in their becoming ignorant and unaware. Consequently, consumer associations took birth in developed countries, mainly in Europe and United States.

Consumerism in India

There is no doubt that consumer is a backbone of all economic activities, therefore his interest should receive first priority. But today Indian consumer is one of the most neglected sections of the society. He faces a plethora of problems affecting his rights and interests. He is very often cheated in a number of ways such as, adulteration, over pricing, short weights and measures, fraudulent advertisements, deceptive packaging, black marketing and poor sales services.

Consumer Guidance Society of India (CGSI), which was started in April 1966, by nine housewives and social workers, has a regular programme for testing the food items and consumer durables.

According to the CGSI, quality has not yet become a heritage in India upon which National reputation can be built.

Fortunately, consumer production is now a widely accepted phenomenons in the country. A number of legal and institutional arrangements developed over the years directly or indirectly aim at safeguarding the interest of consumers.

Further, the Government has brought into effect a progressive and comprehensive legislation in the form of consumer protection Act 1986.

The Government is also making efforts with the help of certain departments, voluntary organisations and media, to educate the general consumer regarding their rights as a consumer.

The Government departments and organizations usually hold talks, exhibitions, seminars, workshops and open discussion with the consumers giving them useful recommendations to increase their awareness for accurate buying policies.

The printed media *viz.*, newspapers, academic journals, magazines etc., often carry information which if properly noted could increase the consumer awareness.

Consumerism in India has already crossed its first and second stages, that is crystallization and organization stages. Though the latter has not been completely surpassed, the Indian movement has also stepped into the third stage that is institutionalization.

Sufficient consumer protection laws has been introduced and Government intervention at both Central and local levels can be seen very well.

Conclusion

The development of consumerism in a country like the consumers are highly aware about their consumer rights as well as towards their surroundings and their claims along with strong consumer organisations to raise voices against market malpractices, which indicates that consumerism has acquired a level of maturity in the developed country.

REFERENCES

- Dr. Atul Dhyani *"Indian Journal of Marketing"* (Consumerism: Gobal *vs.* Indian Perspectives)
- Dr. S.B. Sadar *"Indian Journal of Marketing"* (Consumerism)
- V. Seshadri *"Consumerism"* Mittal publications.
- P. Sivapradlism and S. Rajamohan *"Consumer Empavement"* Kanishka Publishers and Distributors.
- David L. Lowdon & Albert and T. Della Bitta *"Consumer Behaviour"* Tata McGraw-Hill Publishing Company Ltd., New Delhi.

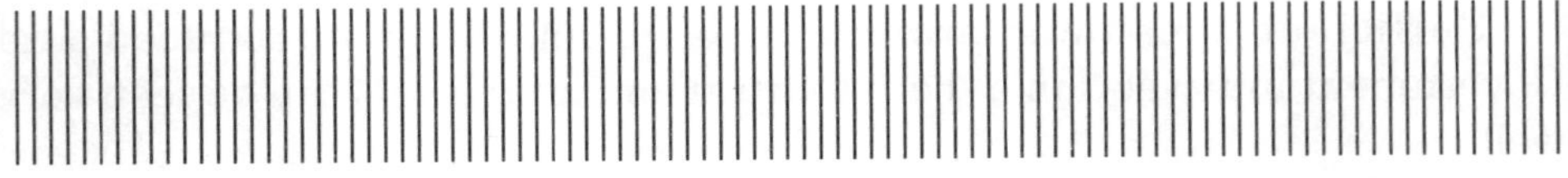

CHAPTER

3

Psychological Aspects of Consumerism

—Dr. O.M. Haja Mohideen

Introduction

Consumerism has a broad definition and can include a range of buying and business behaviours, so finally consumerism is a 'kind of behaviour' and that is how it is important to psychology and psychologists. Consumerism is about individuals or groups and how they select or buy secure and use or dispose products and services so that they can satisfy their needs of consumption and the practice of consumerism would also have a significant effect on society. The study of consumer behaviour in a systematic and even a scientific manner would be the basis of the psychology of consumers and consumerism. The psychology of consumerism could be considered from two different aspects—one from a marketing or the business viewpoint in which consumerism is seen as essential since it helps maintain companies and businesses so the psychology would be based on how to attract consumers whereas the other viewpoint is the behavioural aspect of consumerism or why consumers buy or consume products and services, and what are the reasons of a buying culture and how this could be justified with normal or abnormal behavioural analysis.

Yet we could first try to define consumerism and understand why consumerism is such an important aspect of business and marketing. The term consumerism seems to have both positive and negative connotations as consumerism could mean a culture of possessions and glorification of materialism. Consumerism could however also mean progressively more consumption of goods and products that could benefit the economy and the markets with a heightened buying culture among people although consumerism could also mean the entire gamut of marketing and business activities that finally lead to the buying of products by consumers.

Consumer Psychology from a Marketing Aspect

Consumers buy according to their personal needs and what they feel is necessary and also according to social needs as they follow trends and thus become interested in certain products and services. Certain products appear more important, essential or attractive to consumers and these products tend to have certain value, which makes it easier for companies to sell these products. Businesses and companies are capable of attracting more consumers by using the psychological principles of marketing and consumer behaviour and the key is to create want or the requirement for a product. Businesses and companies understand initial consumer needs through surveys and then they develop new products to attract consumers. Once products are developed, brand image and advertisements help in providing an association between products and companies and when consumers develop an element of familiarity with this association between brand name and product features, they tend to even want the product. In keeping with the demands of competition and consumerism, companies tend to give promotional offers, discounts, sales and low priced products with the aim of attracting more consumers. Considering the marketing perspective, consumerism is advantageous as more consumers and increased buying behaviour would mean more sales of products although the disadvantages of increased consumer spending would be minimal except that increased consumerism would also signal increased competition from other manufacturers.

Thus the most essential features of consumer psychology from a marketing point of view are creating the need for consumerism or for a specific product by advertising specific and unusual features of the product, developing the association between brands and products and offering attractive options such as discounts and sales to attract not just more consumers but also more sales.

Consumer Psychology from a Behavioural Aspect

From a behavioural perspective, it would be interesting to engage in an analysis of buying behaviour and we can try to understand why consumers buy in the first place. There could be several reasons for buying that arise from social and personal needs, from emotional and financial needs and some of these needs are healthy and positive and in fact essential in our daily life. However, buying behaviour as in *'shopaholics'* would be unpredictable, random, and even unhealthy, from a psychological point of view as excessive buying or consumerism cold indicate bipolar illness or a kind of addiction. However consumerism and specific focus on luxury brands could highlight the almost unhealthy addiction to fashion trends and status symbols in modern times and globalization seems to be encouraging this. Companies and businesses create choices in consumers so consumers already have a 'need' when they engage in buying behaviour. Although this need could be personal and social, the need could also perfectly an emotional need to possess.

From a psychological viewpoint consumerism is about fulfilling our inherent need to control and possess certain objects which could well replace or substitute other possessions. For example, a woman undergoing divorce proceedings may suddenly develop the irresistible need to buy things continually because the need for possessiveness towards a partner has been diverted to other directions.

From a more clinical point of view consumerism could be explained with abnormal psychology and the role of depression, the need to satisfy excessive possessiveness and also the blind faith or dependence on fashion trends and all these are seen as negative aspects of consumer psychology. If consumerism is considered as a positive phenomenon, the advantages of consumerism would be the application of psychological principles in understanding buying behaviour.

Consumerism and the study of consumerism helps us to understand and recognize not just consumer needs and how these needs are created or fulfilled but also the behavior and attitudes of consumers towards products and the business directions or endeavors to understand marketing from a behavioural perspective. The psychology of consumerism is thus about creating needs and associations so consumers develop certain familiarity with the product ideas even before buying them.

Consumerism could be both positive and negative and represent not just a global and globalize culture but also highlight the superficial trends and deeper necessities of individuals across societies and communities.

Thus, Psychology is a quantitative and qualitative measurement of consumerism in order to analyze the lifestyle of the consumers.

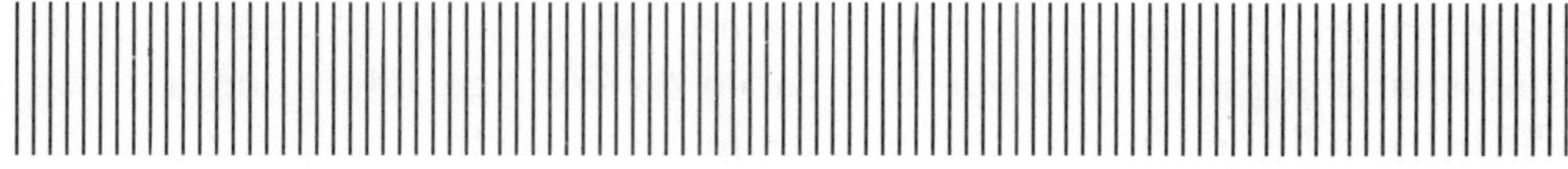

CHAPTER

4

Consumer Psychographics

— Dr. S. Shahul Hameed
— Ms. P. Seethalakshmi

Meaning

Phychographics is commonly known as study of 'lifestyle' of consumers. It plays an important part in building consumer behaviour and helps in the promotion of those products and services which are related to items of personal care, fashion, automobiles, telephone services, alcoholic drinks, newspapers, magazines, food products Re milk, tea, coffee (which are sold by brand names)

The life style depends not only on the regions but also on ones profession. The life style of film actors is entirely different than that of common person. They may like to have pash house, high priced, showy things of glamour which are not part of others life style so that they may be different from others.

Definition

Psychographic considers life experiences basically based on psychology of the group and accordingly decides market strategy and places them in different groups Life style or psychographic can be defined as a "composite measure of the activities a consumer enjoys in and spends time doing, of interest of the consumer and of the opinions held by the consumer".

Psychographics *vs.* Demographics

There is high degree of complementarily in psychographic and demographic analysis. In psychographic studies generally one depends upon lifestyle *i.e.* activities, interests and opinions of an individual while demographics studies and segments the markets based on sex, age, education, income, which are collected by all the countries in census data.

Demographic data is available on sex, marital status, occupation race, religion, homeownership, age of household members, income levels and the number of income earners in the family, languages. In India all this information has been collected in 2001 census and in post census and throws very useful light on socio-economic aspect of the population. In foreign countries advertisements are "increasingly designed ads that depict in words and / or pictures the essence of a particular target market life style.

For instance Colgate is placing great emphasis in its advertisement aimed at children about strength of tooth and their long life. Similarly Pepsodent of Hindustan Lever also gives almost similar message to children about their tooth paste. These are only examples but how successful they have been is not known because advertisers are not willing to reveal the impact of their ads.

The psychographic may divide life style into traditional, very traditional, non-traditional, modem etc. and through demographic studies they can be further segmented as per age, income, sex, profession etc. Thus two together helps one to know in great detail about the consumer and then attempt can be made to influence their behaviour for a particular product or service.

Psychographics *vs.* Motivational Research

Psychographics is study of life style that exists at a point of time but motivation is the reason for particular life style and thus two are highly interdependent. Motivation studies why a person acts in a particular manner and how that style can be changed. Thus while psychographic studies the existing position, the motivation research studies the reasons for current behaviour and also studies how this behaviour can be changed. In other words "motivation can be described as the driving force with in individuals that impels them to action" whether positive or negative. It is generally stated that motivation is based on goal or need fulfillment.

Types Psychographic Variables

Large numbers of variables are influencing psychographic. In brief they may be divided into three groups namely:

1. Activities
2. Interests
3. Opinions

Activities

Activities relate to research how the time spent by an individual, family or a group on various activities such as working, resting, vacation, hiking, riding, playing, studying, recreating, etc. By asking suitable questions various activities of an individual, household or group are studied and measured. Based on these replies society is divided into various groups. The various activities depend upon social class one belongs, status *i.e.* the level of income, level of education, profession, vocation or calling, area of residence, personality, knowledge, interest among other factors also depend upon age. Young boys or girls or recently married couples may prefer to own a house or spend more on fashion, travel as compared to middle aged person. Old family members interest may be more on quiet simple life as compared to outing.

Interests

The interests also depend upon level of education. A person highly educated may have greater 'rest in reading books of his subject while less educated person may not read books or may prefer go to a movie or watch TV.

Language is another variable which influences ones and families interest. A person from Bengal, Tamil Nadu or Kerala will like to read newspapers, magazines and story books in their state language the language not only influences reading habits but also liking for films, music, dances and so on.

The culture and social set up also decides or at least influences preferences and interests. A person living in South India or Bengal likes traditional music, simple traditional dress while those living in high society may prefer to spend more on fashion, going to clubs, spend more on personal care, cosmetics and modern shorts or jeans. Social class, who prefers to have modem dress, may prefer smoking, drinking and entertaining themselves even with outsiders which may be taboo for some other cultures.

Opinions

The opinion about various activities, products, services, health, fashion, books, beauty, nature of consumptíon, politics, tours, travels, education, nature of education, institute, houses, buses also decides consumer behaviour and so the consumption of various goods and services. Therefore researcher wants to study through formal or informal surveys, opinion poles etc. find out opinion of consumers so that the goods and services may be modified, improved, restructured and innovation may be carried out to introduce new products to satisfy the requirements of various consumers. In these research consumers are asked their personal or family opinion on varied social, economic, political, cultural, personal issues, products and services.

Conclusion

Psychographic is study of life style of consumers based on their activities, interests and opinions. The study of consumers psychographic helps to promote sales especially of those products which relate to personal comforts, personal care, fashion etc. In a country of size and diversity like India the study of consumer psychographic is of great significance in developing products and services, segmenting markets and promoting sales. Since the life style depends upon large number of factors the research also uses demographic and both are interdependent and takes the help of each other. Psychographic researchers depend heavily on demographic data on age, sex, education, profession etc.

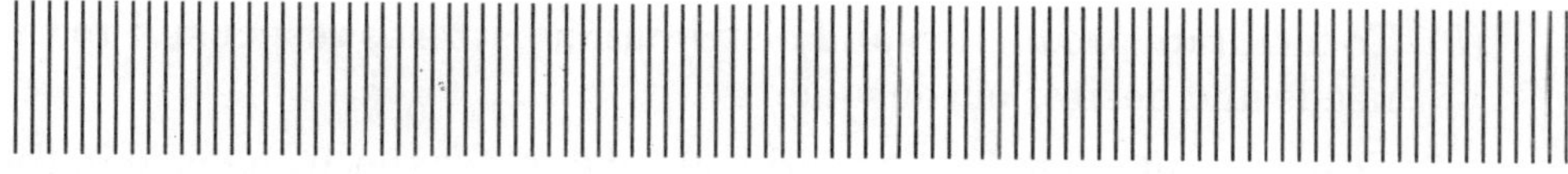

CHAPTER

5

Consumer Protection and UNO

— Dr. M. Nazer
— Ms. Mariam Jenofer

Introduction

In the next millennium, every consumer in his own interest has to realize his role and importance in the right perspective. Each citizen in a democracy derives his power at the time of elections and exercises it through the ballot. In a competitive economic environment the consumer has to exercise his choice either in favour of or against the goods and services. His choice is going to be vital and final. He should realize his importance and prepare himself to exercise his rights with responsibility. It is very often stated "Customer is sovereign and consumer is the King." If that is really so, why do we have the Consumer Protection Act? Why is there a need for protecting the King? Should it not be rightly called "Consumer Sovereignty Act"? It is for the consumers to decide. After all the dictum in democracy is, the citizens get a government they deserve. Similarly the consumers in society get a position in the market depending upon what they do or do not do. It is agreed on all hands that 'consumer empowerment' in India has a long way to go. This is the right time to act. Let us prepare for the next millennium and usher in a new era of 'Consumerism'. When we cross the winter, spring cannot be far behind.

The United Nations Organisation has put forward many guidelines to protect and achieve the goals consumerism. They are:

(*a*) To assist countries in achieving or maintaining adequate protection for their population as consumers;

(*b*) To facilitate production and distribution patterns responsive to the needs and desires of consumers;

(*c*) To encourage high levels of ethical conduct for those engaged in the production and distribution of goods and services to consumers;

(*d*) To assist countries in curbing abusive business practices by all enterprises at the national and international levels which adversely affect consumers;

(*e*) To facilitate the development of independent consumer groups;

(*f*) To further international cooperation in the field of consumer protection;

(*g*) To encourage the development of market conditions which provide consumers with greater choice at lower prices.

It is interesting to note that in spite of U.N. recognition, encouragement from the developed countries and the pro-active role played by the Government, the consumer in India still does not get his due. It is time that he wakes up and realizes his rights. Even the great Hanuman required someone older and wiser to remind him of his potential strength. It will be useful if voluntary consumer organisations take up this role and make way for the realization of the objectives of the U.N. guidelines and the Consumer Protection Act.

GLOBALIZATION, LIBERALIZATION AND CONSUMERISM

Positive Implications

The process of development coupled with increasing liberalization and globalization across the country has enabled consumers to appreciate their increasingly important role in society and governance.

Though it is said it to be 'self reliant' but in present scenario it seems unfeasible to tag along the same. in this day and age the world has transformed into 'global village' not only due to the advancement of trade and commerce but more due to technological advancement. Therefore liberalization is inevitable for a nation-state disposed to develop itself. It is very difficult for any nation to produce everything to satisfy its customer citizens, so the process of globalization and free trade is serving a noble cause for all the probable consumers by satisfying their otherwise unaddressed desires.

Negative Implications

Noam Chomsky, one of the world's noted intellectuals, describes globalization thus: "Insinuation of extension of transnational corporate tyranny.... Their first interest is profit—but much broader than that it is to construct an audience of a particular type...addicted to a certain lifestyle with artificial wants, an audience atomized, separated from one another, fragmented enough so that they don't enter the political arena and disturb the powerful. This, is what all about existing Indian consumer, who is now heading opposite to its own philosophy of consumerism when we compare and contrast it with that of the Gandhiji's which says that "while there is enough on earth for every man's need there is not enough for everyone's greed and that poverty is really the other face of the problem of possessiveness. "It is the consumerist mode of thinking."

Being the consumer of environment and nature today's punter of the third world is really underprivileged of his very deep-seated, fundamental and natural right in the newly evolved monstrous paradigm of globalization in which human well-being is equated with material consumption regardless of the impact of unregulated economic growth on social ties and the environment. 6 per cent of the world's population in America is usurping 40 per cent of the earth's non-renewable fossil fuel resources and non-fuel mining alone produces 1300 million tonnes of garbage annually. If everyone in the world were to enjoy the American standard of consumption, it has been estimated that three planets Earth would be needed.

In the World Economic Forum 1999 meet, Nobel laureate and UNDP Goodwill Ambassador, Nadine Gordimer, condemned the process of globalization for increasing consumption unprecedented, jeopardizing truly human prospects: "While those of us who have been the generations of big consumers need to consume less, for more than one billion of the world's poorest people increased consumption is a matter of life and death and a basic want—the right to freedom from want." She asserted that consumption is necessary for human development "when it enlarges the capabilities of and improves people's lives without adversely affecting the lives of others." This is how globalization turns out fatal for present and probable consumers as well as for national entities also.

Law and Globalize World

The presence of an international or transnational element is likely to make the application of political will, translated into law, extremely difficult. International law does not operate directly on human behaviour, or the behaviour of corporations; the effective actors in international law are nation-states. Rights and remedies acquired under the law of one nation may be recognized and enforced in another nation, but this is not guaranteed. To obtain redress of grievances may be difficult and technically complex quite apart from the practical difficulties of language, location of parties, and finding a party with sufficient assets to justify initiating enforcement procedures.

Since 1960, most developed countries with common law legal systems, the nations of Europe and most recently of Asia have enacted significant consumer protection legislation (For example, Japan, Korea and Taiwan have all recently introduced product liability legislation which is based on the 1985 Product Liability Directive of the European Communities). Such laws are national, and operate only within the geographical limits of the enacting jurisdiction, except where conflict of laws rules permit them to be applied as part of the law of some other country. Attempts to apply such existing laws to activities outside the geographical boundaries of the enacting state might prove ineffective. Examples include marketing and sale of goods or services (including financial services) online through the Internet or satellite TV by suppliers who are in remote areas, often beyond the reach of legal process. If it is impossible to locate production, marketing, distribution and trade in goods and services in a defined physical and juristic locality, no legal control is possible.

Consumer Protection Laws in the Global World

Consumers have sought protection through legislation because the general laws and market forces have failed to provide it. Many consumer protection laws either relate to the terms and conditions of contracts that consumers make with suppliers for the supply of goods and services, or to conduct intended to encourage the making of such contracts (marketing, packaging, advertising and provision of information). Previous laws, especially the law of contracts, assumed that the parties to contracts are legally equal in terms of power and information. In substance, in real markets, almost invariably consumers have markedly less power and information than suppliers. The law deems the action of a consumer in buying a commodity to be the making of a contract—in theory a free, consensual act. In practice, the legal consequences are attributed to the action by the law without any consideration of what the consumer actually knows or wants. The common law of contracts simply cannot afford consumers the protection they probably would seek if they were rational, fully informed, and equal in economic power to the supplier. Because contract law offers an inadequate basis for an equitable legal transaction, it must be modified by legislation in order to afford greater protection to consumers than they can negotiate individually for themselves.

Problem of Legislative Jurisdiction and Its Ways Out

Both public and private international law restricts the power of nation states to provide legal sanctions and remedies. United States anti-trust law provides a good example of Globalization being challenged in its earliest stages. The year, 1892, saw the passage of Anti Trust Laws which made the nascent Industries of the Big Business Era accountable to the people and the Government of the day. Recently, Bill Gates was brought to the book for Anti Trust violations, which turned out to be a big theme for the U S economy in the first tenure of George Bush.

How law, politics and practicalities intersect in ways that destroy international goodwill. Attempts by any single nation to proscribe activities beyond its physical boundaries by people who are neither residents nor citizens are likely to create the problem of legislative jurisdiction. When this happens, a state may enforce its extraterritorial laws within its own boundaries, but other states will steadfastly, block any attempt to enforce those laws within their own territories.

A preferable solution seems to be bilateral or multilateral international agreements under which governments concur that each will make criminal, under its domestic laws, the conduct which all desire to prohibit. This process is sometimes called 'unification' or 'harmonization' of law. If any activities in the Networld are to be made criminal, even though this process seems cumbersome, it may be the only acceptable means available. There are problems of securing agreement of uniform laws.

Suggestions and Annotations

- It is extremely imperative to encourage volunteers, who are gallant, audacious and forthright, concerned in consumer protection movements. Organizations, NGOs, institutions and agencies allied to consumer movements should hearten administrative advocacy in settling consumer disputes so the hitch of case pending and delay in case disposal can be avoided.
- Government should come up with varieties of plans to establish and manage laboratories, equipped with latest available international standard technologies, for testing samples of consumer goods with a view to determining their quality, purity and relative merit. Government should enter into treaties with various countries in order to ensure extra territorial operation of the act.
- Government should be pro active towards the cunning policies of MNCs to exploit the consumer.
- A heavy sum should be taken from the multination companies in the form of security money at the time of their establishment and incorporation.
- Most of the Indian consumers know only COPRA but they are not aware about other laws and statutes which protect their right so

along with the dissemination of consumer protection act, consumer should be made aware about the existence of other laws *i.e.* MRTP, Essential Commodities Act 1955, Bureau of Indian Standard Act 1986 etc.

- Government should make efforts to create a consensus for global consumer policy.
- Judicial activism should be increased in consumer related issues also and parental role should be played by the Supreme Court for consumer redressal agencies.
- Administrative advocacy should be encouraged in order to reduce the burden of consumer redressal agencies.
- Indian consumer suffers from lack of political willingness to enforce consumer rights emphatically. V.R. Krishna Iyer, former Chief Justice of India, expresses himself more stridently:" The country's greatest enemy is GATT and the pro-MNC politics...leading to decolonization of India...Their capacity to corrupt, terrorize, propagandize, destabilize, colonies and subvert...has been the disaster of our country and of many others. And who invites them into our hallowed Bharat? The greats who have taken the oath of office under the secular socialist constitution and worship Gandhi as the Father of the Nation!

Consumer Responsibility

Strange as it may seem, most consumers do not know that the law is on their side. It is for the consumers to enforce the provisions of law by vitalizing enforcement. The machinery is available. It has to be use effectively. Marilyn Ferguson writes in The Aquarian Conspiracy, "Countries like ours are full of people who have all the material comforts they desire, yet lead lives of quiet (and at times noisy) desperation, understanding nothing but the fact that there is a hole inside them and that however much food and drink they pour into it. Therefore, being aware about rights a consumer should also understand his responsibilities for procuring the better outcomes.

How Consumer Fraud Might Be Addressed in the Net World

The globalization of markets makes it very difficult for the laws of nation states to control the excesses of businesses operating outside of their physically defined territories. Computer mediated communication networks afford new opportunities for transnational marketing that may ignore the restrictions afforded by national consumer protection laws. How then could consumers be protected in this new virtual marketplace? A few possibilities are suggested, but none really offers promise of the level of protection which consumers receive under national laws.

First, the most obvious step would be for nations to seek bilateral treaties that establish reciprocal arrangements for enforcing consumer protection laws between nation-states that have similar laws.

Secondly, the most effective means, but most difficult to accomplish would be an international agreement concerning the rights of consumers online, similar to the international agreements governing transnational postal services and telecommunications.

Thirdly, the World Trade Organization might determine that consumer fraud online constituted a threat to the viability of international trade. As sanctions may be imposed upon non-conforming nation-states.

Fourthly, individual nation-states may enforce their own consumer protection laws unilaterally by inhibiting the travel of offending parties foreclosing entry into their territories.

Fifthly, Information Service Providers and Internet Access Providers may themselves unite to establish industry norms for appropriate behaviour in offering consumer transactions over their systems.

Sixthly, major commercial interests that choose to offer products online may establish industry organizations that purport to guarantee an optimum level of consumer protection for purchasers of their products.

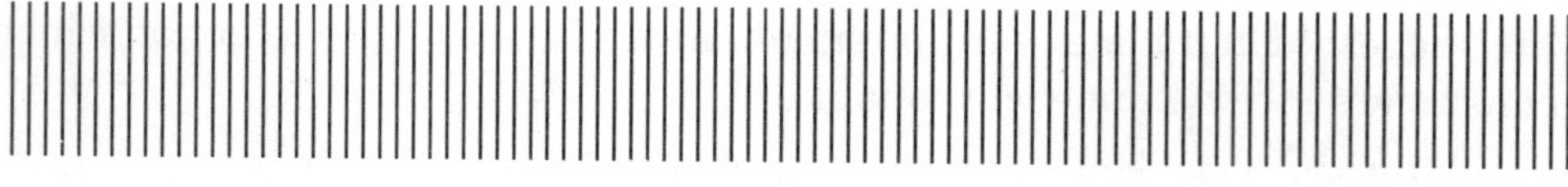

CHAPTER

6

Protection of Consumer Rights

— Dr. N. Abdul Jaleel

— J. Manivannan

Introduction

India is a country, which never fell behind in introducing progressive legislation—we were among the first in the world to introduce universal adult franchise for women. Gandhi had rightly said, *"A customer is the most important visitor on our premises. He is not dependent on us. We are dependent on him. He is not an interruption in our work—he is the purpose of it. We are not doing him a favour by serving him. He is doing us a favour by giving us the opportunity to serve him."*

Consumers are the largest economic group in any country. They are the central point of all economic activity. But the very same consumers are the most voiceless group especially in India. Today the consumers have no power to order what he desires. An average Indian consumer is poor, illiterate, ignorant, apathetic or just defeatist and he continues to be at the receiving end. He is the forgotten man of modern economy. He is the least organized and the most centrifugal element in the circle of investment, production, sale and the consumption and he is generally taken for granted as one who has to buy anyhow in order to live.

Birth of Consumers' Day

Considering the importance of Kennedy's speech to the US Congress on this day, and the resultant law, the International Consumer Federation took a decision in 1982 to observe 15 March as the World Consumer Rights

Day from 1983. Peculiar though it may sound, 15 March is not observed as a special day in the world's largest and most pulsating consumer society—the US. But at home in India the Government, adopted 15 March as the National Consumer's Day.

Consumer and Consumerism

A consumer is a buyer of commodities from a seller. *For the purpose of 'goods', a consumer means a person belonging to some categories like:* (*i*) One who buys or agrees to buy any goods for a consideration which has been paid or promised or partly paid and partly promised or under any system of deferred payment; (*ii*) It includes any user of such goods other than the person who actually buys goods and such use is made with the approval of the purchaser. *For the purpose of 'services', a consumer means a person belonging to some categories like:* (*i*) One who hires or avails of any service or services for a consideration which has been paid or promised or partly paid and partly promised or under any system of deferred payment; (*ii*) It includes any beneficiary of such service other than the one who actually hires or avails of the service for consideration and such services are availed with the approval of such person.

Consumerism depends solely upon the factors of age, taste, preferences and psychology of the buyers. Therefore, there is an urgent need to make the consumers aware of their rights at a time when our society itself has adapted to a consumeristic way of life.

Consumer Rights

Consumer rights are an integral part of our lives as these rights are supposed to be the guiding force for a consumer in buying a commodity. Based upon the provisions of these rights a consumer decides whether his/her rights are protected or not. In India, Consumer Protection Rights Act was passed in the year 1986 to safeguard and protect the common interests of the consumers by ensuring them their rights. Consumer rights are well-defined and well documented because many government and voluntary organizations have worked in tandem to uphold the validity of these rights through district consumer courts in the country. Under the Consumer Protection Act 1986, a consumer is guaranteed the following rights:

- Right to be protected against the marketing of goods and services which are hazardous to life and property;
- Right to be informed about the quality, quantity, potency, purity, standard and price of goods or services so as to protect the consumer against unfair trade practices;
- Right to be assured, wherever possible, access to a variety of goods and services at competitive prices;

- Right to seek redressal against unfair trade practices and unscrupulous exploitation of consumers;
- Right to consumer education.

Protection of Consumer Rights

Often an aggrieved consumer is clueless as to where to complain or whom to approach for lodging the complaint whenever his/her rights are violated. Thus, the consumers are deprived of justice due to their ignorance. This stands as a hindrance in the way of getting redressal through the right forum. The consumer issues are always taken up by the district consumer courts.

The main objective of the Consumer Protection Act is to ensure speedy and effective justice to the afflicted consumers and promote consumer movements through voluntary organizations. This Act is applied to all goods and services and it covers all the sectors, namely, government, private and co-operative.

Who Can Complain?

- An affected consumer.
- Any voluntary consumer organization registered under the Societies Act or Companies' Act 1956.
- The Central and State Governments.

Essentials of a Complaint

- The complaints must contain facts and allegations in writing.
- The complainant or his/her authorized agent should file the complaints.
- The complaint ought to have suffered injury or loss due to unfair trade practice, defective goods and deficiency of services or excessive price of goods.
- The relief sought for should be stated.
- The documents if any to get orders for one or more of the relief.

Relief Available to Consumers

Depending on the nature of relief by the consumer and facts, the Redressal Forum may arrange to get orders for one or more of the relief.

- Removal of defects from the goods.
- Replacement of the goods.
- Refund of the money.

- Award compensation for the loss or injury suffered.
- Removal of defects or deficiencies in service.
- Discontinue the unfair trade practice or the restrictive trade practice or not to repeat it.
- Not to offer the hazardous goods for sale.
- Withdraw the hazardous goods from being offered for sale.

Conclusion

In the next millennium, every consumer in his own interest has to realize his role and importance in the right perspective. Each citizen in a democracy derives his power at the time of elections and exercises it through the ballot. In a competitive economic environment the consumer has to exercise his choice either in favour of or against the goods and services. His choice is going to be vital and final. He should realize his importance and prepare himself to exercise his rights with responsibility. It is very often stated "Customer is sovereign and consumer is the King." If that is really so, why do we have the Consumer Protection Act? Why is there a need for protecting the King? Should it not be rightly called "Consumer Sovereignty Act"? It is for the consumers to decide.

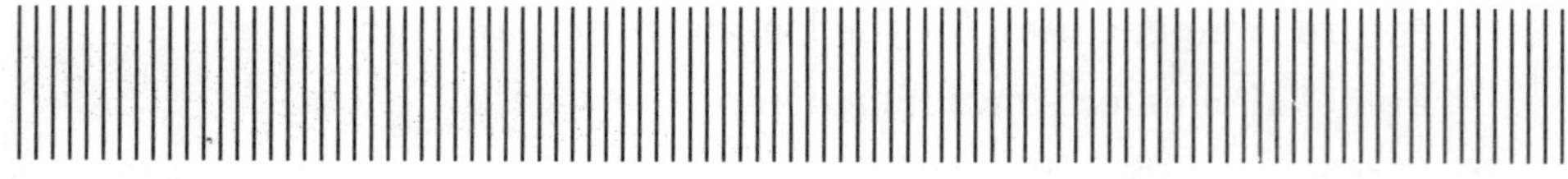

CHAPTER

7

A Forum for Consumer Redressal

— Dr. A. Jalal
— Dr. K. Murali Selvam

Introduction

Few years ago, consumer action in India was virtually unheard of. It consisted of some action by individuals, usually addressing their own grievances. Even this was greatly limited by the resources available with these individuals. There was little organised effort or attempts to take up wider issues that affected classes of consumers or the general public.

All this changed in the Eighties with the Supreme Court-led concept of public interest litigation. It gave individuals and the newly formed consumer groups, access to the law and introduced in their work the broad public interest perspective.

Several important legislative changes took place during this period. Significant were the amendments to the Monopolies and Restrictive Trade Practices Act (hereafter 'MRTP Act') and the Essential Commodities Acts, and the introduction of the Environment Protection Act and the Consumer Protection Act. These changes shifted the focus of law from merely regulating the private and public sectors to actively protecting consumer interests.

The Consumer Protection Act, 1986 (hereafter 'the Act') is a remarkable piece of legislation for its focus and clear objective, the minimal technical and legalistic procedures, providing access to redressal systems and the composition of courts with a majority of non-legal background members.

Consumers

All of us are consumers of goods and services. For the purpose of the Consumer Protection Act, the word 'consumer' has been defined separately for 'goods' and 'services'.

For the purpose of 'goods', a consumer means a person belonging to the following categories:

(*i*) One who buys or agrees to buy any goods for a consideration which has been paid or promised or partly paid and partly promised or under any system of deferred payment;

(*ii*) It includes any user of such goods other than the person who actually buys goods and such use is made with the approval of the purchaser.

For the purpose of 'services', a 'consumer' means a person belonging to the following categories:

(*i*) One who hires or avails of any service or services for a consideration which has been paid or promised or partly paid and partly promised or under any system of deferred payment;

(*ii*) It includes any beneficiary of such service other than the one who actually hires or avails of the service for consideration and such services are availed with the approval of such person.

Consumer Rights Available

- *Right to a safe consumer environment:* The right to be protected against the marketing of goods hazardous to life and property.
- *Right to information:* The right to be informed about quality, quantity, purity and price to protect against unfair trade practice.
- *Right to choice:* The right to be assured access to a variety of goods.
- Right to seek redressal against unfair trade practice.
- Right to be heard and assured that consumer interests will receive due consideration in an appropriate forum.
- Right to consumer education.

Complaints

Under the Act, a consumer or any registered voluntary consumer association or any Central or State Government can make a complaint. A 'consumer' is a person who buys any goods or hires any service for consideration, paid or promised or partly paid or under deferred payment. This includes any user of such goods or services when such use is made with the approval of the person who paid or partly paid etc. However, goods obtained for commercial purposes or for resale are not covered under the Act.

Complaints can be made against (*a*) unfair trade practices by which complainants suffer loss or damage; (*b*) goods that suffer from one or more defects; or (*c*) deficient service.

The procedure adopted by the Forum or Commission on receipt of a complaint is to refer a copy of the complaint to the Opposite Party directing them to file their version within thirty days or such extended period not exceeding fifteen days at a time.

Based on its findings, the Forum or Commission can grant a direction to the Opposite Party to remove the defect, replace the goods free of defect, or refund the charges paid for the goods or service and to pay compensation for the loss or injury suffered by the complainant. Such directions are to be treated as if it was a decree of a court, and non-compliance can amount to imprisonment.

Delays

The biggest problem with the Consumer Forums and Commissions is one of inordinate delays. Even though a time period of three months has been recommended for the disposal of complaints (five months, when laboratory analysis is required), hardly any Forum or Commission complies with this recommendation. This can be remedied by not permitting any adjournments and by allowing the presence of a lawyer only with the consent of the forum and the Opposite Party.

Difficulty in Executing Orders

Consumers face enormous difficulty in executing the orders of the Consumer Forum and Commission. This is because the Consumer Forum cannot attach properties of those not complying with their orders; they can only issue arrest warrants. Right now to attach the properties of defaulters, the case is transferred to the nearest civil court and the process of recovery is tedious. This can be remedied if power to attach is given to the Consumer Forum, along with the power to appoint a Receiver.

Specific Limitations in the 1986 Act

Several provisions of the Act, when implemented, strictly work against the interests of consumers at large. For example, an association of flat owners cannot file a compliant against the builder of their apartment, since they are not recognised under the Act as being a collective of consumers.

They are required to file individual cases against the builder. Similarly, the prohibition on filing a complaint against defective goods purchased "for commercial purposes", prohibit a tailor from filing a complaint against a company that supplies him a defective sewing machine. This works against the intent of the Act. Suitable amendments to the Act and interpreting the Act as a beneficial legislation will remedy these problems.

OTHER LAWS THAT IMPACT CONSUMERS

Essential Commodities Act

Any complaint of hoarding or unfair trade practice against the thirty-four commodities listed as essential commodities under this Act can be preferred to the special courts established under the Act.

Standards of Weights and Measures Act and Rules

This Act prescribes standards for the weights and measures used in trade. These standards ought to be certified by the Bureau of Indian Standards (BIS) and contain the 'ISI' mark. This also prescribes rules for packaged commodities. The rules explain the details that a package should contain—like the maximum retail price (MRP), weight of the commodity, date of manufacture and expiry.

Prevention of Food Adulteration Act

This Act contains stringent provisions against adulterators of food articles. The Act also prescribes a set of officers to check the quality and quantity of food in public establishments.

Reactions to the Act

Traditionally, the relationship between private business and the consumer movement has not been smooth. While on one hand, we have several consumer-unfriendly private businesses, we also have frivolous (consumer) litigators. As a result each views the other with suspicion. However, there are several private sector players who place consumer interests as a priority. These manufacturers and service providers normally resolve individual complaints on their own. However, this is on a case-to-case basis. Unfortunately, the law is not strong enough to protect consumers from fly-by-night operators or intentional defaulters. This is one large lacuna in consumer protection mechanisms and continues to plague consumer attitude towards a private sector manufacturer or service provider.

The activities of consumer groups and the functioning of the various Forums and Commissions under the Act has, without doubt, raised the general level of consumer awareness in the entire country. Due to the stronger presence of consumers and markets in urban India, consumer action is by and large an urban consumer-led activity.

Redressal

The right to redressal means the right to a fair settlement of just claims, not only economic but also social and political. The socio-political dimension of the issue stems from the fact that in a stratified society (polity) like India, vulnerable sections may not have real access to justice. It includes the right to receive compensation for misrepresentation of shoddy goods or unsatisfactory services and the availability of acceptable forms of legal aid or redress for small claims where necessary.

What Do the Guidelines Say?

The Guidelines provides a framework for the governments to use in elaborating and strengthening consumer protection policies and legislation. One of the major objectives of the Guidelines is that the governments should establish or maintain legal and administrative measures to enable consumers to obtain redress through formal and informal procedures that are expeditious, fair, inexpensive and accessible. Another objective is to encourage all enterprises to resolve consumer disputes including advisory services and informal complaint handling mechanisms. The third objective is that the information on available redress and other dispute resolving procedures should be made available to consumers.

What is the Situation in India?

In India, until the Consumer Protection Act (COPRA), 1986, consumers had to rely upon a number of legislations but none provided effective remedy against violation of consumers' rights. COPRA was designed with the specific purpose of protecting consumers' rights and providing a simple quasi-judicial dispute resolution system for resolution of complaints. The rationale of the Act is to take the system of redressal to the people's doorstep.

Why is It So?

The first and foremost problem is that, most state governments do not evince requisite enthusiasm and attention in promptly implementing the provisions of the Act by carrying out their mandatory obligation of establishing properly functioning District Forums and State Commission. Secondly, even with the existence of justice delivery system, the system is plagued by systemic problems resulting in inordinate delays. Apart from these, consumers are also reluctant to make use of the redressal system. One major reason is the absence of proper guidance from voluntary organisations and fear of exploitation by lawyers.

What are the Solutions?

In Section 2 (1) (d) of COPRA, the definition of consumer is limited and restricted in its scope and ambit. In a welfare state like India, the government is the biggest provider of services, especially to the poor.

The exemption of these services, on the ground of want of consideration results in a defeat of the purpose of the right to redressal. Therefore, the definition of the word 'consumer' should be inclusive to encompass all such services so as to make equal access to justice a living reality.

Secondly, there should be a Product Liability Law to save consumers from ill effects, and to proof 'fault' in the product and 'negligence' of the manufacturer. Such law should relieve consumers from the obligation of establishing negligence.

Thirdly, there should be speedy redressal of cases. And for this, three things have to be done on a priority basis-improve the institutions, upgrade the quality of the personnel, and simplify the procedures.

In order to fulfill the objective of effective consumer redressal, the following legislative and administrative measures are to be taken:

- strengthen the existing forums for consumer disputes;
- adopt legislation for alternative dispute resolution or binding arbitration;
- co-regulation with mandatory participation of public interest groups;
- encourage business to establish ombudsman schemes to avoid costly and time consuming litigation;
- business to establish consumer cells under their Chief Executives;
- chambers to
- pursue the adoption of voluntary codes;
- consumer complaints cells;
- voluntary arbitration mechanisms; and
- most importantly, information dissemination about these measures.

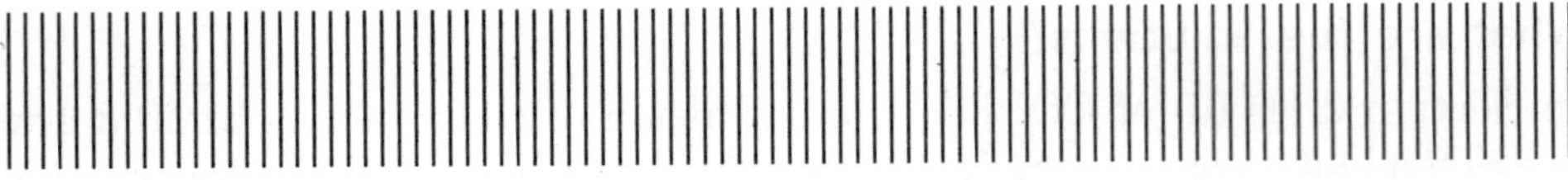

CHAPTER

8

Consumer Protection

Legislative Measures and Consumer Rights

— Dr. A. Peer Mohideen
— P. Kumaravel

Introduction

A consumer is defined as any person who buys any product or hires or avails of any service. The product or service must be paid for either wholly or partly, or may have to be paid later. The services covered by the Consumer Protection Act include supply of electricity, banking, financing, alien, repairs, transport, communication, construction, medical treatment etc.

Under the consumer protection Act, the complaints could be:

- A consumer
- Any voluntary consumer association registered under the companies Act 1956 or under any other law for the time being in force or,
- The Central Government or any State Government, who or which makes a complaint.

Defect and Deficiency

Defect means any fault, imperfection or shortcoming in the quality, quantity, potency, purity or standard which required to be maintained by or under any law for the time being in force under any contract, express or implied, or as is claimed by the trader in any manner whatsoever in relation to any goods.

Deficiency means any fault, imperfection, shortcoming or inadequacy in the quality, nature and manner of performance which is required to be maintained by or under any law for the time being in force or has been undertaken to be performed by a person in pursuance of a contract or otherwise in relation to any service.

The remedies available to a dissatisfied consumer through the redressal machinery are as under:

- Removal of defects in goods
- Replacement of goods with new goods of similar description which shall be free from any defects
- Return of price by the seller or manufacturer
- Payment of compensation if the consumer has suffered any loss or injury
- Remove the defects or deficiency in the services
- Discontinue the unfair/restrictive trade practices, and not to repeat them
- Not to offer the hazardous goods for sale
- Withdraw the hazardous goods from being offered for sale
- Provide for adequate costs to parties

Unfair Trade Practices

Unfair trade practices under Consumer Protection Act has been defined a trade practices which for the purpose of promoting the sale use or supply of any goods or for the provision of any service, adopt any unfair method or unfair or deceptive practices it is:

- Falsely representation that the goods are of a particular standard, quality, quantity, grade composition, style or model;
- Falsely represent any rebuilt, second hand, renovated, reconditioned or old goods as new goods.
- Makes false or misleading representation concerning the need for or the usefulness of any goods or services.

Amendment of the Consumer Protection Act

In 1986, the Consumer Protection Act was passed "to provide for the better protection of the interests of consumers and for the purpose to make provisions for the establishment of consumers councils and other authorities for the settlement of the consumers disputes and for matters connected therewith".

Sailent Features of the Consumer Protection Act, 1986

Social welfare legislation	— highly social welfare
Effective provision and safeguard	— to safeguard against the exploitation
Special consumer courts	— it enforcement of the rights of the consumer
Convenient procedure	— the complaint presents the grievance
Time limit	— a time limit for the disposal of cases
Clan Action	— the complaints relating to unfair trade practices
Price	— A complaint against the excess prices
Consumer councils	— to settle the disputes

Basic Objectives of TE Act

- Provide better protection to consumers
- Provide for the establishment of consumer council and other authorities
- Establish suitable machinery specially consumer councils to settle disputes.

Consumer Protection Act

The issues relating to consumer welfare affects the entire 1986 million people since everyone is a consumer in one way or the other. Ensuring consumer welfare is the responsibility of the government. Accepting this, policies have been framed and the Consumer Protection Act, 1986, was introduced. A separate Department of Consumer Affairs was also created in the Central and State Governments to exclusively focus on ensuring the rights of consumers as enshrined in the Act. This Act has been regarded as the most progressive, comprehensive and unique piece of legislation. In the last international conference on consumer protection held in Malaysia in 1997, the Indian Consumer Protection Act was described as one "which has set in motion a revolution in the fields of consumer rights, the parallel of which has not been seen anywhere else in the world."

The special feature of this Act is to provide speedy and inexpensive redressal to the grievance of the consumer and provide him relief of a specific nature and award compensation wherever appropriate. The aim of the Act is also to ensure the rights of the consumer, viz. the right of choice, safety, information, redressal, public hearing and consumer education.

The Act defines the consumer as one who purchases goods and services for his/her use. The user of such goods and service with the permission of the buyer is also a consumer. However, a person is not a consumer if he purchases goods and services for resale purpose.

The most important feature of the Act is the provision for setting up a three-tier quasi-judicial machinery popularly known as 'consumer courts' at national, state and district levels. The apex court, National Commission functions in Delhi. Every State Government has a State Commission. The third tier is in each district and is called district forum. As on January 2009, there are 543 district forum. All these courts have handled nearly 13 lakh cases of which about 10 lakhs cases have been disposed of. The disposal of 77 per cent of the cases is not a mean achievement. However, it should be noted that only 27 per cent of the total cases have been disposed of within the prescribed period of 90 days or 150 days (where testing is required). This fact really causes concern for the Government and the consumers in general. The National Commission has identified the reasons for the slow disposal and have come out with suggestions for amending the Act with a view to improving the disposal rate within the time limit prescribed in the Act. The Government has been contemplating a number of amendments to the Act and these amendments will be brought out in the next session of Parliament.

The consumer movement in India is as old as trade and commerce. In Kautilya's Arthashastra, there are references to the concept of consumer protection against exploitation by the trade and industry, short weighment and measures, adulteration and punishment for these offences. However, there was no organised and systematic movement actually safeguarding the interests of the consumers. Prior to independence, the main laws under which the consumer interests were considered were the Indian Penal Code, Agricultural Production, Grading and Marketing Act, 1937, Drugs and Cosmetics Act, 1940. Even though different parts of India exhibited different levels of awareness, in general, the level of awareness was pretty low.

The U.N. guidelines for consumer protection are meant to achieve the following objectives:

- To assist countries in achieving or maintaining adequate protection for their population as consumers;
- To facilitate production and distribution patterns responsive to the needs and desires of consumers;
- To encourage high levels of ethical conduct for those engaged in the production and distribution of goods and services to consumers;
- To assist countries in curbing abusive business practices by all

enterprises at the national and international levels which adversely affect consumers;

- To facilitate the development of independent consumer groups;
- To further international cooperation in the field of consumer protection;
- To encourage the development of market conditions which provide consumers with greater choice at lower prices.

Consumer Welfare Fund

The Central Excise and Salt Act, 1944 (1 of 1944) was amended in 1991 to enable the Central Government to create the Consumer Welfare Fund where the money, which is not refundable to the manufacturers etc., shall be credited. The money credited to the Fund is to be utilized by the Central Government for the welfare of the consumers in accordance with the Rules framed.

Consumer Welfare fund rules were notified on 25th November, 1992. Subsequently on the recommendations of the Central Consumer Protection Council, the Rules were further mended on 27th January, 1994 to make them more broad based. The rules were further amended on 16.06.94, 16.01.95 and 13.6.2002.The fund has been set up by the Department of Revenue. However, the Ministry of Consumer Affairs, Food and Public Distribution will operate it. The overall objective of the consumer Welfare Fund is to provide financial assistance to promote and protect the welfare of the consumers and strengthen the voluntary consumer movement in the country particularly in the rural areas.

National Consumer Helpline

A National Consumer Helpline project has been established in collaboration with Delhi University , Department of Commerce. Consumers can call from any where in India to the number *1600-11-4000* from *MTNL/BSNL* lines free of charge and get advice regarding their problem as a consumer. The Helpline has been formally launched on 15.3.2005 on the World Consumer Rights Day and is functional on all working days from 9.30 A.M to 5.30 P.M. A Facilitation Center of the Help Line is also functioning at the Reception, Gate No: 6 of Krishi Bhawan from 9.30am to 5.30 am.

Rights of Consumers

The act provides the following rights to a consumer:

Right to Safety

This is the right to be protected against the marketing of goods and services which are hazardous to life and property.

Right to be Informed

This means the right to be informed about the quality, quantity, potency, purity, standard and price of goods and services, as the case may be, so as to protect the consumer against unfair trade practices.

Right to Choose

It means the right to be assured, wherever possible, access to a variety of goods and services at competitive prices.

Right to be Heard

It means the consumer's interests will receive due consideration at appropriate forums. It also includes right to be represented in various forums formed to consider the welfare of consumers.

Right to Consumer Redressal

It means the right to seek redressel against unfair practices or restrictive trade practices or unscrupulous exploitation of consumers. It also include right to fair settlemement of the genuine grievance of consumer.

Conclusion

The consumer is wealth of the business and important of economic of the nation. The consumer protection Act, 1986 provide the consumer forum for the settlement of disputes and prevent the consumer against the unfair trade practices.

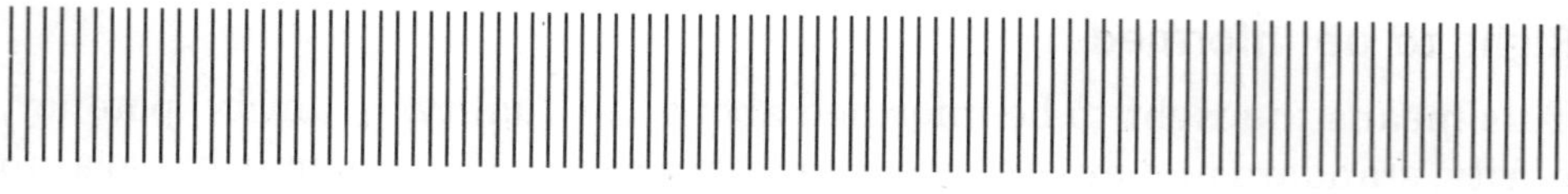

CHAPTER

9

Total Quality Management and Customer Satisfaction

— Dr. A. Mohamed Siddique
— Dr. A. Mohamed Nazar

INTRODUCTION

Total Quality Management

Total Quality Management is a Management Philosophy that seeks to integrate all organizational functions (marketing, finance, design, engineering production and customer service etc.) to focus on meeting customer needs and organizational objectives.

Evolution Pattern of Quality Managtement

Phases of Quality Movement/ Identifying Characteristic	Inspection	Statistical Quality Control	Quality Assurance	Strategic Quality Management
1	2	3	4	5
Primary Concern	Detection	Control	Co-ordination	Strategic view
Emphasis	Product Uniformity	Product uniformity with reduced inspection	Entire production chain	Market and consumer needs
Methods	Gauging and Measurement	Statistical tools and techniques	Programmes and systems	Strategic planning and setting

...(Contd.)

1	2	3	4	5
Role of Quality Professionals	Inspection, Acceptance, Sampling	Trouble shooting and the application of statistical Methods	Quality Measurement, Planning, Programme design	Goal Setting, Education, Training and consultation
Who has Responsibility for Quality	Inspection Department	Manufacturing, Engineering Departments	All Departments	Everyone in the organization.
Orientation and Approach	Inspects in Quality	Controls in Quality	Builds in Quality	Manages in Quality

Principles of Total Quality Management

- Delight the Customer
- Management by fact
- People-based Management
- Continuous Improvement

Delight the Customer

This focuses on the External customer and asks 'what would delight them' 'Delight' means being best at what really mattes most to the customers and this can change over time. Being in touch with these changes and always satisfying the customer are on integral part of TQM.

Management by Fact

Knowing the current Quality standards of the product or service in customer's hands is the first stage of being able to improve.

People-based Management

The more people feel involved, the greater will be their commitment to customer satisfaction systems, standards and technologies themselves will not provide quality. The role of people is extremely important in the continuous improvement of quality with in an organization.

Continuous Improvement

TQM is not a short-term activity that will finish when a set target has been achieved. It is not a programme or a project. It is a management process that recognizes that however we may improve, our competitors will continue to improve and customers will expect more and more from us.

Elements of TQM

- Senior Management Commitment
- Improvement Orientation
- Customer Focus
- Company-wide improvement
- Commitment to training and education
- Ownership of the process
- Emphasis on measurement and review
- Teamwork

An Integrated TQM Model

- Customer Focus
- Management Commitment
- Total Participation
- Statistical Quality Control
- Systematic Problem-solving Process

Customer Focus

The customer may be ultimate consumer external to the organization or an internal user receiving an internal service.

Management Commitment

Commitment can be in the form of changing attitudes, expectations and establishing systems for quality measurement and control.

Total Participation

People at the grass root level produce the goods and services that benefit the end customer. Participation is also a means by which intangibles such as morale, sense of belonging and responsibility.

Statistical Quality Control

Use of various statistical techniques to analyse the collected data and solve various problems.

Systematic Problem-solving Process

It is based on the customer focus element and relies on the Plan-Do-Check-Act-Cycle to improve the whole business process.

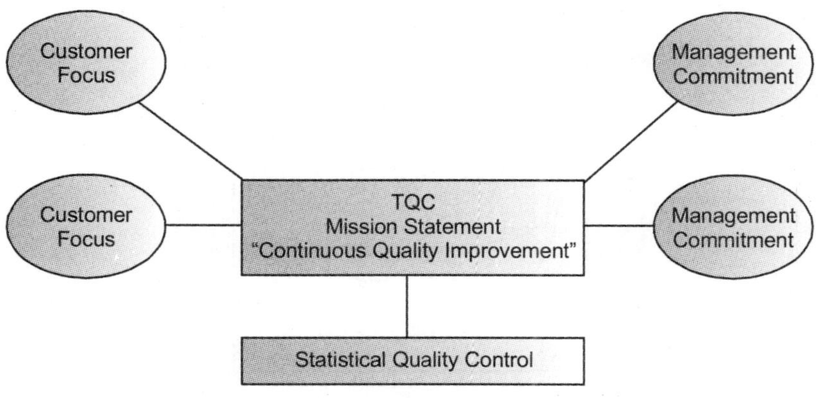

An Integrated TQM Model

Prerequisties for Implementing TQM

- The ten commandments of TQM
- The four Pillars of TQM
- The 4'c'S of TQM

The Ten Commandments of TQM

(1) Approach - Management Led
(2) Method - Prevention not Detection (of defects)
(3) Objective - Total Customer Satisfaction
(4) Measure - The Costs of Quality
(5) Standard - Right First Time
(6) Scope - Ownership and Commitment
(7) Theme - Continuous Improvement
(8) Ability - Training and Education
(9) Communication - Co-operation and Teamwork
(10) Reward - Recognition and Pride

The Four Pillars of TQM

⇒ P1 = Satisfying Customers
⇒ P2 = Systems/Process
⇒ P3 = People
⇒ P4 = Improvement Tools

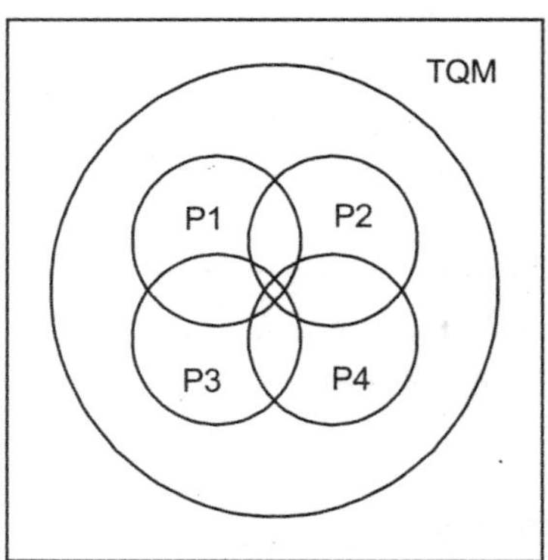

P1—Satisfying Customers

TQM aims not just to meet customer requirements but also to achieve customer satisfaction.

P2—System1 Process

Establishing a system such as ISO 9000 is the initial building block. TQM relies on an effective Quality Management System which ensures that preventive measures are in place and the culture.

P3—People

Management Commitment, training, teamwork, leadership, Motivation, Empowerment etc. would have a vital and complementary role.

P4—Improvement Tools

TQM recognizes the need for continuous Improvement and uses a set of tools.

The 4 'C' S of TQM

⇒ Commitment

⇒ Competence

⇒ Communication

⇒ Continuous Improvement

Commitment

Commitment to quality at work is defined as a desire personal or organizational choice to follow on an agreed-upon plan of action.

Competence

Competence includes certain specific measurable skills, sound education. Good Intuitive Judgment, an ability to apply related knowledge to solve problems and a responsible attitude.

Communication

The purpose of Communication is to achieve mutual understanding.

Quality Communication Model

Sender	Measure	Receiver	Feedback
Strategy Direction Goals	Standards Requirement expectations training	Interpretation Implementation Participation	Ideas Suggestion

Continuous Improvement

Continuous Improvement is a programme, a philosophy and a strategy to improve the quality of gods and services of an organization.

Management Practitioners

- ⇒ It is an Institution-wide process to develop a culture of continuous improvement to achieve customer satisfaction.
- ⇒ It is a management philosophy that seeks continuous improvement through Internal and External Quality Improvement.
- ⇒ It is a Strategy for improving product and service Quality.
- ⇒ It focuses on prevention of problems
- ⇒ TQM culture is formed by the beliefs, values, rules and climate of the organization.

Model for Evaluating TQM Implementation in Services

TQM in service sector such as hotels and banks. These are: (*a*) Transformation leadership; (*b*) customer orientation; (*c*) HRM; (*d*) Organizational culture,

Core Concepts of TQM

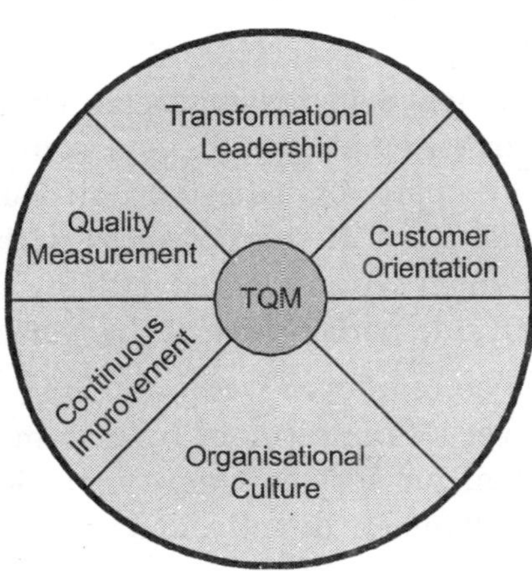

(*e*) Continuous improvement; and (*f*) Quality Measurement. The underlying assumption is that realization of these core concepts is facilitated through the implementation of the peripheral, supporting percepts. One of the peripheral precepts is measurement of customer satisfaction, a dominant theme in services marketing literature, with the dim of increasing customer loyalty and retention.

Transformational Leadership

In Service organizations, there is a high degree of employee-customer Interaction. Employees play on important role in service delivery. In order to provide effective service they need proper guidance. There is a need for a leader to motivate the employees to perform better at work. Therefore, they should lay emphasis on recruitment and selection, training and development, performance appraisal, reward and compensation of service sector employee's quality of supervision influences job satisfaction of employees and their services.

Performance

Southwest Airlines has made a high place in the list of fortune 500 companies by maintaining an excellent employee-customer relations, organizational training and strong leadership as source employee motivation.

Leaders who Inspire, Motivate, and energize their followers to attain higher levels of performance are called transformational leaders. Four components, known as the four I's, make up transformational leadership: (*a*) Idealized Influence; (*b*) Inspiration Motivation; (*c*) Intellectual Stimulation; and (*d*) Individualized Consideration. Transformational leaders Inculcate change in their organization's culture with a vision of share values that help in fostering a sense of purpose and belongingness to the organization.

Customer Orientation

Today's business Environment is increasingly characterized by globalization. In customer-oriented firms, employees have a sense of belonging to the organization to achieve customer satisfaction. Customer Orientation emphasizes the Establishment of relationships with the customers and feedback Mechanisms, which are associated with high levels of satisfaction at work and more favourable perceptions of the working environment.

Organizations focus on employee well-being and satisfaction, because that determines employee's Commitment to customer service. Employee Commitment is Essential for service Quality. In Service organizations, employees interact with customers directly, and they know the current needs and requirement of customers. Therefore, employee's Job Satisfaction and organizational commitment are important dimensions in a firm adopting TQM.

Human Resource Management

A firm's HRM practices create an environment to elicit customer-oriented behaviour from employees. Service firms need to deal with a number of HRM Issues such as recruitment and selection, training and education, performance appraisal, reward and compensation. TQM literature has paid little attention to the Impact of recruitment and selection of employees. TQM practices are primarily intended to improve the quality of products or services.

The Human Resource of the firm needs to be continuously enhanced through training and development. Training and education enhance the skills and knowledge of the existing employees so that the organizational competency needs are met. To ensure courteous, caring, responsive, and empathetic service, training in interpersonal skills is necessary. Employees need to acquire effective communication skills essential for a service-oriented employee. An organization's HRM practices create both economic and Social Exchange relationship with employees and these employees in turn are likely to exhibit better service to its customers.

Organizational Culture

The team 'organizational culture' refers to a system of shared values and beliefs. Culture in places of work is important in generating employee commitment researchers have made an attempt to find the effects of organizational culture on the delivery of quality service it enables people to adopt a common vision of the organization and its goals to achieve a shared target that contributes to the overall delivery of high quality service.

Organizations have become more customer-centric and employees are being given more responsibilities. Employees come to the workplace with a set of beliefs, values and behaviour such as: (*a*) to make their relationships better; (*b*) to bring more creativity and innovation work; and (*c*) to raise the standard of work. Employees expect organizations to cultivate some type of spirituality within their members in order to produce high quality products and services.

Continuous Improvement

Continuous improvement is about learning from the current processes and products to improve them in the future. This process is the object of study of learning theory quite a number of learning theories are available in the literature—(*e.g*) goal setting, reinforcement, and Modeling. Continuous improvement means commitment to constant examination of technical and administrative processes in search of better methods.

Therefore, continuous improvement of technical as well as the physical assets of an organization helps in achieving customer satisfaction. In the present competitive market scenario, customers are more demanding and are aware of the latest trends in the market. If they do not find the product or service offered by a company to be innovative and appealing, they will definitely switch over to the competitor's brand.

Quality Measurement

There are various methods of quality measurement such as statistical process control, benchmarking and customer satisfaction. Measurement of customer satisfaction forms the core building blocks of Quality Management. Measurement of customer satisfaction is a way how firms measure their quality.

Customer satisfaction is a post-consumption experience which compares perceived quality with expected quality. It measured how products and services supplied by a company meet customer's expectations. It is a key performance indicator of a firm. Customer satisfaction depends on service quality, price, timeliness, efficiency and physical environment of the firm.

Conclusion

TQM emphasizes on customer-oriented service processes for the implementation of TQM, certain core concepts of TQM are identified. These are transformational leadership, customer orientation, organizational culture, management of human resources, continuous improvement and quality measurement. Service delivery occurs through human interactions. Therefore, human issues involved with service delivery are considered to be the best predictors of TQM in the service organization.

TQM Implementation can improve the competitive abilities of the firm and provide strategic advantages in the marketplace. TQM implementation leads to improvements in quality, Productivity, Improvement in employee relations operating procedures, customer satisfaction and financial performance of the firms. Managers can use the relationships and interdependencies among the core concepts as a starting point to determine the performance within the organization and monitor company-wide improvements in TQM programmes.

"Taking care of Total Quality Management are areas that need, "Do the right things, right the first time and every time"

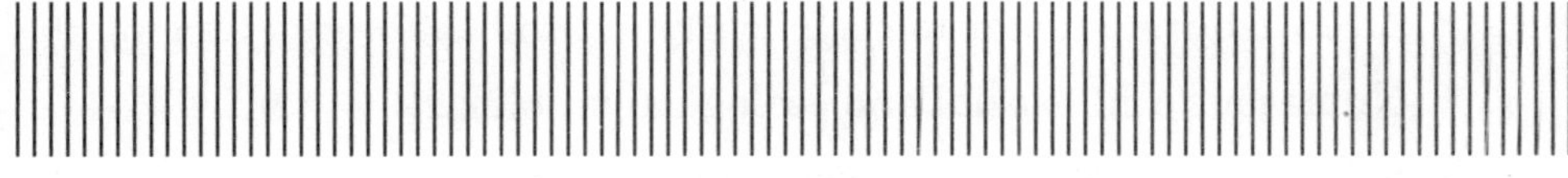

CHAPTER

10

Consumerism and Waste Products

— A. Raja Mohamed
— Dr. P. Ganapathy

Consumer: A consumer is someone who consumes anything that is required by him. A consumer is someone who buys and uses goods and services. Consumers are not only found in human society but also in other societies.

Consumerism: Consumerism refers to the process of consuming anything available in the world. Consumerism also encompasses the evolving set of activities of government business enterprise and independent consumer organization that are designed to protect the rights and interests of consumers. Hence consumerism is a global problem affecting every section of the society.

Product is something that is made, grown or obtained in large quantities so that it can be sold. Production is the basis for consumption. Production increases when the demand for a particular product increases. This increase in production is sustainable only when the quality of the product is maintained; the price is regulated and advertising claims are fair.

Waste product: Waste product is the product which is thrown after a short-period of time usage.

What are the Problems and Causes of Consumerism and Waste Product?

Today's perpetual growth causes the following problems:

- Destructive in the long-run to the environment;

- A contributing factor to the poverty around the world; and
- Numerous other social and ecological problems.

Today's many products produced are luxurious and are non-degradable which takes years to be decomposed. A high rate of consumption leads to pollution and waste product.

Today's 20 per cent of the world richest consume 86% of the world's total resources. In my point of views the 86% of the resources won't be consumed properly by only 20 per cent of the population, so in result there would be waste products as they are consuming and then throwing them away after a short-period of time usage, and finally such kind of process lead to pollution and environmental problems.

At the same time it is inequality as well. The resources are not divided properly among people; they are neither saved nor consumed properly. Due to economic growth, migration is also taking place every where in the world. Many people move from on country to another country and from rural areas to urban areas, in order to improve and have a high standard of living.

This migration of people causes of slums in the cities, different types of pollution and pressure on natural resources such as land, water, food and other resources. In fact the three factors such as population, technology and consumption are responsible for the environment.

How to Solve These Problems?

If we do the following things, we will have a prosperous and bright future:

Population: We need to control population growth. This is the very basic and important step to be taken into consideration. Laws are to be passed for the prevention of population growth.

Consumption: Once we control population growth, the consumption rate would fall down itself, beyond this, still we have to control more the consumption rate by passing some laws.

Technology: We should stop at this stage some of the irrelevant and unimportant products, in order to stabilize the environment. Why do we have to have weapons, different kinds and models of vehicles and many more things like that?

If we enable to do so, so we would be contributing to two major things:

Environment: We would conserve the nature and its resources, so the coming generations can live in peace and enjoy it. Beyond sentient creatures, everything else in the nature has its own intrinsic value, and rights of being staying as a vital component of the nature.

Poverty: We would help those who live under absolute poverty by distributing every thing equally and not consuming a high rate of resources. Beyond of equal distribution and less consuming, we should reuse, recycle and even stop and save, using some of scarce and non-renewable resources in order to avoid waste products.

Efficient consumerism is the most essential element to minimize waste and to promote the economy of a nation. Inefficient consumerism results in the following problems:

- Uncontrolled manufacture of foods leading to inferior quality;
- Rampant adulteration leading to health and hygiene problems;
- Improper services resulting in dissatisfaction and stress;
- Production of lots of waste leads to depletion of natural resources and environmental imbalance.

Suggestions for efficient consumerism:

- Standards should be verified before buying or accepting a product from market;
- In every possible way waste must be minimized;
- Waste minerals have to be recycled;
- Strict laws must be implemented.

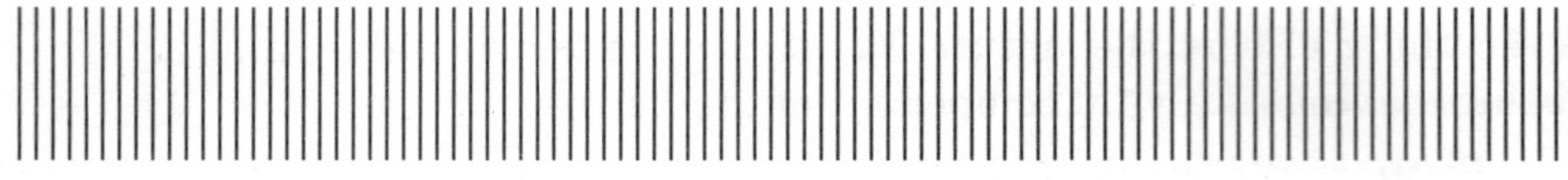

CHAPTER

11

The Extent of Consumer Awareness

— Dr. A. Babu Hussain Sherriff

The Process of development along with the expanding globalization and Liberalization process has increased the number of consumer related issues. Consumer protection has earned an important place in the political, economic and social agendas of many nations. In India, the Government has taken many steps including legislative, to protect consumers.

Education is a life long process of constantly acquiring relevant information, knowledge and skills. Consumer education is an important part of this process and is a basic consumer right that must be introduced at the school level. Consumers by definition include all citizens who are, by and large the biggest group, who are affected by almost all government, public or private decisions. The most important step in consumer education is awareness of consumer rights. However, consumer education is incomplete without the responsibilities and duties of consumers, and this influences individual behaviour to a great extent.

Consumer awareness is making the consumer aware of His/Her rights.

Consumer awareness is a marketing term. It means that consumers note or are aware of products or services, its characteristics and the other marketing P's (place to buy, price, and promotion).

Usually commercials and ads increase consumer awareness, as well as 'word of mouth' (a comment from someone you know about a product or service).

We need it so we will not be misled by producers, it explains if what we buy is worth to our money and not harmful to us and to environment.

Many people are ignorant of their rights to get protected against the exploitation by so many others. So when there is a forum for such redress of grievances there seems to be no such exploitation by many; and becomes a rare one. So in order to get a clear picture of the level of exploitation of consumers, the awareness is required.

Role of producers proper labeling, full information, health warnings, handling information, expiration date, etc. keep to requirements, norms, standards label products according requirements, providing true facts. They have to produce and deliver the goods/services of right quality at right price at right time at right place at right quantity with right face.

If they are providing a service they should carry it out with due skill and care. They must also make sure that any materials they provide as part of this service are fit for the purpose.

It is also illegal for a supplier to cut off, or threaten to cut off, supply to a reseller (wholesale or retail) because they have been discounting goods or advertising discounts below prices set by the supplier.

Consumer Awareness and Suggested Measures to Increase Consumer Awareness

The need for empowerment of consumers as a class cannot be over emphasized and is already well recognized all over the world. The advancement of technology and advent of sophisticated gadgets in the market and aggressive marketing strategies in the era of globalization have not only thrown open a wide choice, for the consumer but all the same also rendered the consumer vulnerable to a plethora of problems concomitant to such rapid changes. There is an urgent and increasing necessity to educate and motivate the consumer to be wary of the quality of the products, and also the possible deficiencies in the services of the growing sector of public utilities.

In short, the consumer should be empowered with respect to his rights as a consumer. He should be equipped to be vigilant with a discerning eye so as to be able to protect himself from any wrongful act on the part of the trader. In order to be able to position the consumer in such a state, there is every need not only to evolve legal remedies but also provide reliable and exhaustive information, which he can access without much effort and expense.

Recognizing the importance of the problem, the Government of India and State Government have initiated steps to introduce dispute redressal mechanism by way of Consumer Protection Act, but a lot more has to be done in the area of creating awareness on the part of the consumer to facilitate his seeking suitable remedy wherever there is a need. This becomes more important in the rural areas, where there is wide spread illiteracy.

But one should never forget that God only helps those who help themselves. You can never be beaten unless you admit that you have lost similarly no one can deceive you unless you let him do so. Thus, it is time for the consumers to wake up and realize that nothing will happen by sitting hands on hands, more than talking of action, one should believe in implementing or doing it. Howsoever one may try it is impractical to erase theft, fraud etc. form our society. In this case the only option left is to take preventive measures.

- The first and the foremost step for a consumer to prevent himself from cheating is to keep his eyes and ears open. Know or be aware of what is happening around you. Read the cases of various scams, thefts, burglaries, phishing scams etc. in that are highlighted in your local newspaper and also seen on television. This will keep you informed and conscious of what is going on and what can unfortunately even happen with you.
- Learn from the mistakes of your neighbours. If a shopkeeper has given a malfunctioning gadget to your neighbor, do not make the mistake of going to that shop. If somebody stole important mails from their mailbox, do make it a point to collect all your crucial mails directly from the post office.
- Never reveal personal identity to a stranger. You go for a morning walk and a man over their tries to be extra amiable even asks you to come home for lunch etc. does not imply that he wants your friendship or that he is a genuine person. So do not disclose your residence, telephone numbers, your workplace numbers etc. to him unless you gather complete information from a known person about him. Avoid giving personal details on phone. If you receive calls from unknown place that offers you some benefits and asks for your particulars, don't be carried away by that. Tell your particulars only when you are sure that the call is genuine and that there is no other way out.
- Do not rely much on courier services. If you an access to the place where you have to deliver the parcel, take out some time and go yourself.
- Do not hand over your credit or debit cards even to your friends. It is foolish to trust someone blindly nowadays. Never tell your friends

or colleagues to check your mails while you are holidaying with your family. It is not wise to let others know your password and mails.

- When you are out for shopping in the market, do not carry much cash. Keep the tentative amount and credit or debit card in case of emergency. This will not only help you do a regulated shopping but will also save you from many pitfalls.
- Before purchasing any commodity, always read the manufacturing date, the expiry date and the MRP carefully.
- Never forget to take all the bills and an assurance for the warranty period. Take the bills for each and every thing you buy and it is advisable to take things on a longer warranty basis even if you have to pay a little more for it.
- If while coming back home you lose your wallet, call up the police and register your complaint. This can protect you from the illegal use your documents by the one who picks them up. It is better that you de not carry your essentials every time you move out of the house.
- Keep all the emergency numbers (like the social security unit of your area, the police station number etc.) stored in your mobile phone. Also what is vital for your security is to keep a back up record in a diary of all the essential numbers in your phone and addresses. This will facilitate you with all the information in case you lose your mobile phone.

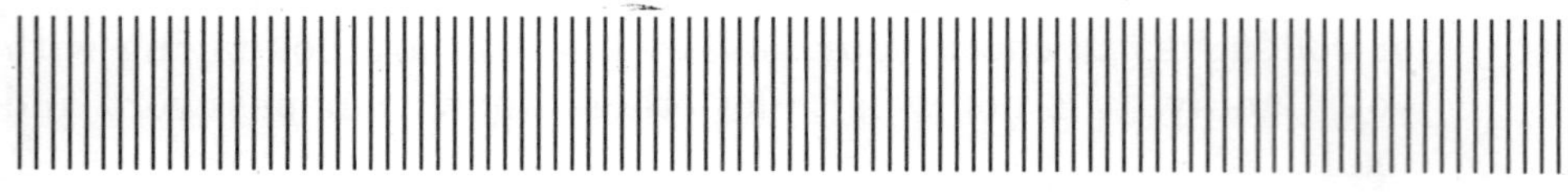

CHAPTER

12

Consumer Awareness in India
An Overview

— Mrs. A. Ayesha Mariam

Anyone who consumes goods is a consumer. Consumers get exploited in the market. They respond to advertisements and buy goods. Generally advertisements do not give all the information that a consumer needs to know or wants to know about a product.

Some of the common methods of exploitation are:

1. Under weight and under measurements—not measured or weighed correctly
2. Substandard Quality—defective home appliances and medicines beyond expiry date
3. High prices—charging above the retail price
4. Duplicate Articles—selling fake items in the name of the original
5. Adulteration and Impurity—is done to get higher profits
6. Lack of safety Devices—absence of inbuilt safeguards in appliances
7. Artificial Scarcity—hoarding and black marketing
8. False and Incomplete Information—misleading information on quality, durability, and safety.
9. Unsatisfactory after sales Service—high cost items like electronics and cars require constant and regular service.
10. Rough behaviour and Undue conditions—harassment in getting LPG connection or a telephone connection..

Factors causing exploitation of Consumers

1. Limited Information—providing full and correct information will help in the choice
2. Limited Supplies—when goods and services are in short supply then price shoots up
3. Limited Competition.—single producer may manipulate the market in terms of price and stocks.
4. Low Literacy.—illiteracy leads to exploitation. Hence Consumer Awareness is essential.

Rise of Consumer Awareness

Even though we are talking more about the Consumer Awareness today, it was written and discussed by our ancestors. *Chanakya* of the Ancient India, who was the Prime Minister of Chandra Gupta the Mauryan Emperor, was the earliest to write in his *Arthasastra* about the need for Consumer awareness and protection. With the growth of private sector there is a greater need for discipline and regulation of the market. Consumers must be aware of the sale and purchase of goods, the health and security aspects also. Ensuring the safety of food items sold in the market is essential these days.

Legal measures for consumer safety and consumer awareness must be uniform, and transparent in terms of prices, quality of goods, and stocks. Consumers must have the tools to combat malpractices and protect their rights.

Rights and Duties of Consumers

As codified under the Indian Laws the Consumers have the following

Rights

1. *Right to Safety*—to protect against hazardous goods
2. *Right to be Informed*—about price, quality, purity
3. *Right to Choose*—access to a variety of goods and services at competitive prices.
4. *Right to be Heard*—consumers interest and welfare must be taken care of
5. *Right to seek Redressal*—protection against unfair trade practices and settling genuine grievances.
6. *Right to Consumer Education*—Knowledge about goods and issues related to consumers.

Duties

1. Get a bill for every important purchase and also the Warranty card
2. Check the ISI mark or AGMARK on the goods
3. Form consumer awareness groups
4. Make a complaint on genuine grievances
5. Consumers must know to exercise their rights

Consumer Protection Measures

1. Legislation concerning Consumer Rights

The Consumer Protection Act 1986 provides for consumer disputes redressal at the state and national level. With the help of this law the agencies can solve grievances in a speedy, simple and inexpensive manner. A separate department of consumer affairs was set up at the state and Central Government. A three tier system of consumer courts at the National, State and District levels were set up. These agencies have done good work by handling lakhs of cases.

2. Public Distribution System

To protect the poor from price rise and black marketing the government food security to the poor by supplying essentials through the ration or Fair price shops.

3. Standardization of Products

These are done to assure the quality of products. The ISI stamp on goods is placed by the Bureau of Indian standards. This caters to industrial and consumer goods. These goods can be trusted to confirm to specific standards. AGMARK is meant for Agricultural products.

At the International level the International Organisation for Standardization (ISO) located in Geneva sets common standards. The FAO and WHO provide food standards.

Legal Formalities for Filing a Complaint

The complaint can be written on plain paper. The supporting documents like the warranty card must be attached. A lawyer is not required. We can argue our case.

Some suggestions to protect the consumer rights:

1. Compulsory sealed packing should be introduced for all food items which will prevent adulteration. The procedure as per the packing Act should be followed in packing the materials.

2. Appropriate centres should be established at all market yards or district headquarters to enable the consumer to test the goods purchased by them and check the weight and measures.
3. Government machinery should insist on the issue of receipts to the consumer. It should also be made accessible to consumers wherever required.
4. A Citizens' Charter and Public Utilities Commission for the country should be established effectively by the government, so as to improve the quality, choice, standards and value of public services.
5. A Centre for Consumer Protection should be established at the University level, with the objective of creating consumer awareness among the students. It should familiarize the students with the legal rights for consumers and procedures for redressal of consumer grievances. The centre should impart consumer education and undertake research and extension activities. Financial assistance should be provided on a project basis by the Department of Consumer Affairs, Government of India, through the UGC or directly.

The Awareness of Consumers to be Improved

1. Consumers should be educated to visit two or more shops before purchasing any product and they should be made to understand the significance of demanding receipts for the payments made.
2. Consumers should be educated to join voluntarily the consumer co-operatives as members and use the society to safeguard their interests by availing the services at reasonable cost.
3. Consumer awareness should be created both in rural and urban areas by highlighting the rights of consumers, remedies available when cheated, the manner of lodging a complaint, the addresses of district forum, State and National Commissions.
4. A Consumer Guidance Centre should be set up by all business and government departments to maintain a close liaison with consumers.
5. Business enterprises should accept consumer protection as their '*Social Responsibility*' and they should welcome the complaints of consumers and take step to redressing them.
6. Frequent exhibitions and demonstrations should be organised in many public places to highlight the consumers, the consumer's rights, the unfair trade practices of the traders and so on.
8. There should be a consumer education campaign through various communication media such as posters, publication, radio, television, films, lectures, seminars, workshop training and so on.
9. Educational institutions should introduce consumer education as the subject in their academic curricula.

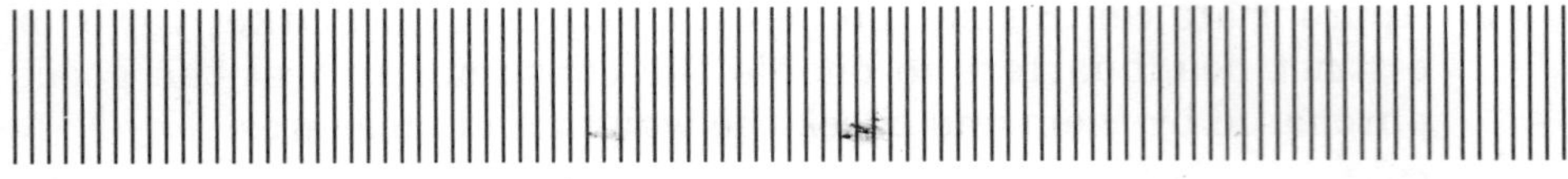

CHAPTER

13

Consumer Psychology Selling the Wireless Technology Dream

— Dr. N. Chithra
— S. Abudhahir

Introduction

Wireless' has become the buzzword of today, no longer causing us to think of our favorite radio shows, but instead to focus upon the freedom and convenience that new wireless technology can provide. This change in concept is largely due to the skill of the marketers who have dedicated themselves to finding the best way possible to sell the wireless dream to the consumer. What they have discovered, through trial and error, is that the people who most wanted wireless solutions in their lives needed to be *told* that they wanted them and that a description of what the technology could do was, to many, useless unless put into an everyday lifestyle context.

The Consumer Decision Making Process

It's important to bear in mind that one of the key aspects of consumer psychology lies in the decision-making process. This comes about as an attempt to 'solve problems'. A *problem,* in the consumer psychology sense, can be described as "a need or desire that is, as yet, unfulfilled." For example, a businesswoman may want to reach her office in under thirty minutes by car, but is subject to constant traffic delays which slow her down. In this instance, a service that could offer a personalized daily route planner to steer her clear of any traffic hold-ups would be of particular value, as it would fulfill a need by solving her particular problem.

Major and Minor Problems

Problems can be major or minor. Major problems such as unemployment have an impact upon minor problems and push them into the background. This, of course, means that unforeseen changes to the economy can consequently have a huge knock-on effect upon product sales, no matter how many consumer problems they may appear to solve during times of economic growth.

Problem Recognition

Consumers will often create their own problems by drawing internal comparisons upon what their life is and what they want it to be. Discrepancies will undoubtedly be found in some areas and, once the consumer has pinpointed these, a psychological balancing act will take place to determine whether the weight or difference is great enough to justify action being taken. If justification is made, then either consciously or unconsciously the consumer will begin to search for solutions, usually in the form of a product or service.

Active and Inactive Problems

There are two primary types of problems in consumer psychology: *active* and *inactive*. An active problem is one that requires immediate attention; for example, you have a toothache and you need to relieve the pain without delay. With an inactive problem on the other hand, the consumer may not be aware that their situation is indeed a problem; for example, they may not realize that they could double their modem speed by using a particular plug-in device.

Links to Maslow

Maslow taught us through his *hierarchy of needs* theory that active problems follow a strict order of internal significance. In other words, once we have satisfied our primary instinctive need for food, warmth and shelter, our psyche is free to attain higher levels of satisfaction such as those relating to self-esteem and a sense of belonging. The search for attainment of these higher-level needs initially falls into our category of inactive problems, as they are not considered a necessary part of our internal life-style model and exist, for the most part, on a subconscious level. Necessity is born only when our inactive needs are stimulated and enhanced by both our external and internal perception of the world around us. Our search for fulfilment of these needs then becomes an active problem when their characteristics become seen as necessary to our life-style.

Lifestyle Model Reinforcement

Furthermore, active problems are often effectively stimulated and reinforced by marketers in their drive to provide prospective purchasers with the perfect *lifestyle-model,* that is, a glimpse into the perfect lifestyle where the attributes of your product are seen to be key to finding a better way of life. The power of the life-style model lies in its subconscious link to the feelings of fulfillment and acceptance being sought by the consumer. Good technology marketers know that inactive problems are the ones most commonly used to introduce new products into the marketplace. Indeed, the marketer will often create a problem for the consumer that is initially inactive, but then gradually grows in significance to the consumer through repeated media exposure routes, until it becomes an active problem that requires immediate attention.

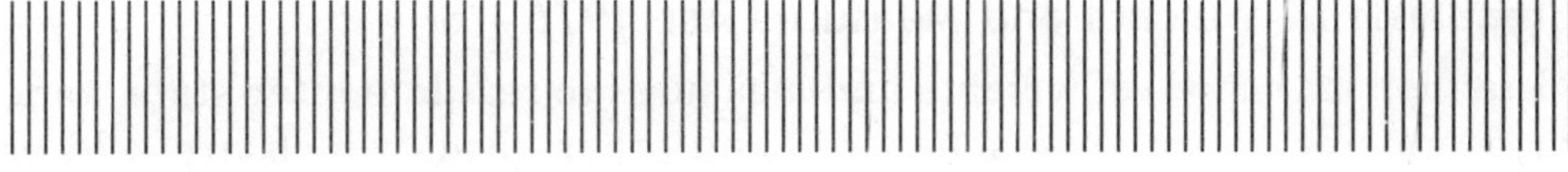

CHAPTER

14

Legal Measures of Consumer Protection

— Mrs. M. Paritha Begam

Definition

The consumer is an important part of economic system in any country and every individual is a consumer. Thus on Ist March 2001 in India there were 102 crore consumers which are cared by the government through various acts, regulatory authorities and administrative actions and Central and state governments have been very thoughtful to safeguard the interest of consumers even before independence but the level of protection and their rights awareness has been evolved over a long period.

Consumer Protection Before 1986 Act

Before Consumer Protection Act was enacted in 1986 there were following main laws to protect the consumers:

- Defense of India Rules
- Trade Marks Act, 1969
- Essential Commodities Act, 1955
- Monopoly and Restrictive Trade Practices Act 1969 which was throughly amended after 1991 and unfair trade practices were included in it.
- Standards of Weights and Measures Act, 1951
- AG Mark Act
- Food Adulteration Act

Standards of Weights and Measures Act 1976

Establish standards of weights and measures to regulate inter-state trade or commerce in weights, measures and other goods which are sold or distributed by weights, measure or number". The basic objective of the Act is that con-sumer gets the quantity as agreed and is not cheated in this regard but the Act has tried to achieve other objectives too which will be clear from the following description.

Trade and Merchandise Marks Act

This Act aims to provide for the registration and better protection of trademarks and for the prevention of the use of fraudulent marks on merchandizes. After valid registration of a trade mark the registration gives to the registered proprietor of the trade mark the exclusive right to the use of the trade mark in relation to goods in respect of which the trade mark is registered.

Trade Mark Act 1999

To amend and consolidate the law relating to trade marks to provide for registration and better protection of the trade marks for goods and services and for the prevention of the use of fraudulent marks.

ISI Marks

Bureau of Indian Standards has prescribed standards for large number of products with regard to specifications of materials to be used, processes to be applied. Standards have been fixed for strength, finish, safety etc. In some cases like electrical appliances use of ISI standards has been made compulsory for the protection of user. Thus ISI marks assure that the goods are having the quality as prescribed in the standards of Bureau of Indian Standards.

AG Mark

AG MARK for agricultural products which is mark that goods are as per standards laid down. These standard have been fixed for almost all the agricultural products including wheat, rice, spices, ghee etc.

Food Adulteration Act

This Act has been passed to ensure that consumer gets unadultered products be it wheat, rice, pulses, spices, milk, vegetable oils or other food products etc. If some one is found guilty there is severe punishment which is vehemently opposed by trade and industry and their associations. First they object to the standards fixed and secondly to severe punishment even when one, is selling packed goods.

Laws to Control Price and Distribution

The government controls prices and distribution system through various laws amongst which following are most important.

Industrial (Development and Regulation) Act 1951

To provide for the develop-ment and regulation of certain industries as specified in the first schedule which includes almost all industries metallurgical, fuels, boilers and steam generating plants, prime mover, electrical equipment, telecommunications, transportation, industrial machinery processing industries, vegetable oils and *vanaspati*, soaps, cosmetics and toilet preparations, rubber goods, leather goods, glue and *gelatine*, glass, ceramics, cement and gypsum products, timber products, *defence* industries and miscellaneous industries.

Essential Commodities Act

Essential Commodities Act 1955 was enacted in 1955 "to provide in the interests of the general public for the control of the production, supply and distribution, of and trade and commerce in certain commodities" as per preamble of the Act. The Act has been amended from time to time specially in 198 The essential commodities have been defined in the act which means cattle fodder, including oil cakes and other concentrates. coal including coke and other derivatives, component parts and acces-sories of automobiles, cotton and woollen textiles, drugs, foodstuffs, including edible oils seeds and oils, iron and steel, including manufactured products of iron and steel paper including newsprint, raw cotton, whether ginned or unginned and cotton seed and raw jute.

Monopolies and Restrictive Trade Practices Commission

Monopolistic trade practice is which has or likely to have the effect of:

1. Maintaining prices at an unreasonable level by limiting, reducing or otherwise controlling the production, supply or distribution of goods of any description or the supply of any services or in any other manner.
2. Unreasonably preventing or lessen competition in the production, supply or distribution of any goods or in the supply of any services.
3. Limiting technical development or capital investment to the common detriment or allowing the quality of any good produced, supplied or distributed, or any service rendered, in India to deteriorate.

Restrictive trade practice means a trade practice which has, or may have the effect of preventing or distorting or restricting competition in any manner and in particular:

I. Which tends to obstruct the flow of capital or resources into the stream of production; or

II. Which tends to bring about manipulation of prices, or conditions of delivery or to effect the flow of supplies in the market relating to goods or services in such manner as to impose on the consumer unjustified costs or restrictions.

Consumer Protection Act (COPRA)

1986 the Consumer Protection Act was passed to provide for the better protection of the interest of consumers and for that purpose to make provisions for the establishment of consumers councils and other authorities for the settlement of the consumers dis-putes and for matters connected therewith.

Conclusion

The objectives of state policy are to ensure that transactions are fair and consumer must be provided full information and nothing should be concealed. Secondly, there should be discrimination against any class based on sex, race, colour, region, income level, religion, culture, caste or for any other reason. Similarly various regulatory authorities have taken greater interest to protect consumers; still the level of protection in India is much lower than in developed countries because of lack of consumer movement.

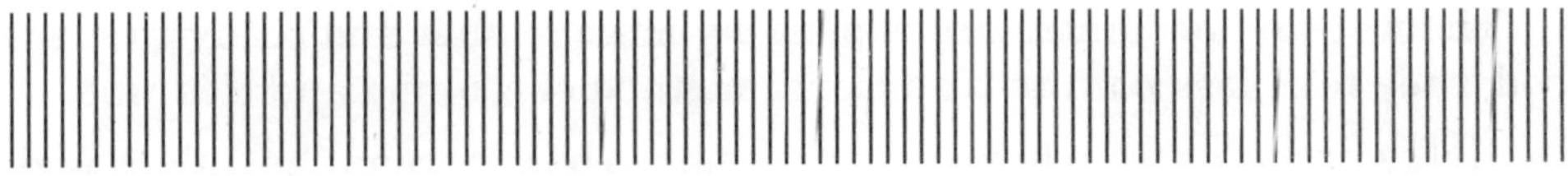

CHAPTER

15

Changing Trends in Indian Consumer Behaviour

—Dr. V. Balasubramanian

Introduction

Increasing Awareness of Indian Consumers

Over the years, as a result of the increasing literacy in the country, exposure to the west, satellite television, foreign magazines and newspapers, there is a significant increase of consumer awareness among the Indians.

Today more and more consumers are selective on the quality of the products/services.

This awareness has made the Indian consumers seek more and more reliable sources for purchases such as organized retail chains that have a corporate background and where the accountability is more pronounced. The consumer also seeks to purchase from a place where his/her feedback is more valued.

Indian consumers are now more aware and discerning, and are knowledgeable about technology, products and the market and are beginning to demand benefits beyond just availability of a range of products that came from 'trusted' manufacturers.

The Indian consumers are price sensitive and prefer to buy value for money products.

Bulk Purchasing

Urbanization is taking place in India at a dramatic pace and is influencing the life style and buying behaviour of the consumers.

The working urbanites are depending more on fast and ready-to-serve food, they take less pain in traditional method of cooking and cleaning.

Bulk purchases from hyper stores seems to be the trend these days with purchasing becoming more of a once-a-week affair, rather than frequent visits to the neighbourhood market/store/vendor.

The popular growing shopping trend among urbanities is purchasing from super markets to hyper stores.

Trendy Lifestyles

The current urban middle and upper class Indian consumer buying behaviour to a large extent has western influence. There is an increase in positive attitude towards western trends. The Indian consumer has become much more open-minded and experimental in his/her perspective. There is now an exponential growth of western trend reaching the Indian consumer by way of the media and Indians working abroad.

Foreign brands have gained wide consumer acceptance in India, they include items such as:

- Beverages
- Packed food
- Ready to eat food
- Pre-cooked food
- Canned food
- Personal care products
- Audio/video products
- Garment and apparel
- Footwear
- Sportswear
- Toys
- Gift items

Foreign brands vie increasingly with domestic brands for the growing market in India. Foreign made furniture is well accepted by the Indian consumers. Malaysian, Chinese, Italian furniture are growing in popularity in India.

Indian consumers have also developed lifestyles which have emerged from changing attitudes and mind sets; exposure to western influences and a need for self-gratification. Beauty parlours in cities, eateries, designer wear, watches, hi-tech products are a few instances which reflect these changes.

Buyer's Market in the Making

The sellers' market is slowly moving towards becoming the buyers' market.

Since, India's economic liberalization policies were initiated in 1991, many new product offerings have entered the Indian market and product variety has also increased manifold.

Import licensing restrictions are being eliminated and tariffs significantly reduced and this has led to large range of consumer goods made available in India.

Indian consumers have always preferred foreign goods and with the liberalization, they now have a choice of foreign products vis-à-vis the local products.

Consumer Spending Behaviour

The Indian consumer spending has increased from US$ 133.60 in 1992-93 to US$ 350.74 in 2002-03, a compound annual growth of 10.13 per cent at current prices.

The way Indian consumers are spending their money on various items has changed in recent years. The share being spent on the basis (food and beverages) has fallen from 54.07 per cent in 1992-93 to 44.8 per cent in 2002-03. Other items have increased in importance, for example, medical and healthcare spending has increased from 3.5 per cent to 8.5 per cent of total expenditure over the same period, a compound growth rate of 19.71 per cent. Similarly spending on transport and communication has grown at 13.2 per cent.

While the Compound Annual Growth Rate (CAGR) in total consumer spending has been around 12 per cent a year over the past decade, there have been sharp ups and downs. Consumer expenditure has been in tandem with the annual GDP growth.

For rural India, per capita 30 days' consumer expenditure of US$ 12.34 was split up into US$ 6.78, on an average, for food, and US$ 5.56 for non-food. Food expenditure included US$ 2.25 for cereals and cereal substitutes, and US$ 2.37 for milk, milk products, vegetables, edible oil and US$ 2.16 on others. Non-food expenditure included US$ 1.11 for fuel and light, and another US$1.00 for clothing, footwear and US$3.45 on other non-food expenditure.

For the urban sector, average Monthly Per Capita Consumer Expenditure (MPCE) of US$ 23.53 was split up into US$ 10.00 for food and US$ 13.53 for non-food. Of food expenditure, US$ 2.37 went towards cereals and cereal substitutes while US$ 3.67 was spent on milk, milk products, vegetables and edible oil and US$3.96 on other food items. US$ 2.11 was spent per person per month on fuel and light, and US$ 1.65 on clothing and footwear and US$9.77 on other non-food items.

Urban expenditure levels per capita exceeded rural levels for all the product groups, except on cereals and cereal substitutes. The average monthly per capita expenditures on cereals and cereal substitutes for rural and urban areas are very close to each other.

The gap between rural and urban averages of MPCE was of the order of US$ 11.16. The item-groups viz. milk and milk products, beverages etc, fuel and light, education, miscellaneous consumer goods and services, conveyance and rent contributed to the gap significantly.

Non-food expenditure per person in the urban sector was more than double of that for the rural sector, where it was about US$ 5.55.

In India, the higher income group (>US$2,465) spends more amount of their income on luxury goods and trendy products than fact moving consumer products.

The middle income group (US$1,162–US$1,190) spends more on consumer expendables than the rich.

Combined the middle and the lower income group provide 60 per cent of the value of the Indian market.

Conclusion

Top class, middle class and lower class are income related classifications of the population and each of this class has its own consumption pattern.

For the Indian market, Malaysian exporters/manufacturers should see the substantial middle class and base the market demand/projections on this roughly estimated at 250 million people with substantial disposable income.

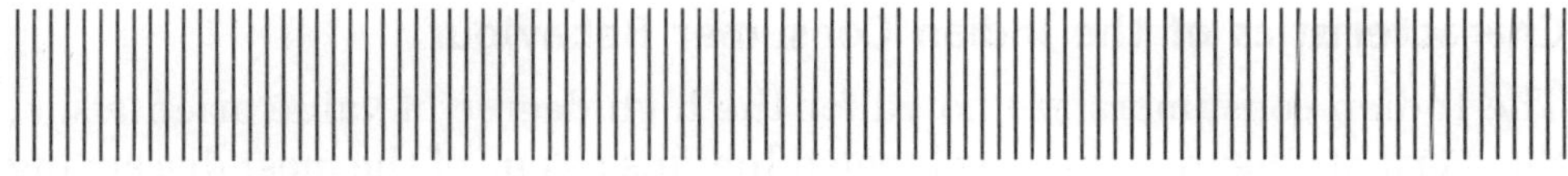

CHAPTER

16

Product Market Study

Consumer Behaviour in India

—Dr. P. Mohamed Sirajudeen

Introduction

This study on Indian consumer behaviour is aimed at helping International businessmen to get a better understanding of the Indian market place thus enabling them to embark on selected strategies to effectively reach the Indian consumers.

India is a big country with 28 states, over one billion people and 120 dialects/languages.

From the market perspective, people of India comprise different segments of consumers, based on class, status, and income.

An important and recent development in India's consumerism is the emergence of the rural market for several basic consumer goods. Three-fourths of India's population lives in rural areas, and contribute one-third of the national income. This rural population is spread all over India, in close to 0.6 million villages.

India is a lucrative market even though the per capita income in India is low and it remains a huge market, even for costly products.

Among the total 164.8 million households in India, 80.7 million households comes under low income group (<US$ 581), followed by 50.4 million lower middle income households (US$ 581 to US$ 1162), 19.7 million middle income group (US$ 1162 to US$ 1190), 8.2 million upper middle income group (US$ 1790 to US$ 2465) and 5.8 million high income group (>US$ 2465).

Characteristics of the Indian Consumer Behaviour

The Indian consumers are noted for the high degree of value orientation. Such orientation to value has labeled Indians as one of the most discerning consumers in the world. Even, luxury brands have to design a unique pricing strategy in order to get a foothold in the Indian market.

Indian consumers have a high degree of family orientation. This orientation in fact, extends to the extended family and friends as well. Brands with identities that support family values tend to be popular and accepted easily in the Indian market.

Indian consumers are also associated with values of nurturing, care and affection. These values are far more dominant that values of ambition and achievement. Product which communicate feelings and emotions gel with the Indian consumers.

Apart from psychology and economics, the role of history and tradition in shaping the Indian consumer behavior is quite unique. Perhaps, only in India, one sees traditional products along side modern products. For example, hair oils and tooth powder existing with shampoos and toothpaste.

Different Segments of Indian Consumers

The Socialites

Socialites belong to the upper class. They prefer to shop in specialty stores, go to clubs on weekends, and spend a good amount on luxury goods. They are always looking for something different. They are the darlings of exclusive establishments. They go for high value, exclusive products. Socialites are also very brand conscious and would go only for the best known in the market.

The Conservatives

The Conservatives belong to the middle class. The conservative segment is the reflection of the true Indian culture. They are traditional in their outlook, cautious in their approach towards purchases; spend more time with family than in partying and focus more on savings than spending. Slow in decision making, they seek a lot of information before making any purchase. They look for durability and functionality but at the same time is also image conscious.

They prefer high value consumer products, but often have to settle for the more affordable one. These habits in turn affect their purchasing habits where they are trying to go for the middle and upper middle level priced products.

The Working Women

The working woman segment is the one, which has seen a tremendous growth in the late nineties. This segment has opened the floodgates for the Indian retailers. The working woman today has grown out of her long-standing image of being the homemaker. Today, she is rubbing shoulders with men, proving herself to be equally good, if not better. Working women have their own mind in decision to purchase the products that appeal to them.

India's Rich People

India's rich can be categorized into five major categories as follows:

The Rich

The rich have income greater than US$11,000/- per annum. Total household having such incomes are 1,058,961. These people are upwardly mobile. Some of them in this category are Double Income No Kids (DINK) households. They spend more on leisure and entertainment-activities than on future looking investments. Across the category, backgrounds are distinctly middle class. They aspire, therefore, to attain the super-rich status.

The Super Rich

The Super Rich have income greater than US$22,000/- per annum. Total number of households is 320,900. There are less DINK families here than in the rich category. The Super Rich are mainly professionals and devoted to consumerism. They buy many durables and are status conscious.

The Ultra Rich

The Ultra Rich have income greater than US$44,000/- per annum. The number of households in this category is 98,289. There is no typical profile of the ultra-rich. There are some DINK households of middle-level executives. Some single earning households are of first generation entrepreneurs. Some rich farmers, who have been rich for a long time, belong to this category.

The Sheer Rich

The Sheer Rich is made up by households having income exceeding US$110,000/- per annum. Such households are 20,863. They do not have a homogenous profile. There are joint families as well as nuclear families in this category. They consume services greatly. They own multiple cars and houses. They aspire to social status and power.

The Obscenely Rich

The Obscenely Rich is made up of households having income exceeding US$222,000/- per annum. There are hardly 6,515 such households in India.

They are first-generation entrepreneurs who have made it big. Some of them are techies. A variety of people belong to this category. They are just equivalent to the rich in the developed countries. They crave for exclusivity in what they buy. Most premium brands are relevant to them.

Rural Consumer

About three quarters of the Indian population are in the rural areas and with the growing middle class, specially in the Indian cities, the spill over effect of the growing urban middle class is also felt in the rural areas.

The Indian rural market has been growing at 3-4% per annum, adding more than 1 million new consumers every year and now accounts for close to 50 per cent of the volume consumption of fast-moving consumer goods (FMCG) in India. The market size of the fast moving consumer goods sector is projected to more than double to US$ 23.25 billion by 2010 from the present US$ 11.16 billion. As a result, it is becoming an important market place for fast moving consumer goods as well as consumer durables.

Increasing Awareness of Indian Consumers

Over the years, as a result of the increasing literacy in the country, exposure to the west, satellite television, foreign magazines and newspapers, there is a significant increase of consumer awareness among the Indians.

Today more and more consumers are selective on the quality of the products/services.

This awareness has made the Indian consumers seek more and more reliable sources for purchases such as organized retail chains that have a corporate background and where the accountability is more pronounced. The consumer also seeks to purchase from a place where his/her feedback is more valued.

Indian consumers are now more aware and discerning, and are knowledgeable about technology, products and the market and are beginning to demand benefits beyond just availability of a range of products that came from 'trusted' manufacturers.

The Indian consumers are price sensitive and prefer to buy value for money products.

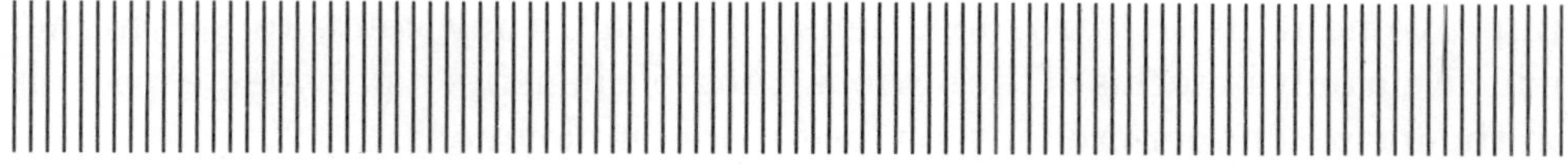

CHAPTER

17

Education, Rights and the Spectre of Consumerism

—S. Chandrasekaran

There can be no doubt that anyone with the intellectual potential and ability to benefit from higher education should have the opportunity to study at that level. No-one should be denied the opportunity on irrelevant grounds such as race, ethnicity, gender, age or poverty. Anti-discrimination laws and policies, wider availability of scholarships and loans, and more flexible forms of study such as part-time programs and distance learning courses, mean nowadays that far more people than before are able to take the opportunity to study in higher education. That is as it should be. A civilized country needs a talented and educated population, not merely for vocational reasons but also because education provides the best means for ensuring that human beings—and the communities and nations they create—live together pleasantly and peacefully.

Unfortunately, however, debates over widening access to higher education have been hijacked by the language of law. The breaking down of barriers of privilege has led to the perception that the experience of higher education is to be enjoyed as of right. This paradigm shift towards a 'rights culture' in education has led to the universities' being haunted by the spectre of consumerism.

The term 'consumerism' denotes the belief that individuals obtain both gratification and social standing primarily through their consumption of tangible products. So far as higher education is concerned, consumerism implies that students cease to see higher education as a vehicle for self-improvement in the broadest sense. Instead, they come to see higher education only in terms of the obvious, tangible benefits it provides, especially in the form of paper credentials for future employment.

The intrusion of a legal paradigm into higher education has laid the foundations for educational consumerism in two respects. First, usage of the language of 'rights' has shifted the focus from the *provision* of education to the existence of a *right* to education. Secondly, as part of a wider development in Western legal culture, rights have become reified. Formerly the idea of a legal right was that it represented a type of relationship between individuals or between an individual and society at large. Now, however, a right has come to be seen as an object or thing to be possessed. 'Having' first the right to an education and, subsequently, the right to advertise a Bachelor's or graduate degree is thus becoming more important than becoming educated.

Instead, therefore, of focusing on how best to provide quality higher education for all those capable of benefiting from it, the rhetoric of public policy regarding universities seems increasingly to focus misguidedly on legal issues of rights. This paradigm shift might be more acceptable if the existence of a 'right' to something automatically meant that that 'thing' itself was provided, but everyone knows that having a right and being able to exercise that right are two very different things. A 'right' means an entitlement; it does not mean the fulfilment of that entitlement. Indeed, most people do not obtain their education because of some putative 'right' but as a result of their good fortune in having reasonably enlightened parents. Moreover, the existence of a 'right' to education also fails to address issues of equity since having a 'right' to education says nothing about the *quality* of the education provided to each individual. As the Association of American Colleges and Universities has recently reported, while there are many top quality higher education programs, there are also many others whose educational value is very much open to doubt.

Some commentators have mistakenly identified this problem as one of 'commodification', arguing the cost of university access effects a cultural cheapening of higher education. This argument is, however, both simplistic and misleading. Education always has been bought and sold. It was the case, for example, at Plato's Academy way back in 387 BC, yet it can hardly be argued that advances in mathematics, astronomy or medicine attributable to advanced study by the Ancient Greeks were cheapened because students had to pay for their education. Indeed, the very model of a modern university was created by the Palace School of the Emperor Charlemagne as long ago as AD 782: again, all students were forced to pay for the privilege. Education has not recently become commodified—it has always been a commodity.

But never before has a student been seen as a consumer. Farrington has pointed out that: "In the mediaeval universities, scholars had particular obligations to fulfil if they were to remain matriculated". Students of a consumerist bent, however, are unlikely to be interested in studying or working at anything which has no clear connection with their grades or future employment prospects. Instead, they are increasingly ready to challenge any grades that are not as high as they feel they require for their chosen career path—regardless of the intrinsic worth of the piece of work produced—since the only purpose which they can identify for higher education is to give them the right to say that they possess a particular qualification. According to this view, students are not obliged to take responsibility for their own learning precisely because they have the *right* to an education—something that entails no obligations on his or her part. It is simply the responsibility of the professor to ensure that the student is educated. But since a right cannot be worthwhile unless it can truly be represented by some tangible 'thing', students demand paper qualifications and transcripts which record good grades. So the right to higher education becomes the right to demand a good degree, regardless of student capability or achievement.

Unfortunately, universities themselves must take some of the blame for this. Universities frequently advertise their 'wares' as though brands on offer in a sort of educational Wal-Mart. In the current era in the United States, for example, all too many college presidents not only describe students inappropriately as customers, but also stand by while their institutions' catalogs describe in detail the supposed utility in the job market of obtaining a degree while singularly failing to explain the inherent worth of the education which it is ostensibly that institution's mission to provide. At the same time, academics not only 'dumb down' courses so that few students can fail them, they are also becoming increasingly wary of giving students bad grades for fear that this will sully the reputation of the institution—because it needs to be known as a place where an easy route to subsequent employment can be found. Sperber has called this a "non-aggression pact... between many faculty members and students" in which "[t]he glue that keeps the pact intact is grade inflation".

The picture is not, however, one of total doom and gloom. Ironically, one of the major obstacles to the unbridled application of consumerism in higher education has proved to be the judiciary. The actual application of legal rights—as opposed to the misplaced rhetoric of rights – simply does not mix well with higher education. Time and time again the courts have emphasised that they will not second-guess matters of academic judgment. It is long overdue for universities to regain their self-confidence and to reassert a true sense of mission. Their function is not to train but to educate; and so far as admissions are concerned, the issue is not one of universal rights but of equity.

REFERENCES

- *The Law of Higher Education* (London: Butterworths, 1994) p. 355.
- *How Undergraduate Education Became College Life—and a Personal Apology'* in R.H. Hersh and J. Merrow, *Declining by Degrees: Higher Education at Risk* (New York: Palgrave Macmillan, 2005) p. 138.

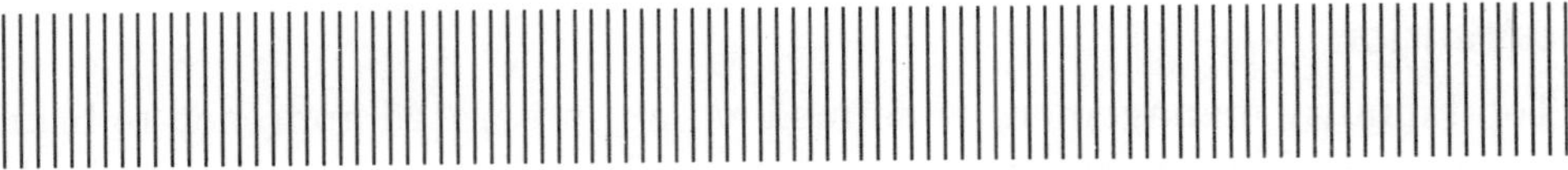

CHAPTER

18

Customer Satisfaction Through Proper Planning and TQM

— Dr. M. Gomatheeswaran
— Dr. T. Sivagnanasithi

Introduction

Total quality management may yet be regarded as a passing fed. However, the underlying themes of management being addressed by those who are striving to define and move to a new paradigm are not lads. These themes include the importance of understanding customer needs formulating strategies to provide value to customers and continuously improving organizational system to provide that value. Let's take a closer look at each of these themes:

Evoluation of TQM

It's evaluation from 1900's is given below:

1900	:	Quality was controlled by the operator
1925	:	with more advanced assembly line and mass production, quality become the responsibility of a form an
1950	:	There came a separate inspection department which was responsible for quality
1970	:	Use of statistical quality control tools for controlling quality became popular
1985	:	Concept of total quality control
1990	:	TQC and company wide control became more popular
2000	:	Total quality management and international standard like ISO 9000.

Definition

Total quality management is defined as "an integrated approach to bring continuous improvement in products and services using proper tools, technology and training to meet customer's expectations on a continuous basis.

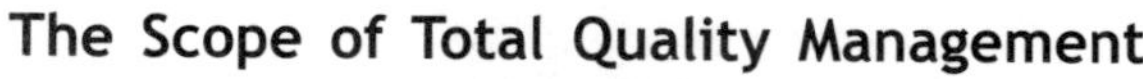

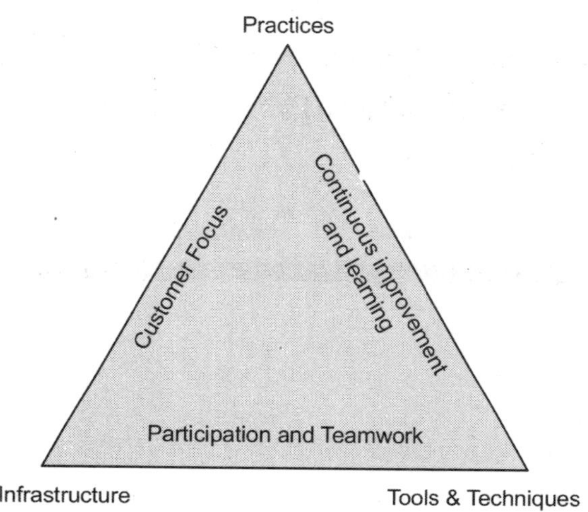

Infrastructure

Infrastructure refers to the basic systems of management that are necessary too function as a high-performing organization.

Practices

Practices are those activities that occur with in a management system to achieve high performance objectives.

Tools

Tools include various graphical and statistical methods to plan work activities, collect data, analyse results, monitor progress and solve problems.

Basic Concepts of TQM

- Effective involvement and utilization of the entire workforce
- Continuous improvement of the business and production process
- Treating suppliers as partners
- Establish performance measures for the processes

Principles of TQM

Total quality management stresses on three principals:

- Customer satisfaction
- Employee involvement
- Continuous improvement in quality

Customer Satisfaction

Customer satisfaction is a relative concept that various from one customer to another. Also a customer may be satisfied with today's product but not satisfied in future.

Employee Involvement

Employees must be involved in quality management by encouraging them to use quality control tools and techniques to track performance and identity areas needing improvement.

Continuous Improvement

It is a never ending process and is driven by knowledge and problem-solving.

Benefits of TQM

Tangible Benefits

Better product Quality

Productivity improvement

Reduced quality cost

Increased market

Increased profitability

Reduced employee grievances

Intangible Benefits

Effective team work

Job interest

Customer satisfaction

Better company image

Enhanced problem-solving capacity

Necessity for TQM

- TQM adds value to the services offered to the customers

- All personnel are involved, which improves motivation and commitment
- TQM provides assurance that performance and processed are well understand
- TQM is economic in the long term to both the company and its customers

Leadership and Strategic Planning for TQM

Leadership

Leadership is the ability to positive influence people and systems under one's authority to have a meaningful impact and achieve important results. Leaders may seek to motivate employees and develop enthusiasm for quality and rhetoric but actions speak louder than words.

Strategic Planning

Strategic business planning drives the quality improvement throughout the organisation. Strategic planning helps to anticipate many changes such as customer's expectations new business opportunities, technology developments new customer segment community / societal expectations, evolving regulatory requirements and thrust by competitors.

Leadership and Strategic Planning for TQM

One of the critical aspects of leadership is strategic planning. Strategic planning enables and could be fire to 10 yrs in the future.

A strategic is a plan that integrates organisations major goals, policies and action sequence in to cohesive whole formal strategies contain three elements:

(*a*) Goals to be achieved;

(*b*) Polices that guide or limit action; and

(*c*) Action sequence or programmes that accomplish the goals.

Effect strategies revolve around the key concepts or thrust areas such as customer satisfaction-which provide focus. Strategic planning helps to build strong posture to enable the organization achieve its goals despite unforeseeable external forces.

Human Resource Management for TQM

Nowadays, the total quality movement has caused business to look more closely at the human side of work the focus on customer satisfaction and flexibility to meet over changing customer demands has brought new approaches to work design and employee development HRM is addressed with in a quality environment, focusing on the design and management of high performance work systems.

Organising for TQM

Quality or lack of quality, impact the entire organization from supplier to customer and from product design to maintenance. A successful set of activities begins with an organizational environment that fosters quality, followed by an understanding of the principles of quality and then an effort to engage employees in the necessary activities to implement quality. When things are done well, the organization typically satisfies its customers and obtains a competitive advantage, the ultimate goal of winning the customers.

Quality Measurement

There are various methods of quality measurement such as statistical process control, bench marking and customer satisfaction measurement of customer satisfaction forms the core building blocks of quality management. Measurement of customer satisfaction is a way how firms measure their quality. Customer satisfaction is a post-consumption experience which compares perceived quality with expected quality. It measures how products are services supplied by a company meet customer expectations. It is a key performance indicator of a firm. Customer satisfaction depends on service quality, price, timeless, efficiency and physical environment of their firm.

Conclusion

In the future there will be two kinds of companies, those who have implemented and those who have not implemented the TQM. For the implementation of TQM—certain concepts of TQM are identified. There are transformational leadership, strategic planning, HRM, TQM doesn't measure customer satisfaction directly but there are certain key dimension related to the human factors of the enterprise that would play a prominent role.

REFERENCES

- *Shridhara Bhat, "Total Quality Management"*
- Dr.D.D Sharma, *"Total Quality Management"*
- Bounds yorks ADAMS RANNEY, *"Total Quality Management"*
- G.R BASOTIA, *"Total Quality Management"*
- JAMES W. Cotada, *"TQM for Information System Management"*

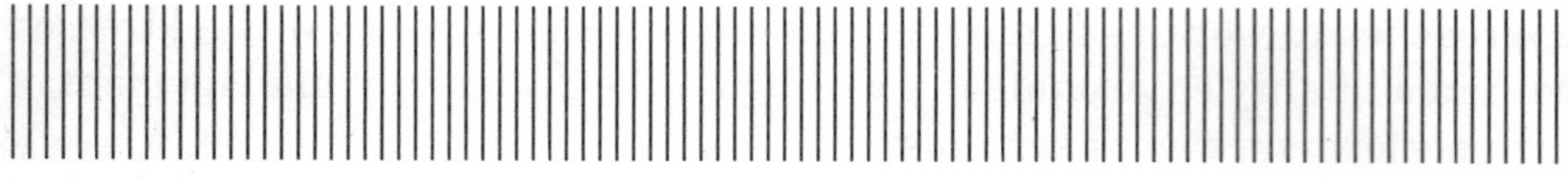

CHAPTER

19

Consumer Satisfaction and Total Quality Management

—Dr. S. Sivasankaran

Introduction

Total quality management (TQM) ought to go beyond the traditional meaning of the quality of a product or service; it should include not only customer satisfaction, but also efficiency, productivity, quality of work life, commitment and loyalty within the organization. It is also about more than just listening to the customer, which means that the organization ought to integrate its quality performance targets within its corporate social responsibility strategy—that is, to analyze more the 'big picture', which incorporates the important notion that the perceptions of the customer ought to equate to those of the supplier. Inevitably, quality and its continuous improvement take time. What is required is a long-term commitment to the fundamentals to be perceived more as a process than a one-off plan. Thus, the two basic elements highlighted are: (1) to ascertain a sound formula based on a careful examination of an organization's past performance and future goals; and (2) to install a sophisticated programmed of training for all levels of the organization, emanating from the leadership. Total quality management is a key ingredient towards achieving business excellence, but must embrace an all-inclusive approach.

Total Quality Management is an approach to the art of management that originated in Japanese industry in the 1950's and has become steadily more popular in the West since the early 1980's. Total Quality is a description of the culture, attitude and organization of a company that aims to provide, and continue to provide, its customers with products and services that satisfy their needs. The culture requires quality in all aspects of the company's operations, with things being done right first time, and defects and waste eradicated from operations.

Many companies have difficulties in implementing TQM. Surveys by consulting firms have found that only 20-36 per cent of companies that have undertaken TQM have achieved either significant or even tangible improvements in quality, productivity, competitiveness or financial return. As a result many people are skeptical about TQM. However, when you look at successful companies you find a much higher percentage of successful TQM implementation.

Some useful messages from results of TQM implementations:

- if you want to be a first-rate company, don't focus on the second-rate companies who can't handle TQM, look at the world-class companies that have adopted it;
- the most effective way to spend TQM introduction funds is by training top management, people involved in new product development, and people involved with customers;
- it's much easier to introduce EDM/PDM in a company with a TQM culture than in one without TQM. People in companies that have implemented TQM are more likely to have the basic understanding necessary for implementing EDM/PDM. For example, they are more likely to view EDM/PDM as an information and workflow management system supporting the entire product life cycle then as a departmental solution for the management of CAD data.

Important aspects of TQM include customer-driven quality, top management leadership and commitment, continuous improvement, fast response, actions based on facts, employee participation, and a TQM culture.

Customer-driven Quality

TQM has a customer-first orientation. The customer, not internal activities and constraints, comes first. Customer satisfaction is seen as the company's highest priority. The company believes it will only be successful if customers are satisfied. The TQM company is sensitive to customer requirements and responds rapidly to them. In the TQM context, 'being sensitive to customer requirements' goes beyond defect and error reduction, and merely meeting specifications or reducing customer complaints. The concept of requirements is expanded to take in not only product and service attributes that meet basic requirements, but also those that enhance and differentiate them for competitive advantage.

Each part of the company is involved in Total Quality, operating as a customer to some functions and as a supplier to others. The Engineering Department is a supplier to downstream functions such as Manufacturing and Field Service, and has to treat these internal customers with the same sensitivity and responsiveness as it would external customers.

TQM Leadership from Top Management

TQM is a way of life for a company. It has to be introduced and led by top management. This is a key point. Attempts to implement TQM often fail because top management doesn't lead and get committed - instead it delegates and pays lip service. Commitment and personal involvement is required from top management in creating and deploying clear quality values and goals consistent with the objectives of the company, and in creating and deploying well defined systems, methods and performance measures for achieving those goals. These systems and methods guide all quality activities and encourage participation by all employees. The development and use of performance indicators is linked, directly or indirectly, to customer requirements and satisfaction, and to management and employee remuneration.

Continuous Improvement

Continuous improvement of all operations and activities is at the heart of TQM. Once it is recognized that customer satisfaction can only be obtained by providing a high-quality product, continuous improvement of the quality of the product is seen as the only way to maintain a high level of customer satisfaction. As well as recognizing the link between product quality and customer satisfaction, TQM also recognizes that product quality is the result of process quality. As a result, there is a focus on continuous improvement of the company's processes. This will lead to an improvement in process quality. In turn this will lead to an improvement in product quality, and to an increase in customer satisfaction. Improvement cycles are encouraged for all the company's activities such as product development, use of EDM/PDM, and the way customer relationships are managed. This implies that all activities include measurement and monitoring of cycle time and responsiveness as a basis for seeking opportunities for improvement.

Elimination of waste is a major component of the continuous improvement approach. There is also a strong emphasis on prevention rather than detection, and an emphasis on quality at the design stage. The customer-driven approach helps to prevent errors and achieve defect-free production. When problems do occur within the product development process, they are generally discovered and resolved before they can get to the next internal customer.

Fast Response

To achieve customer satisfaction, the company has to respond rapidly to customer needs. This implies short product and service introduction cycles. These can be achieved with customer-driven and process-oriented product development because the resulting simplicity and efficiency greatly reduce the time involved. Simplicity is gained through concurrent product and process development. Efficiencies are realized from the elimination of non-value-adding effort such as re-design. The result is a dramatic improvement in the elapsed time from product concept to first shipment.

Actions Based on Facts

The statistical analysis of engineering and manufacturing facts is an important part of TQM. Facts and analysis provide the basis for planning, review and performance tracking, improvement of operations, and comparison of performance with competitors. The TQM approach is based on the use of objective data, and provides a rational rather than an emotional basis for decision making. The statistical approach to process management in both engineering and manufacturing recognizes that most problems are system-related, and are not caused by particular employees. In practice, data is collected and put in the hands of the people who are in the best position to analyze it and then take the appropriate action to reduce costs and prevent non-conformance. Usually these people are not managers but workers in the process. If the right information is not available, then the analysis, whether it be of shop floor data, or engineering test results, can't take place, errors can't be identified, and so errors can't be corrected.

Employee Participation

A successful TQM environment requires a committed and well-trained work force that participates fully in quality improvement activities. Such participation is reinforced by reward and recognition systems which emphasize the achievement of quality objectives. On-going education and training of all employees supports the drive for quality. Employees are encouraged to take more responsibility, communicate more effectively, act creatively, and innovate. As people behave the way they are measured and remunerated, TQM links remuneration to customer satisfaction metrics.

A TQM Culture

It's not easy to introduce TQM. An open, cooperative culture has to be created by management. Employees have to be made to feel that they are responsible for customer satisfaction. They are not going to feel this if they are excluded from the development of visions, strategies, and plans. It's important they participate in these activities. They are unlikely to behave in a responsible way if they see management behaving irresponsibly—Saying one thing and doing the opposite.

Product Development in a TQM

Product development in a TQM environment is very different to product development in a non-TQM environment. Without a TQM approach, product development is usually carried on in a conflictual atmosphere where each department acts independently. Short-term results drive behaviour so scrap, changes, work-arounds, waste, and rework are normal practice. Management focuses on supervising individuals, and fire-fighting is necessary rewarded. Product development in a TQM environment is customer-driven and focussed on quality. Teams are process-oriented, and interact with their internal customers to deliver the required results. Management's focus is on controlling the overall process, and rewarding teamwork.

Awards for Quality Achievement

The Deming Prize has been awarded annually since 1951 by the Japanese Union of Scientists and Engineers in recognition of outstanding achievement in quality strategy, management and execution. Since 1988 a similar award (the Malcolm Baldrige National Quality Award) has been awarded in the US. Early winners of the Baldrige Award include AT&T (1992), IBM (1990), Milliken (1989), Motorola (1988), Texas Instruments (1992) and Xerox (1989).

Conclusion

Total Quality is a description of the culture, attitude and organization of a company that aims to provide, and continue to provide, its customers with products and services that satisfy their needs. The culture requires quality in all aspects of the company's operations, with things being done right first time, and defects and waste eradicated from operations.

Quality is the outcome of all activities that take place within an organization; that all functions and all employees have to participate in the improvement process; that organizations need both quality systems and a quality culture.".

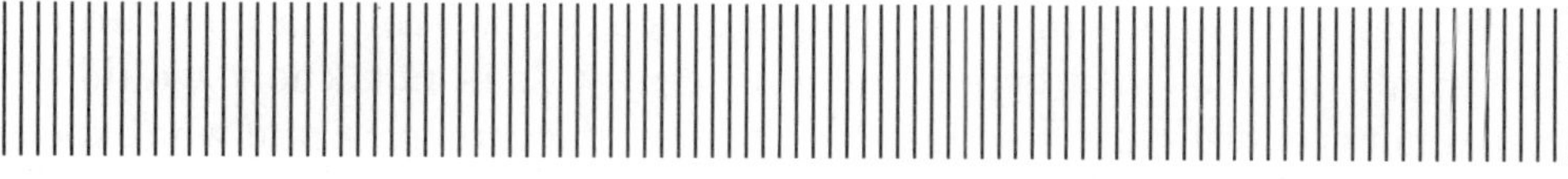

CHAPTER

20

Changing Scenario of Consumerism

— Dr. Mrs. K. Mahuthammal

ABSTRACT

Consumerism is concerned with protecting consumers from all organizations with which there is an exchange relationship. There are consumer problems associated with hospitals, libraries, schools, police forces, and various government agencies, as well as with business firms. Consumerism is a movement that promotes the interest of buyers of goods and services. It strives to protect the consumer from unsafe or low quality products, fraudulent, advertising, labelling, packaging and business practices that limit competition. It promotes adequate information about the producer so that consumer can take wise decisions in purchasing goods and services. This chapter highlight origin and growth of consumerism need for consumerism, scope of Area of business firms, Area of non-profit organizations, Area affecting quality of life in consumerism, uses of consumerism, causes of consumerism as a social movement historical perspective, consumerism in India.

Introduction

Consumerism is a phenomenon that has managed to stay in the limelight in many industrialized nations that recently went through an economic crisis. Although consumerism has been on the scene for many decades in one form or another, the term consumerism appears to be uniquely associated with the past decade.

"Consumerism means that consumer looks upon the manufacturer as somebody who is interested but who really does not know would the consumers realities are. He regarded the manufacture lives, and who expects the consumer to be able to make distinctions provide some insight into this current phenomenon referred to as consumerism.

Consumerism is the outcome of a complex interplay of forces—political ideology, production class relations, international trade, and economic theory cultural and moral values."

—*Yiannus Gabriel and Tim Lang*

"Consumerism is a social movement seeking to augment the rights and powers of buyers in relation to sellers." It is an organized movement of concerned citizens and government to enhance the right and power of buyers in relation to sellers

—*Philip Kotler*

Origin and Growth of Consumerism

During the late 1800's and early 1900's the sale of many impure and unsafe products led to an increase of consumer interest in legislation to bring about standard of quality. Formation of the national consumer league in the USA in the year 1899 was an indication of the growing strength of the consumer movement. This book led to the passing of federal food and drug act of 1906.

They also marketed many low quality products. In the late 1980's the congress passed the first anti-trust and anti-monopoly laws to protect consumers from the powerful firms. Business also began to advertise extensively to distinguish their products from those of other companies.

In 1929, consumer's research, a pioneer in product testing, was founded to provide testing and rating services for consumers.

Today's consumer groups play a larger role than ever before in supporting the inputs of consumers. Ralph Nader founded an organization in the name of the public citizen, which conduces research on products, works to influence congress and state legislatures and develops educational programmes for consumers.

Consumerism

The term consumerism was first coined by business men in the middle of 1960's as they through of the consumer movement as another 'Ism' like socialism and communism, threatening capitalism. The philosophy of marketing is based on consumer. The consumer is not only the heart of marketing but also the controller of marketing functions.

Consumerism is a movement that promotes the interest of buyers of goods and services. It strives to protect the consumer from unsafe or low quality products, fraudulent advertising, labeling, packaging and business practices that limit competition. It promotes adequate information about the producer so that consumer can take wise decisions in purchasing goods and services. Consumerism also tries to inform consumers of the effective means of obtaining compensation for damage or inconvenience caused by defective products and services.

Need for Consumerism

In an economic sense consumption means use of things for satisfaction of human wants. Today, consumption is viewed more than an economic act since the industry views consumers as groups. As Jacques observes "consumption is no longer viewed as primarily an individual economic like production". It is seen as a social process with social consequences. "The rapid globalization of production and market gives new twists to consumption patterns, involving economic cultural, environmental and moral aspects". Consumerism or consumer movement has to take care of a life excessively pre-occupied with consumption.

Consumers, being malleable creatures are often over-managed and controlled. They are in a week bargaining position. Consumerism serves as a bargaining agent for the consumers.

Rising income enhances the purchasing power of the consumers and their propensity to attain higher standard of living for which they need consumer information. "Consumers as individuals have little opportunity to gain relevant information for themselves and they are, therefore, dependent on independent consumer organizations, investigative journalists and the provisions of official information." It is also pointed out that "consumer information means knowing what your rights are and being confident enough to exercise them", it gives consumers the to redress. Hence, there is need for consumerism.

The consumer has genuine reason to belives that he is being exploited either by way of paying higher prices or taking defective goods. He is taken for a ride by misleading advertisements. Juran classified the grievances of the consumer under three heads as follows:

Scope of Consumerism

"According to William Stanton, consumerism at present covers the following three areas of consumer dissatisfaction and remedial efforts there at:

Area of Business Firms

The first perhaps the original consumer dissatisfaction generates from the area of direct exchange relationship between consumers and business firms. Thus, the core of the marketing concept is to ensure of the marketing concept is to ensure consumer satisfaction by the selling firms.

Area of Non-profit Organisations

The second area of consumer dissatisfaction comprises non-profile organizations such as government agencies, etc., with which there is an exchange relationship.

Area Affecting Quality of Life

The third area comprises environmental matters affecting the quality of life. For example air pollution, water pollution, water pollution etc.

Uses of Consumerism

Well-organised and dynamic consumerism may be expected to produce the following results.

Consumerism will provide feed back for the business. It will enable producers to understand the consumer's needs and wants. This will assist in the more effective implementation of the marketing concept or societal marketing concept, depending upon the nature of consumerism.

Producers will be able to enlist the support of consumers to minimise the imperfections in distribution. Several times the supply position is made worse by hoarding and black marketing by traders. The sellers have a tendency to charge a price which is higher than the actual by giving some reason or the other.

Consumerism as a Social Movement—Historical Perspective

Consumerism is also one of the many form of social movements. It also passes through a few developments stages, as does social movement. He not only restricted himself to his production but also started learning the advantages of other commodities. With the change in society industrial development took place, due to this not only did industry come up but even the number of cities and towns went up. This brought about employment facilities and marketing methods were established.

In the early 1900's Upton Sixlair's writings, and ethical drug scandals, exposed the shocking sanitary conditions prevailing in the packing plants of Chicogo. During the 1930's consumerism started getting maximum consumer attention resulting in understanding of the phenomenon. Research work began to be devoted to this field and thus came the evolution of the concept of consumerism.

Consumerism in India

Any attempt to trace the origin of consumer movement in India will take us back to the beginning of the trade and commerce. "In *Kautilya's Arthashastra* there use references to the concept of consumer protection against exploitation by the trade and industry short weighment and measures, adulteration and punishment for these offences. However history of consumer movement in India can be traced to the beginning of the 20th century. It is said to begin with the "formation of passengers and traffic relief Association and the women graduates union, Bombay during 1915". But the consumer movement started gaining momentum only in nineteen sixteen Indian consumers are passive and tolerant and like *sadhus* they believe in fascism and attributed the receipt of defective goods to their fate or ill luck.

Passive by nature most Indian consumers have had to put up with adulterated food, faculty weights, under measures, spurious and hazardous drugs, exorbitant prices, endemic shortages leading to blade marketing and profiteering substandard products, useless guarantees, callous and indifferent services from public utilities and a list of others ills.

Indian consumers have to face problems as I sing out of unfair trade practices, spiraling prices, misleading advertisements, poor quality of products, etc. The business has the responsibility of providing goods and services needed by the consumers at fair prices and guarding against adulteration, poor quality, defective advertisement and lack of service and courtesy.

But the altitude of business towards consumers has been found to be indifferent. Whatever be the native of market, the competition or monopoly, the worst affected is the consumer. "Where there is monopoly, the consumer is of course helpless and where there is competition, he is at the mercy of advertising.

The competitive movement is characterized by laissez faire *i.e.,* the least interference by Government in economic matters. Under the competitive selling the business is concerned with the study of the tastes and preferences of the consumers and strives to satisfy them. In other words, the altitude of business towards consumer is indifferent and the tastes and preferences of the consumers are irrelevant, unless they are compelled to sell under competitive conditions.

Conclusion

The development of consumerism in a country whether it is developed or less developed depends on its economic environment and its major components. Therefore, it is clear that consumerism has not developed as much in the developing countries in the developed.

REFERENCES

- Atul Dhyani, *"Indian Journal of Marketing"* (Consumerism).
- David L.Loudon and Albert J. Della Bitta Tata McGraw-Hill Publishing Company Ltd.
- P. Sivaprakasam, S. Rajamohan, *"Consumer Empowernment",* Kaniska Publisher's.
- V. Seshadri, *'Consumerism',* Mittal Publications.

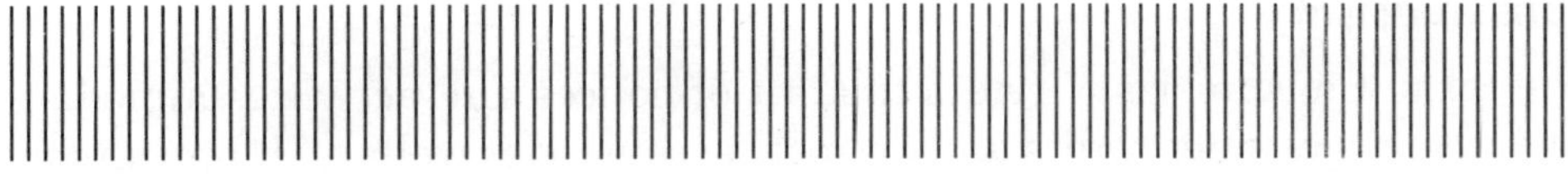

CHAPTER

21

E-marketing and Consumerism

—Srinivasa Rao Boyine

ABSTRACT

The development of World Wide Web (www) has been the most exciting phenomenon since the last decade. It has influenced all spheres of life. It has undoubtedly enhanced the efficiency and effectiveness of various communication and information related activities in many ways. Moreover World Wide Web has generated enormous opportunities for the business sector. This chapter highlights the scope of consumerism, Need for consumerism, Uses of consumerism, E-marketing features, process of E-marketing, E-marketing environment, E-marketing of guidelines, The rise of E-marketing, New product strategies for E-marketing.

E-marketing

E-marketing is the application of a broad range of information technologies for.

- Transforming marketing strategies to create more customer value through more effective segmentation, targeting, differentiation, and positioning strategies.
- More efficiently planning and executing the conception, distribution, promotion, and pricing of goods, services, and ideas.
- Creating exchanges that satisfy individual consumer and organizational customer's objectives.

Consumerism

The term 'Consumerism' refers to a set of polices and activities aimed at protecting consumer rights and promoting consumer welfare. It appears to rise when there is consumer's discontent, Ignorance and unfavourable economic conditions.

Scope of Consumerism

(1) Area of business firms:

The first and per laps the original consumer dissatisfaction generates from the area of direct exchange relationship between consumers and business firms.

(2) Area of Non-Profit organizations:

The second area of consumer dissatisfaction comprises non-profit organizations such as government hospitals, government school, several other government agencies etc.

(3) Area affecting quality of life:

The third area comprises environmental matters affecting the quality of life. For example, air pollution, weather pollution etc.

Need for Consumerism

The need for consumerism has been primarily due to the indifference of the business community, Consumers have not only been called upon to pay higher prices but also have to settle at lower quality, spurious , duplicate and adulterated products that are being sold through misleading and powerful advertisement media.

Uses of Consumerism

(*i*) Producers and sellers will not take the consumer for granted, when consumers strive to Protect their right, business will be compelled to show its unfair trade practices.

(*ii*) Consumers will provide feed back for the business. It will enable the producers to Understand the consumer's needs and wants this will assist in the move effective implementation of the marketing concept or societal marketing concept, depending upon the nature of consumerism.

Features of E-marketing

- E-marketing is technology based and mainly depends on the internet for marketing a particular product.

- The marketer does not market his product through physical shops but through virtual shop.
- Any information related to a specific product is instantly made available to the prospective consumers through the internet.
- E-marketing is that the marketer can make use of various audio and video effects to communicate about the product or service.
- E-marketing is an effective and efficient marketing process through the website, which is capable to providing the same information to many prospective customers at the same time.

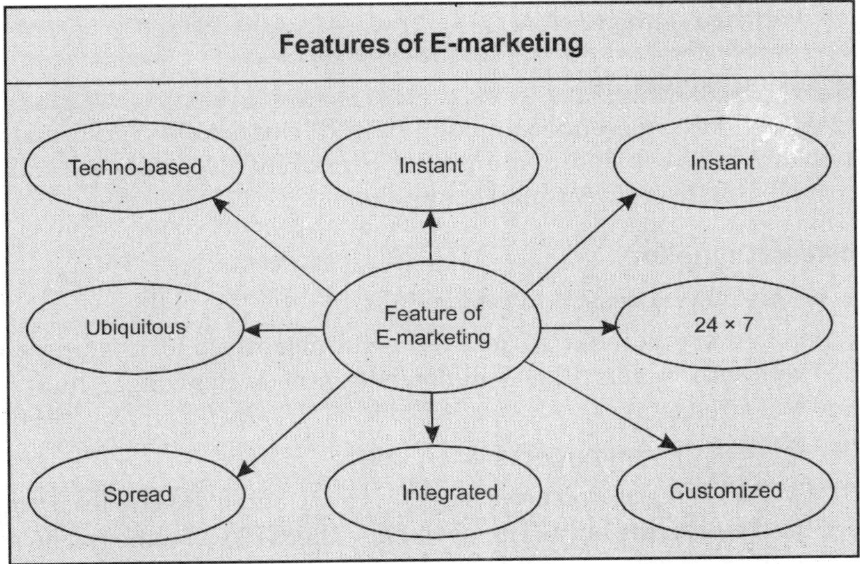

Process of E-marketing

The process of e-marketing is simple and haggles free. The customer can get the product delivered at the door step on the website of the marketer the customer can find all the information related to the mode of placing an order and making payment.

Customer is satisfied with the attributes of the product, He places an order through registration on the marketer's site or via e-mail or phone some marketers demand for advance payment through cash on delivery mode like value paid parcel (VPP)

The marketer also provides after sales service in some cases or as per the requirement, Thus e-marketing is simple and easy the both seller and the buyer.

E-marketing Environment

The marketing environment is ever changing providing plenty of opportunities to develop new products, new markets and new media to communicate with customers, plus new channels to reach business partners, At the same time, The environment poses competitive, economic and other threads.

Factors that affect E-marketing Environment

— Legal Factors

— Technological Factors

— Market-related Factors

E-marketing Guidelines

If a company does an e-mail campaign right, It can not only build customer relationship but reap additional profits E-mail involves only a fraction of the cost of 'd-mail' or direct-mail, campaign.

Important Guidelines

Give the customer a reason to respond:

Campaign should offer surfers powerful incentives for reading e-mail pitches and online ads, like e-mail trivia games, Scavenger hunts and instant-win sweepstakes.

Personalize the content of your e-mails:

IBM's "Focussing on you news Digest" is distributed directly to customers office e-mail delivering only "The news they choose". Customers who agree to receive the newsletter select from topics listed on an interest profile.

The Rise of E-marketing

Internet has efficiently enhanced the quantity and quality of information transfer and improved the accessibility to the information

The credit for the development of e-marketing, which is also known of electronic or online marketing, goes to the expansion of the internet services through www.

E-marketing is the process of selling products or services through virtual shops. A virtual shop is nothing but the website of any marketer, Where all the in formation pertaining to the product or service is displayed on the website.

Today a website is the most important marketing tool. Most of the marketers are currently marketing their goods and services through e-marketing.

New Product Strategies for E-marketing

Many new products such as Netscape, Yahoo! And classmates.com, were introduced by "one-pony" firms. Built around the firm's first successful product other firms, such as Microsoft added internet products to an already successful product mix, This section explores product mix strategies to aid marketer in integrating offline and online offerings.

Conclusion

It can be said that selling through website is emerging as an affective marketing tool. The e-marketing phenomenon is definitely getting support from technological development, In the future, it is expected that there will be more virtual marketers and the competition will provide added advantages to the customers. Consumerism is concerned with protecting consumers from all organizations with which there is an exchange relationship.

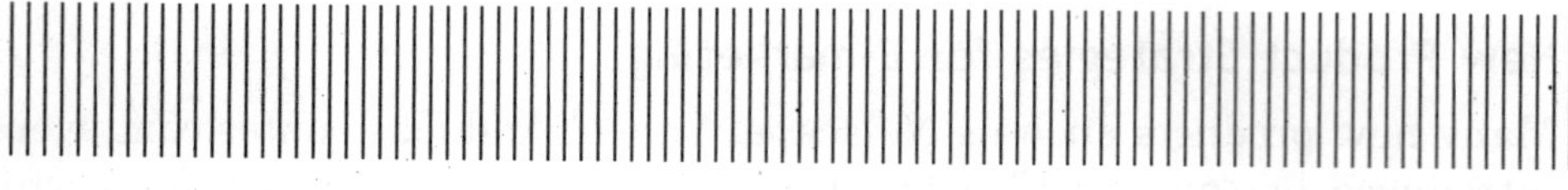

CHAPTER

22

The Ever-changing Scenario of Consumerism

— Mr. K. Neelamegam

Introduction

Every Year Ides of Mars (March 15) is observed as the World Consumer Rights Day. John F. Kennedy, the then President of the United States of America, stamp its approval on a Consumer Bill of Rights. The historical decision marked the beginning of the new era of Consumerism in the USA. The bill was aimed at establishing certain standards of ethical conduct for those engaged in the production and distribution of goods and services to the consumers and also to curb such business practices at the national and international levels, which adversely affected consumers.

Subsequently, these rights were adapted in the UN draft guidelines for consumer protection. Governments were called upon to develop and strengthen their consumer protection policies in line with these principles.

The four basic rights, advocated by President Kennedy, which came to be regarded as the *'Core of Consumerism'*, are as follows:

1. Right to Safety
2. Right to be informed
3. Right to Choose
4. Right to be Heard

International Organisation of Consumer Unions (IOCU) pitched in with three more rights along with the four above. They are:

5. Right to Redressal of Grievances
6. Right to Healthy Environment
7. Right to basic Needs

Emergence of Consumerism

It is evident that the consumer movement originated in the west. The reasons for emergence and growth of consumerism are embedded in the history of industrialization and fast economic growth of those countries. The high growth western economies percolated down to the developing countries of Asia, Africa and Latin America. Some of the important reasons for the emergence of consumerism in US and later on elsewhere are as follows:

- Rise in disposable income and education sensitized people to the values of quality of life beyond the values of material gains;
- Increased complexities of marketing techniques, the technology and product complexity demand better awareness on the part of consumer;
- Increased exploitation of the environment and diminishing natural resource caused concern among the people;
- Consumers by and large were highly disorganized and individually they had a very weak bargaining power. In order to assert their rights and secure a better deal it was necessary for them to get united.

The present day concept of consumerism is of relatively new origin. The terminology came into common parlance only after the US Congress passed the bill of consumer rights in the late sixties.

The concept of consumerism involves the actions of individuals and organizations in response to consumers' dissatisfaction arising out of exchange relationship. To some extent, it is also viewed as an attempt to preserve the free enterprise economy by making the market work better.

Who is a Consumer?

Consumers are the largest economic group in any country. Irrespective of the system of governance, consumer is the prime concern of all the economic activities.

A consumer may be defined as 'One who consumes goods whether manufactured by business units or created by nature and utilities and services offered by the Government, business or a non-business organization.'

Why Consumer Needs Protection?

Consumers of any product or service are scattered over a vast territory and they are highly disorganized. Individually they have a very weak bargaining power. Many consumers, especially in the developing countries, are literate, ignorant and usually lack information to make intelligent purchases. Often, they are not in a position to protect their interests while dealing with fully organized united and well informed professional sellers.

Businessmen usually take advantage of the general apathy, indifference and helplessness of consumers and adopt anti-consumer policies to earn larger profits. Consumer movements and consumer protection activities cannot have a firm and strong foundation unless there is a general awakening and consciousness about consumer rights in the public. In principle, a consumer in the market place can be protected by three different approaches:

1. Through legislation;
2. Self-regulation by the business community; and
3. Through consumerism, that is self-help.

Objectives of Consumerism

Consumerism is a multifaceted concept aimed at achieving the following diverse objectives:

1. To restore the balance in the buyer-seller relations in the market place;
2. To safeguard consumer rights;
3. To represent consumer interests before the Government and pressurize it to provide meaningful consumer protection through legislation;
4. To organize consumer resistance against unfair trade practices and to create strong public opinion in favour of fair trade practices;
5. To collaborate with the Government and business concerns for consumer protection;
6. To undertake programmes of consumer education, consumer information and comparative testing.

Strong Voluntary and Non-Government Organisations (NGOs) should take lead in this regard rather than depending solely on the Government for this cause.

Consumerism in India

Consumers in India are a highly neglected and ill-treated lot. Till recently, markets for most essential products and services were sellers' markets allowing the manufacturers and traders to keep their one up position in the market *vis-à-vis* the consumers. The extent of consumer neglect is evident from:

- The adulterated food people eat
- The Spurious, unsafe and substandard products (durable as well as non- durable) sold openly in the market
- The repeated shortage of essential commodities, accompanied by black marketing and profiteering
- The hazardous drugs that are pushed through Over The Counter (OTC) sales
- The misleading, unethical, and manipulative ads consumers are bombarded with
- The humiliation, indignity and harassment people are subjected by the public sector organizations such as railways, banks, telephone department, electricity boards, and Government hospitals like
- The polluted water and air most of us drink and breath
- The unfair treatment meted out to people by many service operators, mobile phone and credit card Companies, cable TV operators and the like

In fact, the plight of Indian consumer is worse as compared to any other country because:

- They have no voice in the decision-making process related to the goods and services produced for their consumption
- In a vast country like India it is rather difficult to organize the consumers
- A majority of population is illiterate and ignorant
- Poverty, lack of education, lack of information and traditional outlook of suffering in silence deters them form doing anything for their own rights
- Proliferation of brands and misleading advertisements make it difficult for the people to make a right choice of the product.

Unfortunately, the plethora of consumer protection laws has turned out to be a close preserve of the bureaucracy. The legal armory in this regard, consists about 30 laws meant for protecting the consumer directly or indirectly besides the statutory orders that can be enforced under the rule making power of the Government at all levels. Yet, the kind of protection the gullible consumer is in need of is illusive.

A list of important laws acts meant for protecting the consumers' rights in India is as follows:

- Indian Contract Act, 1872
- Dangerous Drugs Act, 1932
- Sale of Goods Act, 1932
- Agricultural Produce (Grading and Marketing) Act, 1950
- Drugs and Cosmetics Act, 1940
- Drugs Control Act, 1950
- Emblems and Names (Prevention of improper use) Act, 1950
- Standards of Weights and Measures Act, 1952
- Drugs and Magic Remedies (Objectionable Advertisement) Act, 1954
- Prevention of Food Adulteration Act, 1954
- The Essential Commodities Act, 1955
- Trade and Merchandise Marks Act, 1958
- Essential Service Maintenance Act, 1968
- The Monopolies and Restrictive Trade Practices Act, 1969
- Hire Purchase Act, 1972
- Cigarettes (Regulation of Production, Supply and Distribution) Act, 1975
- Standards of Weights and Measures (Packaged Commodities) Rules, 1977
- Prevention of Black Marketing, Maintenance of Supplies of Essential Commodities Act, 1980
- Bureau of Indian Standards Act, 1986
- Consumer Protection Act, 1986

This is however not an exhaustive list because there are many other product-specific acts also that could protect the economic interests of consumers, friendly.

The Consumer Protection Act

The consumer Protection Act, 1986, was enforced to provide better protection of consumers' rights in the country. The Act intends to ensure simple, speedy and inexpensive redressal of consumers' grievances. However as it was enacted somewhat in haste and several lacunae were found in actual application. The salient features of the 1986 Act are summed up as follows:

1. The Act applies to all goods and services unless specifically exempted by the Central Government;

2. It covers all sectors whether private, public or co-operative;
3. The provisions of the Act are compensatory in nature;
4. It sanctifies various rights of the consumers;
5. To provide simple, speedy and inexpensive redressal of consumer grievances, the Act envisages the creation of three-tier quasi-judicial machinery at the national, state, and district levels;
6. The Act envisages establishment of consumer protection councils at the central and the state levels with the main objective of promoting and protecting the rights of consumers;
7. There is no fee for filing a complaint and one can send it by post also.

Depending upon the nature of the relief sought by the consumer and facts, Redressal Forums may give orders for one or more of the following relief:

- Removal of the defects from the goods;
- Replacement of goods;
- Refund of the price paid; and/or
- Award of compensation for the loss or injury suffered.

From the point of consumer protection the progressive amendments effected the Ordinance amended in 1993 are significant.

Consumer Dispute Redressal Agencies

The consumer Protection Act 1986 seeks to establish following forums to look into and resolve consumer grievances. They are:

- District Consumer Dispute Redressal Forum
- State Commission
- National Commission

Consumerism in India: Future Scenario

Through consumer movement in India is yet to gain its full momentum, growing consumerism may manifest its impact on trade and industry in the following ways in not so distant future:

As Indian customer is getting exposed to better quality products and services his expectations are also rising fast. The firms in future will be required to produce safer, effective and aesthetically designed user-friendly products to satisfy the needs of discerning consumers. The growing intolerance towards substandard and unsafe products is a healthy symptom in this regard. It should ring the warning-bell for those so for not concerned about the safety and quality of goods produced or marketed by them.

The manufacture was held responsible for the mishap because the label on the product did not warn consumers about any such possibility. The time is not vary far when consumers in India would also follow suit and demand damages for physical injuries or mental torture from the producers of poor quality or defective products.

The public and the courts will probably more forcefully question unfair and arbitrary business performance causing damage to the environment. The growing awareness among the people would compel business houses to be more careful about pollution and adopt effective measures to prevent any damage to the environment. The social responsibility concept may also find its due place in business practices of Indian firms.

Despite liberalized economic policies, business in future will have to operate more under scrutiny of government, the press and public interest groups. Business units will be required to adopt necessary safety measures for the general public and also for their workers. Stringent punitive measures might be introduced to prevent child labour, not paying the minimum wages and violating other business norms. Public interest groups may come down heavily on the firms resorting to misleading advertising, and making unsubstantiated claims in business communications. Firms will also be required to provide the service necessary for making effective use of products marketed by them.

Mass production industries and service organizations will probably be more affected by growing consumerism as compared to the industrial goods producers or smaller firms operating in niche markets.

The creditability of existing business organizations and their ethical assumptions may come under public evaluation rather more forcefully. Meaning that, public opinion could question even the internal procedures and value systems of business firms as they affect the society and the individuals. This may probably damage the philosophy and practice of management in many ways.

Conclusion

A survey conducted by 'Consumer Action Group' revealed that due to higher media exposure and rise in literacy levels, public-expectation from various products and services as well as peoples' perception of quality, service and corporate responsibility are changing fast (*The Economic Times*, Jan 26, 1993). In future, this may call for a different marketing approach, especially for mass consumption goods, domestic appliances, utilities and personal services. Growing consumerism is bound to throw up several new challenges for the marketers in the next few years.

For business firms, gone are the days of arbitrary decisions, they will have to learn to live with consumerism. Business leaders accustomed to operating in sellers' market may find themselves in an uncomfortable situation in the new environment. Changes in the socio cultural and the business environment that have largely been responsible for the advent of consumerism are here to stay and the bad news for such firms is that they are irreversible.

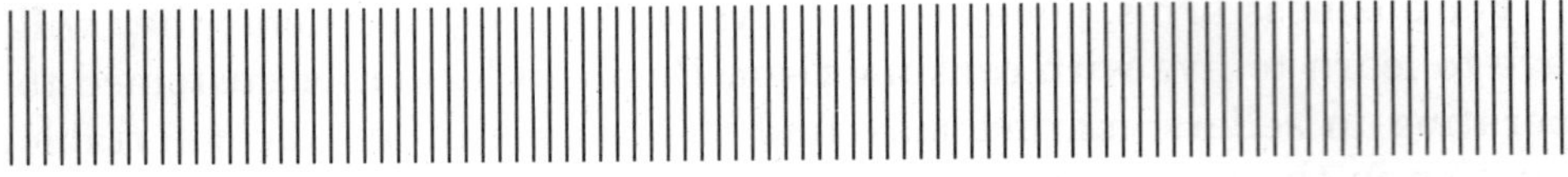

CHAPTER

23

Surveillance of the Firms and Total Quality Management

—Dr. G. Ganesan
— Ms. S. Vijayalakshmi

Introduction

Total Quality Management is an enhancement to the traditional way of doing business. It is a proven technique to guarantee survival in world class competition.

Analyzing the three words:

Total: Made up of the whole

Quality: Degree of excellence a product or service provides.

Management: Act, art or manner of handling, controlling, directing, etc.

Therefore, TQM is the art of managing the whole to achieve excellence. It is set of guiding principles that represent the foundation of a continuously improving organization. It is the application of quantitative methods and human resources to improve all the processes with an organization and exceed customer needs now and in future. TQM concepts that enable the Japanese industries become popular and it is originated in US. In the middle of 1990's ISO 9000 standard were popularized and accepted worldwide as a means to achieve quality.

Objectives

Aims to examine the role of TQM towards enhancing customer satisfaction.

Methodology

This presentation based on secondary data and collected from Books, Journals and Websites.

Definition of TQM

TQM is customer oriented definition.

Armend V.Feigenbaum argues that "*total quality control is necessary to achieve productivity, Market penetration and Competitive advantage. Quality begins by identifying the customers requirements and ends with a product or service in the hands of a satisfied customer*"

TQM refers to a quest for quality that involves everybody in the organization. The two key aspects of TQM are:

1. *A never ending push to improve* continuous improvement (KAIZEN)
2. *Customer satisfaction* meeting on exceeding the customers' expectation.

TQM is a management philosophy that seeks to integrate all organizational functions (marketing, finance, design, engineering, production, customer service etc) to focus on meeting customer needs and organizational objectives.

Importance of Implementing TQM

In the last decade, that there was a great pressure on companies to go for ISO 9000 certificate. For companies who wanted to adopt TQM, the ISO Certification was one of the routes to get into the mode. ISO certified company does not necessarily become TQM Company. Yet, it is the first step towards evolving into a TQM company.

TQM is now becoming recognized as a generic management tool just as applicable in service and public sector organization. The simple objective of TQM is "Do the right things; right the first time; every time".

The Total Quality Management Principles

TQM Principles provide guidance on the application and it produces benefits for customers, owners, people, suppliers and society at large.

- *Customer Focussed Organization:* Organizations depend on their customers and therefore should understand current and future customer needs, meet customer requirements and strive to exceed customer expectations.
- *Leadership:* Leadership establishes unity of purpose and direction of organization. They should create and maintain the interval

environment in which people can become fully involved in achieving the organization's objectives.

- *Involvement of People:* People at all levels are the essence of an organization and their full involvement enables their abilities to be used for the organization's benefit.
- *Process Approach:* A desired result is achieved more efficiently when related resources and activities are managed as a process.
- *System Approach to Management:* Identifying, understanding and managing a system of interrelated processes for a given objective improves the organization's effectiveness and efficiency.
- *Continual Improvement:* Continual improvement should be a permanent objective of the organization.
- *Factual approach to Decision Making:* Effective decisions and actions are based on the analysis of data and information.
- *Mutually Beneficial Supplier Relationships:* An organization and its suppliers are independent, and a mutually beneficial relationship enhances the ability to create value.

Customer Satisfaction Measures and Measurement

The first and major TQM principle is to satisfy the customer—the person who pays for the product or service. Customers want to get their money's worth from a product or service they purchase. The whole idea of TQM is to keep the customers happy and satisfied. The companies are aiming one step above customer satisfaction, *i.e.,* 'Customer delight'. If the customers are provided with more than what they expect from the product, it results in delight. It should be remembered that the customers are given top priority in the TQM implemented organizations. Requirements of TQM award Malcolm Baldrige National Quality Award (MBNQA) focus on continuous quality improvement and highest priority (*i.e.,* 300 Points) given to Customer Satisfaction.

To achieve the customer satisfaction the following measures should be followed:

- Understanding the customer needs and expectations by market research, collection of data and information on consumer behaviour and perception, regular survey and by personal contacts;
- Making everybody in the organization aware of customer needs and expectations by organizing workshops on customers and interaction with employees and customers and periodical newsletter;

- Translating customer needs into reality by the product or service offered company;
- Management of relationship with customers by exchange visits, business calls and by proactive actions to resolve any problem.

Customer satisfaction is not an objective statistic but more of feeling or attitude. Although certain statistical pattern of measurement done on the satisfaction level regarding quality of products or service, complaint resolution, comparison with competitors product and services, ethics of business practice, anticipation of needs and co-operation.

The *Teboul Model* describes customer satisfaction as the degree to which the customer's experience of a service or product matches the expectations. This model will lead to same conclusion in both the cases when the customer has low expectation and the product performance is low and high expectation and the product performance is high.

Customer Satisfaction Model

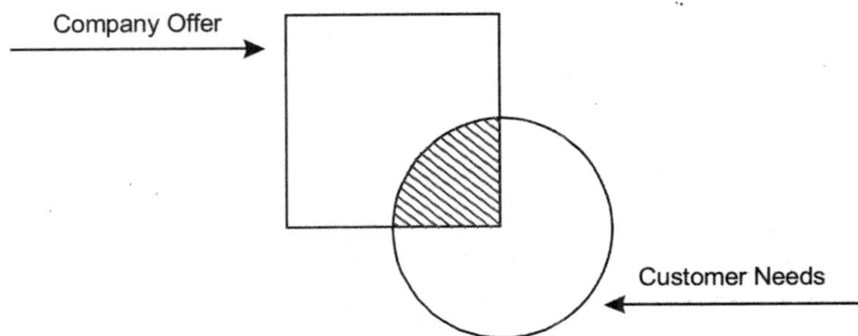

Comment Card: It is used to get simple information at the time of purchase and used in hospitality industry.

Customer Questionnaire: It is popular tool for obtained opinion and perception about an organization and its product and services. In this grading technique is used because it easily produces metric.

Toll-free Telephone Number: It is an effective, cheap and faster respond to the complaint. But it is not reach those who not decide to buy the product and discovered likeable feature of competitors' product.

Customer Visits: It is another way of gathering information and identifying any specific or recurring problems.

Report Card: It is very effective information gathering tool and determines areas for improvement.

Conclusion

The TQM Company believes it will only be successful if customers are satisfied. TQM is a better way to run a business and compete in domestic and world markets. TQM does not occur over night; there are no quick remedies. It takes a long time to build the appropriate emphasis and techniques into the culture. Although the customer is the judge of quality, it will be considered to be measured with reliable data concerning the customer's needs and expectations. Maximize customer satisfaction and retention will give financial result for the concern.

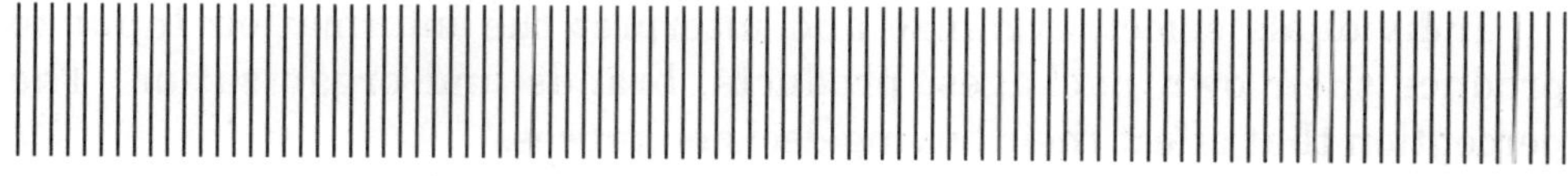

CHAPTER

24
Consumerism and Psychological Aspects

— Mrs. S.P. Manickavasugi

Introduction

Consumer Behaviour is the processes involved when individuals or groups select, purchase, use or dispose of products, service, ideas or experiences to satisfy needs and desires. Consumer Behaviour as the dynamic interaction of affect and cognition, behaviour and the environment by which human beings conduct the exchange aspects of their lives. Consumer Behaviour involves the thoughts and feelings of people experience and the actions they perform in consumption process.

Psychological needs are the fundamental type of consumer needs. Psychographics is an operational technique to measure the lifestyles of the consumers. It measures the Activity, Interest and opinions of the consumers.

Marketers study four factors in order to understand the influence of consumers while making a purchasing decision in psychological aspects of consumers.

Cultural: (Culture, Sub-culture and Social Class)

Social: (Reference groups, Family and Social Roles and Status)

Personal: (Age, Stage in life cycle, Personality and Self-concept)

Psychological: (Motivation, Perception, Learning, Beliefs and Attitudes).

Psychological influence determines people behaviour as consumers. The primary psychological influences on consumer behaviour are Perception, Motives, Learning, Attitudes, Personality, and Self-concept and Life styles.

Individuals select, organize and interpret the information Input to produce their own packages, products, brands and organization. The perception that affect their buying decision process.

Motive is an internal force that derives a person towards those activities, which satisfies his needs or helps him in achieving the goal. Learning refers to changes a person's thought process and behaviour caused by information and experience. Marketers, try to figure out the consumer's learning that influences what they want to buy.

An Attitude of consumers in their evaluation of a product, feelings for a product and behavioural tendencies towards a product. Personality is the set of traits and behaviour that makes a person unique. Self-concept is the person's perception and personality.

Life-style is how one lives. It influences consumer's needs, brand preferences and how and where they purchase. Socialization is the process, which a person acquires the knowledge and skills to function as a consumer. It is partially accomplished through family influences. Reference group is any group that positively or negatively affects a person's values, attitudes or behaviour.

Marketer must examine buyer's levels of involvement and the number of brand available to determine whether consumers are engaging in complex buying behaviour, dissonance-reducing buying behaviour, habitual buying behaviour or variety–seeking buying behaviour. The internal search buyer searches their memories for information about the product that might solve the problem. If they cannot retrieve from memory for enough information for a decision, they seek additional information through external search.

Pyramid of Psychology Aspect of Consumer

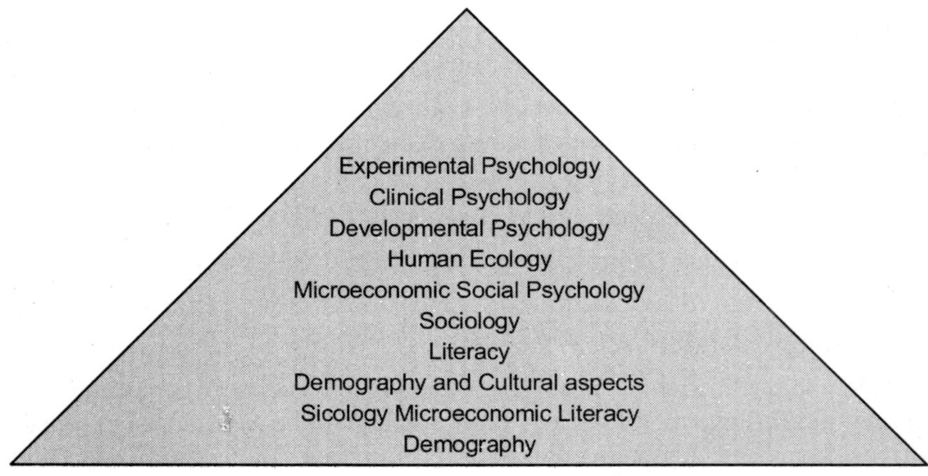

The above pyramid examine that in various aspect the marketer examine the psychological aspects of the consumer for purchasing the product. After purchasing the product, buyers evaluate the product to determine the actual performance meets expected level. The marketer's position is to understand the buyer's behaviour at each stage.

Thus, psychology is the attempt to analyze and measure the lifestyle of the consumers. Psychology aspects help to identify consumer types and to identify the Attitude, Interest and Opinion of consumers.

A set of Psychological process combines with consumer characteristics to result in decision processes and purchase decisions. The marketer's task is to understand what happens in the consumer's consciousness between the arrival of the outside marketing stimuli and the ultimate purchase decision.

Some basic aspects of consumer on Psychological aspects are:

- How the product perceived the consumer?
- What induce the customer to purchase the product?
- Demographic factors influence purchase decision
- Customers buy on particular brand
- Customers' lifestyle influence their decision
- Social factors influence the purchase decision
- Customers' Attitudes towards product.

In order to understand the consumer behaviour the marketer evaluates the psychological aspects on various basis. *E.g.*: Honda engineers took videos of shoppers loading groceries into car trunks to observe their frustration and generate possible solution. Thus, smart companies try to fully understand the customer's buying decision process to their experience in learning, choosing, using and even disposing the product.

Thus the psychological process involve Motivation, Perception, Learning and Memory which play a vital role in understanding how consumers actually make their buying decision. Whereas, marketer must understand and analyze the basic aspect of consumer behaviour.

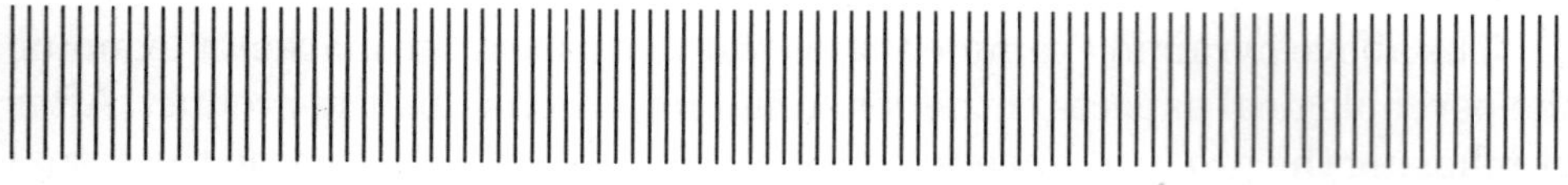

CHAPTER

25
Consumer Protection and Rights

— J. Arul Mani
— N. Manickavasagam

Introduction

Consumer is an important part of economic system. Whatever goods and services are produced or made available must be consumed. Unless there is consumer to consume the goods and services the whole system will come to a halt and collapse. Therefore, consumer is called '*king*' and in many countries he has been given very high and important place in the whole economic system. In India, a number of acts have been passed from to time to time to protect the interest of consumers.

In India, till the middle of 80's it was seller market, actually there was no marketing because consumer was coming to seller rather the opposite which is the trend in countries of west, and Japan where the position is just the opposite as they have to compete with each other to attract customers for all type of goods and services. In India, consumer had to buy what was offered and he had no choice even if the price was high, the quality and service was poor and terms of sales were unattractive and sometime even unreasonable compared to situation prevailing in free economy countries. In USA or Japan, consumer are not required to book a car or LPG gas for cooking or scooter by making a deposit with the company, rather the manufacturer offers credit to the buyer.

The Indian industry and trade completely ignored the consumer even in the matter of after sales and services or keeping to their promise to repair or replacement. Consumer often fed helpless because our laws are very complicated, costly and time consuming and required an advocate to plead the case. Often it was felt wise to get a thing repairs by incurring extra cost rather endless requesting for company engineer to look into it.

In 1986, *The Consumer Protection Act* was passed "to provide for the better protection of the interest of consumers and for that purpose to make provisions for the establishment of consumers' councils and other authorities for the settlement of the consumer disputes and for matters connected therewith".

Salient Features of the Consumer Protection Act, 1988

- The salient features of the Act are given below:
- Social welfare legislation
- Effective provision and safeguards
- Special consumer courts
- Simple, speedy and inexpensive redressal machinery
- Convenient procedures
- Coven goods and services
- Time-limit
- Clean Action
- Check on unfair practices
- Price
- Consumer councils.

Objectives of the Study

- To study the consumer protection through the legislative measures.
- To study the consumer rights in India
- To know the procedure for applying the consumer protection Act.

Basic Objectives of the Act

- Provide better protection to consumers
- Provide for the establishment of consumer council and other authorities
- Establish suitable machinery specially consumer councils to settle disputes.

Consumer Movement through Act

One of the most important milestones in the consumer movement in the country has been the enactment of the Consumer Protection Act, 1986 to better protect the interest of the consumers. This has revolutionized consumer rights. It is one of the most progressive and comprehensive pieces of socio-benevolent legislation covering all goods and services. The Act provides for a separate three-tier quasi-judicial consumer dispute redressal machinery, popularly known as consumer courts, at the national, state and district levels to provide simple, speedy and free redressal against consumers' complaints

Aims and Objectives

- To provide certain important scheduled commodities to the ration card holders at reasonable rates at prescribed quantum.
- To indirectly control open market prices of certain commodities.
- To protect the interests of consumers through enforcement of Weights and Measures Act and rules thereunder.
- To implement Minimum Support Price Scheme of the Central Government to safeguard farmer's interests
- Matters incidental and supplementary to the above objectives.
- To promote and protect the rights of consumers by the way of implementation of Consumer Protection Act.

Functions of the Department

- To implement the Public Distribution System in the State
- To implement Minimum Support Price Scheme.
- To implement Maharashtra Rice (Levy on Rice millers) Order, 1989.
- To implement Mid Day Meal Scheme in association with school education Department.
- To assist implement *"Annapurna"* Scheme of the Central Government.
- Creation and maintenance of storage facilities for PDS.
- Implementation of Consumer Protection Act, 1986

Definition of Consumer

Definition of Consumer as defined in the Consumer Protection Act, 1986, 'Consumer' means any person who—

- Buys any goods for a consideration which has been paid or promised or partly paid and partly promised, or under any system of deferred payment and includes any user of such goods other than the person who buys such goods for consideration paid or promised or partly paid or partly promised, or under any system of deferred payment when such use is made with the approval of such person, but does not include a person who obtains such goods for resale or for any commercial purpose; or

- Hires or avails of any services for a consideration which has been paid or promised or partly paid and partly promised, or under any system of deferred payment and includes any beneficiary of such services other than the person who hires or avails of the services for consideration paid or promised, or partly paid and partly promised, or under any system of deferred payment, when such services are availed of with the approval of the first mentioned person; {Explanation,- For the purposes of sub-clause (i), "commercial purpose" does not include use by a consumer of goods bought and used by him exclusively for the purpose of earning his livelihood, by means of self-employment.

Implementation of Consumer Protection Act

Consumer Protection: This department is nodal department for implementing provisions of the consumer protection Act 1986, and for that purpose following authorities have been established for the redressal of grievances of the Consumers :

- Consumer Disputes Redressal Commission at State Level.
- District Forums at District levels.

State Commission

- The State Commission is established in the year 1989. The President and two other members appointed on this Commission.
- The person, who is or has been a judge of the High Court, is appointed as the President and two other members, who shall be persons of ability, integrity and standing and have adequate knowledge or experience of, or have shown capacity in dealing with problems relating to economics, law, commerce, accountancy, industry, public affairs or administration are appointed.
- Out of the two members, one will be a lady member. The Commission shall have jurisdiction to entertain complaints where the value of the goods or services and compensation, if any, claimed exceeds Rs. 20,00,000/- but does not exceed Rs.100,00,000/-. It also decides the appeals filed against the judgments of the District Forums.

District Forums

- A person who is or has been or is qualified to be a District Judge is appointed as the President and two other Members, who are having qualifications as that of State Commission members; are appointed on the District Forum.

- Out of these two members, one will be a lady member .The Forum shall have jurisdiction to entertain complaints where the value of goods or services and the compensation, if any claimed does not exceed Rs. 20 lakhs.
- In Maharashtra, every district has got one forum and the districts of Mumbai, Pune and Nagpur have additional forums as they have more number of complaints. At present 34 district forums are working in the State.

State Consumer Protection Council

- This Council was initially constituted in the year 1987, for a period of 3 years. This Council consists Members of Parliaments, Members of Legislative Assemblies, representatives of Voluntary Consumer Organizations, Representatives of Trade and Commerce Organization, Government Officials, persons in the Consumer Protection field as well as the journalists.
- The objects of this Council is to promote and protect within the State, the rights of the consumers as laid down in 'Section 6 ' of the Consumer Protection Act, 1986.
- Important Schemes for Consumer Protection
- Every year the Government makes budgetary provisions for the Consumer Welfare Fund and it is spent on the Consumer Protection related matters.
- There are many Voluntary Consumer Organizations. Since, these
- Transitions contribute to the welfare of the consumers and create awareness, such organizations are given assistance for their work.
- The Central Government has started a Scheme under which the Voluntary Consumer Organizations which do commendable work in the Consumer Protection field are granted Rs. 50,000, Rs. 40,000 and Rs. 30,000 along with Merit Certificate.
- Similarly, there is National Youth Scheme under which the Youths between 15-35 years age-group are given Rs. 20,000, Rs. 15,000 and Rs.10,000 along with Merit Certificate for their contribution in consumer field. The State Government recommends, the names received from the Consumer Organizations to the Central Government.

- To create awareness in the School/College students, lecturers are given in each district and for that purpose visiting lecturers are appointed.
- Apart from the above, the Government has created Consumer Protection Cells at District level under the Chairmanship of the Collector. The Cell consists of 17 unofficial members from different Consumer Organizations, representatives of Gas dealers, petrol dealers and Traders' Organizations apart from the Senior Officers at District level connected with consumer goods/services.
- The meetings of the Cell are held every month and the consumer problems are solved on the spot and many other problems are settled after regular follow-up.

John F. Kennedy had equated the rights of the ordinary American consumer with national interest. He gave the American consumer four basic rights:

1. *The Right to Safety*—to be protected against the marketing of goods which are hazardous to health or life.
2. *The Right to Choose*—to be assured, wherever possible, access to a variety of products and services at competitive prices: and in those industries where competition is not workable and Government regulation is substituted, an assurance of satisfactory quality and service at fair prices.
3. *The Right to Information*—to be protected against fraudulent, deceitful or grossly misleading information, advertising, labelling, or other practices, and to be given the facts s/he needs to make an informed choice.
4. *The Right to be Heard*—to be assured that consumer interests will receive full and sympathetic consideration in the formulation of Government policy, and fair and expeditious treatment in its administrative tribunals.

Kennedy recognised that consumers are the largest economic group in the country's economy, affecting and affected by almost every public and private economic decision. But they were also the only important group who were not effectively organised, whose views were not heard.

Therefore, the Federal Government, by nature the highest spokesman for all people, had a special obligation to the consumer's needs. Thirteen years later President Gerald Ford felt that the four rights constituted in Kennedy's Bill of Rights were inadequate for a situation where most consumers are not educated enough to make the right choices. So he added the Right to Consumer Education, as an informed consumer cannot be exploited easily.

While these rights served the interest of the American consumer well enough, they did not cover the whole gamut, because a global consumer did need, apart from them, other well-defined rights like basic needs, a healthy environment and redress.

The Consumers International (CI), former International Organisation of Consumer Unions (IOCU), the umbrella body, for 240 organisations in over 100 countries, expanded the charter of consumers rights contained in the US Bill to eight, which in a logical order reads:

1. Basic Needs
2. Safety
3. Information
4. Choice
5. Representation
6. Redress
7. Consumer Education
8. Healthy Environment

This charter had a universal significance as they symbolized the aspirations of the poor and disadvantaged. On this basis, the United Nations, in April 1985, adopted its Guidelines for Consumer Protection.

Conclusion

The consumer is wealth of the business and important of economic of the nation. The consumer protection Act, 1986 provide the consumer forum for the settlement of disputes and prevent the consumer against the unfair trade practices. The consumer rights have been protected is important for the economic development and environmental factors.

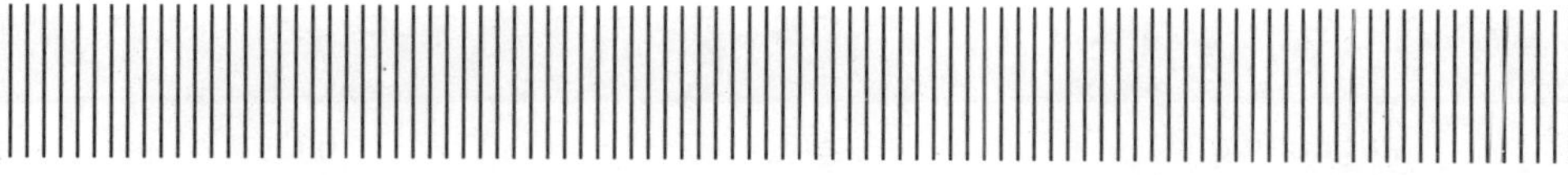

CHAPTER

26
An Overview on Coffee Consumption in India

— Mrs. Malathi

Introduction

Coffee is the most popular drink worldwide with 1.4 billion cups consumed everyday. Coffee was consumed as food, then wine, a medicine and finally beverage. Its use as beverage dates Back 700 years ago. Till the 1960's, coffee was regarded as harmful. Coffee means many things to many people. Coffee was first known in Europe as Arabian wine. Iced coffee in a can has been popular in Japan since 1945. For reducing wrinkles and improving skill, the Japanese have been known to bathe in coffee ground. Caffeinated soaps and lip balm are used by Japanese. The Europeans first added chocolate to their coffee in the 1600's.

Nutritional Values of Coffee Beverage

Coffee contains a very wide range of macro and micro nutrients to our diet and well being.

Table 26.1 : Typical composition of coffee

Component	Mg/litre
1	2
Caffeine	651
Calcium	32
Phosphorus	1.6

...(Contd.)

1	2
Magnesium	61
Sodium	14
Potassium	785
Iron	1.8
Manganese	0.44
Chromium	0.005
Copper	0.20
Selenium	Trace
Zinc	0.09
Thiamine	0.1
Riboflavine	0.1
Phyridoxine	0.1
Nicotinic acid	4.4
B.carotene	0.05

Nutritional Contribution of Coffee

Carbohydrates

Carbohydrates constitute almost half the dry weight of green coffee.

Lipids

The lipid content of green beans vary from 8-18 per cent. Lipid levels are insignificant in filtered and instant coffee.

Nitrogenous Compounds

These include proteins, amino acids, trigonelline and alkaloids. The most abundant alkaloid is caffeine. A cup of coffee contains 30-180mg of caffeine depending on the blend and mode of preparation.

Vitamins and Minerals

Green coffee contains several vitamins including B1, B2, and B6, B12, vitamic and folic acid and riboflavine. Minerals represent about 4 per cent of dry weight. These minerals include calcium, phosphorus, magnesium, sodium, potassium, iron, copper, zinc, selenium and manganese.

Carboxylic Acids

Several aliphatic acids are present in green coffee—mostly citric, malic and quinic acids are present.

Volatile Compounds

Hundreds of compounds in large amounts give coffee its unique flavor and aroma.

Chlorogenic and Caffeic Acids

These acids represent 7 to 10 per cent of dry matter of green coffee. Both are strong antioxidants. Coffee contains high level of antioxidants compared to other commonly consumed beverages.

Medicinal Values of Coffee

Various scientific Experiments and research have established very clearly that coffee is a beverage that has health benefits.

Coffee Reduces the Incidence of Human Diseases

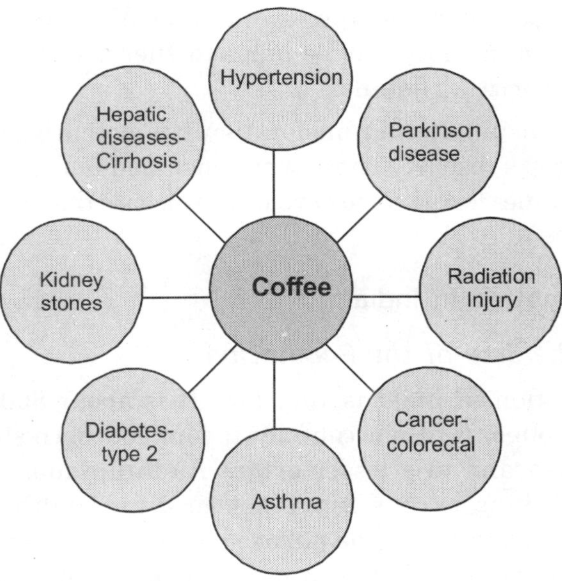

Coffee When Consumed in Moderation has Lot of Health Benefits

A cup of coffee dissolves drowsiness, sharpens wits, stimulates mind, stop headache and prevent cavities.

- Coffee works wonders for long distance runners, cyclists and those who exercise for long periods. They feel less tired afterwards.
- Coffee prevents liver cancer. Coffee drinkers were 41 per cent less likely to have liver cancer than people who don't drink coffee.
- Coffee is good for eyes. Italian researchers have found that having one or two cups of coffee a day could protect from eye tremors.

- Caffeine is used in many medicines, because it improves absorption and increases pain killing effect. A strong cup of coffee can help relieve migraine.
- Four or more cups of coffee a day reduce the risk of gout (a painful joint disorder caused by uric acid in the blood).
- Consumption of coffee helps reduce incidence of gall stones, liver cirrhosis and type 2 diabetes.
- Drinking more than three cups of coffee a day protect older women against some age related memory decline.
- Drinking four or more cups of coffee a day reduces one's risk of colorectal cancer by 24 per cent compared to people who rarely or don't drink coffee.
- 200 mg of caffeine, the amount typically found in two cups of coffee will not only increase the level of alertness but also helps in our short term memory. Coffee helps to energize our self, concentrate and memorize all details.
- Coffee consumption in moderation has potential to reduce risk of Parkinson's disease. Those who consumed four cups of coffee a day are five times less risky to develop the disease than those who consume no coffee.

Coffee Consumption in India

Considering the Size of the Population

Coffee consumption in India is very low. It is about 85000 metric tones annually. The coffee culture is confines to four southern states only, Tamil nadu, Karnataka and to a lesser extent Andhrapradesh and Kerala. In India coffee drinking is considered 'not good for health' a wrong notion spread among the masses by the physicians and it is a habit forming drink and as such youths are not encouraged to drink coffee, so India is one of the lowest per capita coffee consuming country in the world.

The following table shows it clear:

Table 26.2. World-wide coffee consumption (per capita)

Country	(in Kilograms) / year
1	2
Finland	12.0
Sweden	11.5
Norway	11.0

...*(Contd.)*

1	2
Denmark	10.0
Netherlands	10.0
Federal Republic of Germany	8.0
Belgium and Luxembourg	7.2
Switzerland	6.5
France	6.0
Costa Rica	5.4
Italy	4.5
USA	4.4
German Democratic Republic	4.3
Canada	4.2
Brazil	4.2
Columbia	4.2
Hungary	4.0
Spain	3.5
Greece	3.0
U.K.	2.5
Japan	2.4
Australia	2.4
Yugoslavia	2.3
Ethiopia	2.3
Czechoslovakia	2.1
El Salvador	2.1
Guatemala	2.1
Algeria	1.7
Ecuador	1.7
Mexico	1.2
Argentina	1.0
Poland	0.9
Cameroon	0.6
Zaire	0.4
Indonesia	0.4
Kenya	0.3
USSR	0.2
Uganda	0.2
Ivory coast	0.2
India	0.1

With the total production of 4.7 million bags in 2007-08; India has exported 3.5 Million bags leaving only 1.2 million bags for the domestic market.

This is reflected in the following Table.

Year	Production	Consumption	Export (Quantity in Metric tones)
2000-01	301200	60.000	253524
2001-02	300600	64.000	223782
2002-03	275275	68.000	213008
2003-04	270500	70.000	222425
2004-05	275500	75.000	228246
2005-06	274000	80.200	203768
2006-07	288000	85.000	244989
2007-08	262000	90.000	214243

Indian coffee is exported to over 40 countries earning. Foreign exchange of 1598 crores, in the year 2007-08. 70 per cent of our coffee production is exported, only 30 per cent is consumed locally. The majority of the coffee drinkers does not have access to good quality because better quality beans are exported. Coffee is traditionally mixed with chicory and drunk with milk, but the Coffee Board wants to spread the message that 100 per cent coffee- as opposed to the chicory mix, to differentiate pure coffee.

Table 26.4 Per capita consumption of coffee in India

Year	(in Kg/per year)
1951	0.051
1961	0.077
1971	0.069
1981	0.074
1991	0.065
2001	0.062
2002	0.066
2003	0.068
2004	0.069
2005	0.072
2006	0.075
2007	0.08
2008	0.08

The positive benefits of coffee drinking in moderation are largely unknown. The Indian Market for hot beverages is dominated by Tea.

Suggestions to Boost-up Coffee Market in India

- An increase in domestic coffee sales by educating consumers about products and qualities.
- An increase in per capita and total domestic coffee consumption.
- An increase in the types and variety of coffee products offered on the local market.
- An increase in the number of outlets that sell and or serve coffee.
- An increase in the percentage of coffee that remains in the country.
- Most importantly, an improvement in prices received by coffee growers in the local market.
- Use of existing positive coffee and health resources.

Conclusion

In India, no massive market promotion measures have been undertaken like in Norway, Brazil and England to promote the internal market. The mass media shall be utilized to promote demand among the consumers. Medias--Radio, Press and Television shall be utilized to increase the publicity. The only Journal, which gives advertisement to coffee, is Indian coffee which has very limited circulation. Publicity campaign shall cover opening of coffee shops or coffee Houses, coffee fairs, giving price subsidy to coffee Houses, issuing pamphlet especially in rural and Non-Traditional areas of coffee. Our policy towards a larger domestic base needs to be given top priority.

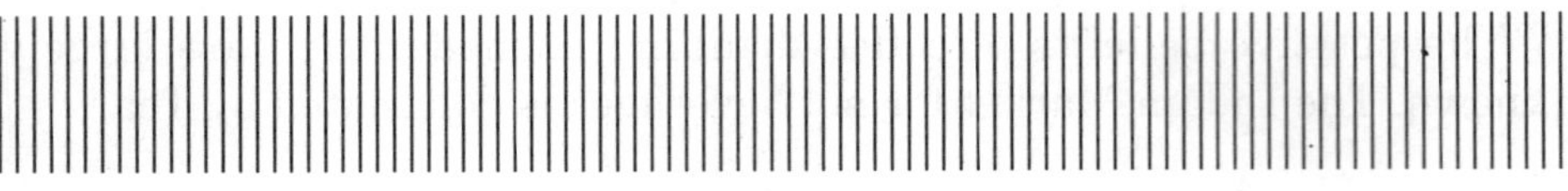

CHAPTER

27

Impact of Consumer Movement in India

— Mr. Al-Ameen

ABSTRACT

This chapter highlights the consumer movement in India 20th century and its objectives role of consumer organizations, consumer boycotts, role of Government, regulatory agencies in consumer movement. It also describes the strength of consumer protection Act in consumer movement. Consumer movement has yet to get going in India; existence of the act has stimulated the creation of much consumer organization across the country. The movement has not blossomed because not all of the organizations are active enough to make an impact, there has hardly been any unified action which would demonstrate their strength, and there has been no active consumer participation in the movements. Consumers claim that the lack of consumer education makes them passive and apathetic and blame consumer courts to which they may take their grievances. Consumer rights organizations, however, counter that they lack sufficient funds and blame the government for their inaction. The Indian consumer movement is elitist and considers the need to focus upon rural consumers, the significant contributions at that organizations have made in laying the foundations for change, the need for consumer education, the need for specialists, the particular need for consumer protection with regard to health-related products and support by voluntary by health groups.

Introduction

The history of consumer movement in India can be traced to the beginning of the 20th century. It is said to begin with the "formation of passengers and traffic relief association and the women graduates union, Bombay during 1915". But the consumer movement started gaining momentum only in 1960's. Indian consumers are passive and tolerant and like sadhus they believe in right-wing and attributed the receipt of defective goods to their fate or ill luck.

"Passive consumers have and to put up with adulterated food, faculty weights, under measures, spurious and hazardous drugs, exorbitant prices, endemic shortages leading to black marketing and profiteering substandard, useless guarantees intensity and indifferent services from public utilities and a list of other ills".

Indian consumers have to face problems arising out of unfair trade practices, spiraling prices, misleading advertisements, poor quality of products, etc. The business has the responsibility of providing goods and services needed by the consumers at fair prices and guarding against adulteration, poor quality, defective advertisement and lack of service and courtesy. But the altitude of business towards consumers has been found to be indifferent whatever be the native of market, the competition or monopoly, the worst affected is the consumer. "Where there is monopoly the consumer is of course helpless and where there is competition, he is at the mercy of advertising.

The competitive movement is characterized by laissez fair *i.e.,* the least interference by Government in economic matters under the competitive selling the business is concerned with the study of the tastes and preferences of the consumers and strives to satisfy them. In other words, the attitude of business towards consumer is indifferent and the tastes and preferences of the consumers are irrelevant, unless they are compelled to sell under competitive conditions.

A few local councils and consumer groups affiliated to it were also set up in Delhi. Another consumer organization popularly known as 'price rise resistance movement' was started in Delhi in the year 1964. It held meetings to protest against rising prices and formed special squads to keep watch on the price trend in different areas of the city.

Consumer movement in India, in the past was weak against the giant manufactures and traders and the fight against unfair trade practices, consumers often lost due to lack of funds and official support. The consumer movement emphasizes co-operative efforts by consumer themselves to protect their rights and interest in the market place against unfair trade practices.

From 1980's onwards, the movement gained momentum. The there were about 230 consumer organisations in the country, of which 45 per cent were in Gujarat, Karnataka, Andhra Pradesh and Tamil Nadu.

Among the cities Delhi with 14 organisations occupies the first place, followed by Ahmedabad, Hyderabad and Bombay.

Objectives of Consumer Movements

The important objectives of the consumer's movement are as follows:

(1) To restore the balance in the buyer-seller relations in the market place;

(2) To protect and promote the consumers interest;

(3) To safeguard consumer rights;

(4) To prevent consumer exploitation by unscrupulous traders;

(5) To represent consumer interest before the Government and pressure the Government to provide a meaningful consumer protection through proper legislation;

(6) To organize consumer resistance against unfair trade pratices and create a strong public opinion in favour of fair trade practices;

(7) To collaborate with Government and business centres for consumer protection;

(8) To undertake programmes of consumer education, consumer information and comparative testing;

(9) To ensure consumer-oriented practices of marketing programme by business enterprises; and

(10) To redress the affected consumer through Government and non-Governmental organisations.

Consumer Movement in Tamil Nadu

Consumers in Tamil Nadu are not getting their due recognition with the result, they are relegated to a very low level and thus they are subjected to economic exploitation on a large scale by unscrupulous businessmen who with selfish motive, indulge in restrictive and unfair trade practices with the consumer exploitation rampant, the consumers are left with no other alternative except to protect their interests.

The first consumer movement was started in 1949 by a Gandhian in Chennai. Sometime later, a consumer protection council was established in Chennai under the leadership of Sri Rajagopalachari. The growth of these organizations was slow till 1980. In 1986, the consumer protection Act was introduced with other allied Acts. The consumer's redressal machinery was introduced at the district, state and National levels.

The Government of Tamil Nadu have constituted consumer redressal forum in all the districts be added by a district judge, will representatives from the public and consumer protection activists, as members the state commission also was established in Chennai headed by a president and a few members. At present, there are 21 District consumer disputes redressal forums.

The voluntary consumer protection organizations number about 30 in Chennai city. There are more than 200 consumer organizations functioning under different names. These organizations have their own federation called "Federation of consumer organizations in Tamil Nadu" (FEDCOT). The federation has 189 voluntary organizations as members. Its head office is located in Chennai. It imparts training to the members of the consumers associations and creates consumer awareness among the public.

THE ROLE OF CONSUMER ORGANISATIONS AND GOVERNMENT

Role of Consumer Organisations

Consumers union, the oldest consumer group which was established in 1936 as a product-testing and consumer education agency, now has a membership of 2 million and publishing consumer reports magazine. It has undertaken broad consumer education programs regarding interest rates, life insurance, product safety, doctor selection and the problems of low-income consumer, consumers regard consumers union as an objective, impartial third party that can assess product quality and consumer complaints through its product-testing facilities.

Consumer Boycotts

One primary means consumer activities and organizations have used to pressure organizations boycotts protesting higher prices, supermarket boycotts were of California grapes to protest grape growers' treatment of migrant workers.

In 1988, thousands of consumers joined action for corporate accountability when it resumed a lapsed six-year boycott of Nestle S.A for violating world Health organization standards on marketing infant formula to developing nations.

Role of Government Organisations

Government framed a legislative measure for protecting the interest of the consumer.

Legislation

In the area of legislation, congress has outlawed.

(1) Deceptive packaging
(2) Required warning labels on cigarettes
(3) Mandated full disclosure of all finance charges in consumer credit agreements
(4) Prohibited the sale of unsafe products to children, and
(5) Required full disclosure of health claims and ingredients for food products.

The most important consumer protection laws passed since 1966 are listed also have a legislative role in protecting consumer rights. State laws have required unit pricing on food products and open dating of perishable foods and drugs. States and local communities have also enforced laws regarding recycling and waste disposal.

REGULATIONS

Federal Regulatory Agencies

It plays a critical role in ensuring consumer rights. The two most important are.

(1) The federal trade commission (FTC)
(2) Food and drug administration (FDA)

Federal Trade Commission (FTC)

The FTC established in 1914 to curb the monopoly powers of big business and unfair trade practices, is also a watch dog over deceptive advertising.

Food and Drug Administration: (FDA)

The FDA, created in 1906 as a result of the outcry over Sinclair's the jungle, sets product standards and requires disclosure of product contents. The federal communications commission (FCC) oversees advertising directed to children.

Since 1991, the FDA has been particularly active in controlling health claims and ensuring accurate labeling as a result of passage of the Nutritional labelling Act in 1990. Board on FDA actions in two-year period. Kraft-general foods had to stop exaggerating the calcium content of its craft singles cheese.

Other Agencies

It established in the 1970's are important

(1) The consumer product safety commission (CPSC)
(2) The environmental protection agency (EPA)

The Consumer Product Safety Commission (CPSC)

It is empowered to set product safety standards to product consumers from risk or injury.

The Environmental Protection Agency (EPA)

It sets controls on industry emissions, toxic wastes and automobile pollution.

Strengthening the Consumer Movement

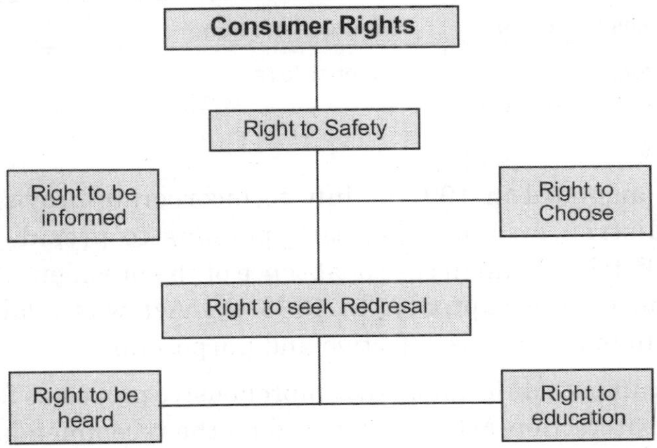

It is generally believed that the consumer movement in India as of today is quite strong when it is compared with other developing countries in Asia, Africa and Latin America. India is a vast country with a very large population of which a sizeable percentage lives below the poverty line. Because of economic inequality, low level of literacy and ignorance, particularly amongst women, the level of consumer awareness is not too high and therefore, the consumer are not able to assert and protect themselves. They easily get exploited by trade and industry and service providers with the liberalization process which started in 1991 the entire economic scenario is undergoing a complete change from a government driven economy to a market-driven economy. Protecting the interests of consumers has, therefore, become one of the paramount concerns of the Government than ever before. Hence, polices are being designed and legislations enacted to protect the consumers interest and grant them the right to safety, right to be informed, right to choose, right to redress, right to healthful and environment and right to privacy.

Consumer Protection Act, 1986

One of the most important milestones in the consumer movement in the country has been the enactment of the consumer protection Act, 1986 to better protect the interest of the consumers. This has revolutionised consumer rights. It is one of the most progressive and comprehensive pieces of socio-benevolent legislation covering all goods and services. The Act established a three-tier redressal forum classified according to the value of claims where complaint can be filed.

Value of Claims	Forum /commission where complaint is to be filed
Up to Rs. 20 lakhs	District forum
Over Rs. 20 lakhs to 1 crore	State commission
More than 1 crore	National level

Amendments

The Act was amended in 1991 mainly to incorporate provisions for the quorum of District forum, appointing persons to preside over State commission/District forum in case of absence of the president to enable the court function uninterruptedly. In 1993 the Act was again amended exhaustively to make it more effective and purposeful.

The Government has formulated comprehensive proposals for amending the consumer protection Act mainly based on the recommendations of the working group and export group set up for the purpose and the wide ranging consultations its had with the representatives of consumer interest, presidents of the national and state commissions and Central Government ministries and departments. These amendments are mainly aimed at facilitating quicker disposal of complaints, enhancing the capability of redressal agencies, strengthening them with more powers, streamlining the procedures and widening the scope of the Act to make it more effective to protect the consumers interest.

The consumer protection (Amendent) bill, 2001 introduced in the Rajya Sabha on 26th April, 2001 among other things address the issues of quicker disposal of complaints, Widening the scope of the Act, Strengthening the consumer courts, streamlining the procedures and a proposal to strengthen the consumer movement. It is also proposed to establish a consumer protection council in every district in order to strengthen the consumer movement at the grassroot level.

Enactment of the Amendment Bill will not only further strengthen the consumer movement in the country but also help the large number of consumers in securing speedy and effective redressal of their complaints.

Governmnet Role

A separate department of consumer affairs was created in 1997 to act as the nodal outfit in the central Government for promoting and protecting the welfare of the consumer. It sets to do this in various ways such as:

(1) Ensuring availability of essential commodities at reasonable prices including monitoring of prices;

(2) Formulating standards of goods and services;

(3) Regulation of weighing and measuring instruments;

(4) Prepacked commodities;

(5) Providing a legislative frame work for safeguarding consumers interest; and

(6) Establishment of machinery for redressal of consumer complaints.

Some of the important measures being taken to strengthen the consumer movement include:

(1) Initiating multimedia publicity programmes to educate the consumers;

(2) Providing financial assistance through consumer welfare fund to the NGO's;

(3) State Governments to generate consumer awareness;

(4) Setting up to district information centres to guide the public;

(5) National awards on consumer protection to encourage outstanding work by women and youth;

(6) Observing national and world consumer rights day to remind the consumer to be vigilant;

(7) Interactions with various interests through central and state consumer protection council to promote;

(8) Protect the rights of the consumers;

(9) Formulation of citizen's charters containing their entitlements to public services;

(10) Standards of performance;

(11) Redressal of grievances for providing an efficient; and

(12) Responsive administration.

Conclusion

Thus social force it originated with the necessary of protecting and promoting the interest of consumers against unethical and unfair trade practices.

Rampant food shortages, hoarding, black marketing, adulteration of edible oil gave birth to the consumer movement in an organized form in 1960's. Till 1970's consumer organizations were largely engaged in writing articles and holding exhibitions. These organizations formed consumer groups to look in to the mal practices in the ration shops and over crowding in the road passenger transport more recently India has witnessed an upsurge in the number of organized consumer groups. There are to day more than 700 consumer groups in the country of which only about 20-25 are well organized and recognized for their work. India has been observing 24 December as National consumers' day as it was on this day that the India parliament enacted COPRA in 1986. India is one country that has exclusive courts for consumer redressal. In 1985 UN adopted the UN guidelines for consumer protection. This was a tool for national to adopt measures to protect consumers and for consumer advocacy groups to press their Government to do so. At the international level it has become the foundation for consumer movement. Today consumer international has 240 organizations from over 100 countries.

The success of the consumer movement mainly depends upon the level of consumer awareness around the country. The Government can only be playing the role of a facilitator or catalyst. The growth of consumer movement is a voluntary effort involving the participation of one all only alert a consumers can protect themselves and the society.

REFERENCES

- Leon G. Schiffman, Lesile Lazar Kanuk *'Consumer Behaviour'.*
- V. Seshadri, *'Consumerism'.*
- P. Sivaprakesam, S. Rajamohan, *'Consumer Empowerment'.*
- C.L. Tyagi, Arun Kumar *'Consumer Behaviour'.*

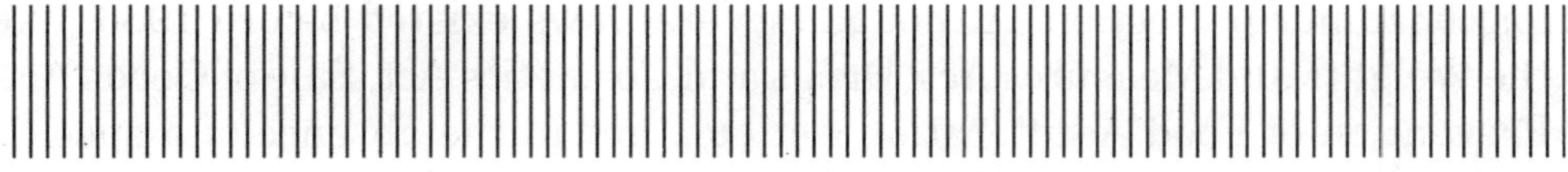

CHAPTER

28

Consumer Awareness and Role of Voluntary Organizations

— Dr. A. Ganesan
— Dr. S. Bhuvaneswari

Introduction

Consumerism is commonly known as consumer protection has gained momentum over the last few decades on account of the formation of a large number of voluntary organizations all over the world. In India, like other developed countries, consumerism started much later, India was among the first countries to enact legislation to protect consumers. The voluntary consumer organizations across the country are there to help consumers to assert their rights. The voluntary consumer organizations work and render their services to meet specific goals which are important for the consuming society as a whole.

Consumer activism in India started way back in 1949 when the housewives of Mumbai raised their voice against the quality of goods sold in the market in 1949 and constituted a consumer protection council for their cause.

India has the distinction of being the only country in the world which has established a parallel judiciary system (by way of consumer courts) to redress consumer grievances. Prior to the Consumer Protection Act, there were many acts already in operation but none of them had the provision of granting any direct relief to consumers. They were penal in nature and the state took action against the defaulters. They, in due course, either paid a penalty and continued following the same practices or managed to escape being penalized all together. Before 1986, there was no comprehensive law for consumer protection. Although, several laws existed before 1986, like the Weights and Measures Act, Drugs and Cosmetics Act, Sale of Goods Act, Prevention of Food Adulteration Act etc., but in the absence of a specific and comprehensive consumer protection law with its own enforcement machinery, consumers throughout the country felt harassed and in fact without remedy.

A sound healthy and efficient consumer organization having support of the people as well as the government can be a powerful force in protecting and safeguarding the rights of the consumers. In India, a vast country, with a large percentage belonging to illiterate class, only a concerted effort of voluntary consumer associations and activists can help make his movement a people's movement.

Consumerism is a social movement which seeks to protect and augment the rights of the consumer in relation to producer. While producer is having the power to design the product, price it and sell it, the consumer at the other end is having the power to reject that particular product. But how far the consumer can exercise his power is questionable. In general consumer often tells that he may not always be fully equipped to exercise that power in his best interest. This may be due to lack of information and misleading information.

This led to 'consumerism' consumer movement is a socio-economic movement which seeks to protect the right of the consumer in relation to the seller. The consumer protection act 1986, that provides the impetus and extremely good opportunity for the aggrieved Indian consumer. The consumer protection act incorporates provisions which ensure consumers with effective safeguards against unfair trade practices indulged in by both the manufacturers and the public utility services. It provides for the consumer protection councils at the central, state level, to uphold, promote and protect consumer rights.

Consumer Rights

1. Rights to safety
2. Right to be informed
3. Right to choose
4. Right to be heard
5. Right to seek redressal
6. Right to be consumer education

Objectives of Consumer Movements

- To restore the better balance between the buyer and seller relations in the market place

- To protect and promote consumer citizen interests
- To safeguard consumer rights
- To prevent exploitation of consumers by unscrupulous traders
- To undertake programmes of consumer education, consumer information and comparative testing and ensure the practices of consumer oriented marketing programmes by business enterprises.

Consumer Protection Council and Forums

Under the provisions of the CPC 1986, there should be consumer councils and a three ties quasi-Judicial Machinery called redressal forums—at National, State and District levels.

About seven hundred consumer forums are functional in India and every state has a State Consumer Dispute Redressal Commission. The National Consumer Redressal Commission (NCDRC) is the apex court in the consumer courts setup and an appeal against the order of this commission can be made with the supreme court only.

The National Commission

This national commission shall consist of 5 members (president and 4 members). A person, who is or has been a judge of the Supreme Court appointed by the Central Government act as the president of the commission. The other members are persons of ability, integrity and standing and adequate knowledge or experience about problems relating to economic, lab, commerce, accountancy industry. One of the 4 members must be a woman. The National Commission can entertain complaints where the value of goods or services and compensation if any is claimed for more than Rs. 1 crore.

State Commission

It consists of 3 members (President and 2 members) A person who is or has been a judge of High Court is appointed by the state government to act as the president of the commission. The other member are persons of ability, integrity and standing and adequate knowledge or experience about problems relating to economics, law, commerce, accountancy industry one of the 2 member must be a woman. The State Commission can entertain complaints where the value of goods or services and compensation if any is claimed from Rs.20 lakhs to 1 crore.

District Level—District Forum

The district Forum consists of a president and 2 members. The president shall be a person who is a district judge or qualified to be a district judge. A member shall be a person of eminence in the field of education, trade and commerce one of the members shall be a lady social worker. The District Forum shall entertain complaints arising from within the district. The District Forum can entertain complaints where the value of goods or services and compensation if any is claimed for upto Rs.20 lakhs.

Reason for Slow Growth of Consumer Movement in India

The progress of consumer movement in India has very slow as compared to that in Western countries and U.S.A. growth of consumer movement may be attributed to the prevailing vicious circles of poverty, high level of illiteracy, insurance, dearth of information flow and general apathy of consumer of India. The consumer movement is very weak and ineffective because the common man is ignorant about the prevalence of legal frame work to protect him. The success of the consumer movement machinery depends upon the level of consumer awareness around the country.

Conclusion

Consumer problem have increased several fold. You may never come to know how much money you pay for services and goods how much should be paid back to you. The right to information act is one tool by which you can have government departments and producers cough up information that they would never otherwise make public. The government should encourage only motivated and dedicated NGOs by acknowledging and highlighting their efforts as well as introducing prestigious awards in the categories of social service.

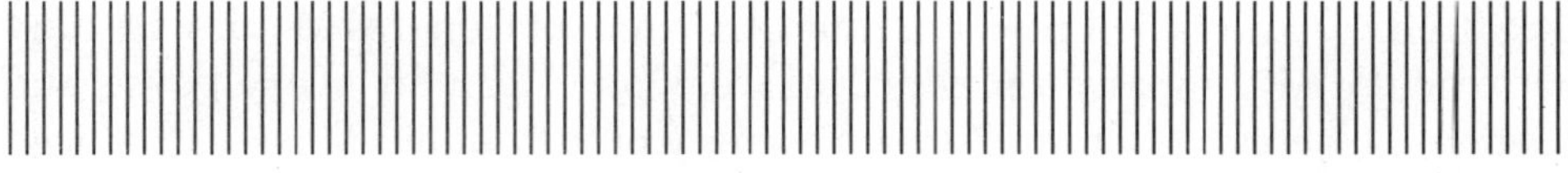

CHAPTER

29
Consumer Behaviour
Global Scenario

— Dr. S. Chitra

Introduction

Consumers are users of goods and services so consumers derive consumption utility from goods and services. Behaviour refers the way of acting or functioning. Consumer behaviour is that subset of human behaviour that is concerned with decision and acts of individuals in purchasing and using products.

The Dictionary of Marketing and Advertising defines consumer behaviour as "observable activities chosen to maximize satisfaction through the attainment of economic goods and services such as choice of retail outlet, preference for particular brands and so on.

Consumer behaviour is not just making a purchase decision or the act of purchasing, it also includes the full range of experiences associated with using or consuming products and services. It also includes the sense of pleasure and satisfaction derived from possessing or collecting 'things'.

Consumer Behaviour—Global Scenario

The field of consumer behaviour is based in the marketing concept, a business orientation that evolved in the 1950's through several approaches referred to as production concept, the product concept and the selling concept.

Though the idea of producing and selling only those goods that match, consumer needs took hold during the 1950's, it was articulated much earlier by Alfred. P. Sloan the President and Chairman of General Motors. In 1924 he articulated company's product strategy as 'A car for every purse and purpose', General Motors offered a variety of affordable Mass—Produced Models from the Aristocratic Cadillac to the Proletarian Chevrolet and took over a large portion of Ford's market share.

Even before evolution of the marketing concept, an intuitive understanding of consumer behaviour was the key to the growth of companies that have remained highly successful even today. So consumer behaviour has become an integral part of strategic market planning. While understanding consumer behaviour is difficult enough for companies marketing within the borders of a single country understanding global consumer is daunting.

Different Categories of Global Consumers

Although consumer in different countries may have some things in common their values, attitudes and behaviours often vary greatly. Consumer behaviour is strongly influenced by culture. There are infact, a variety of perspectives concerning cross-cultural consumer behaviour theory. The four main approaches to cross-cultural consumer behaviour theory are:

Table 29.1 : Cross-cultural Perspectives in Consumer Behaviour Theory

Consumers	Universal	Specific
Universal	1. **GLOBAL PERSPECTIVE** • Consumers are global in preference and behaviour • CB theories are globally applicable.	3. **ETHNIC CONSUMPTION PERSPECTIVE** • Although Consumers are global in preferences you certain products they differ in behaviour • CB theories are not globally applicable
Specific	2. **IMPORTED 'PERSPECTIVE'** • Consumers differ in preference but are global in behaviour. • CB theories are globally applicable.	4. **CULTURAL MEANING PERSPECTIVE** • Consumers differ in preferences and behaviour. • CB theories are not globally applicable.

CB = Consumer Behaviour

The global perspective is rarely used today in its purest form. It continues to be applied in situations where consumer are considered actually to be 'global' but is most appropriate in the case of high technology products that tend to lack a predefined culturally based meaning for consumers.

In the 'imported' perspective, consumers are considered to vary in the types of products that they prefer but to conform generally to the same pattern of behaviour.

The ethnic consumption perspective takes into account the effect of culture on consumer behaviour.

The cultural meaning perspective holds that consumers are cross culturally different in both their preferences for product and their behaviour, An individual's motivations to consume is due not merely to the products specific attributes, but also to the culturally based meaning that are embodied in the product and the consumption act.

Global Consumer Characteristics

In many ways consumer around the world are becoming more alike. Several market segments, like the very wealthy, teenagers and technocrats , even transcend national borders. Yet, despite the decreasing importance of geography as a basis of distinguishing consumers, the average consumers are different around the world, so a study of consumers in major regional markets of the world is imperative.

1. Consumer Behaviour in Europe

Europe consists of 23 countries. There are 340 million car-buying, clothes-washing, and grocery shopping consumers in Europe. Relatively affluent they buy more brand name items than people in any other part of the world. . Europeans are bound by tradition as to the foods, they eat, the way they conduct business, and the way they shop. Though Europeans may be brand conscious 99 per cent of those brands are still national, if not strictly local, in their appeal.

2. Consumer Behaviour in France

The French believe in status and often do not mingle between the groups. France has a very established and updated infrastructure system that supports its direct marketing ventures. Currently, It has the second largest direct mail market in Europe. Television home shopping is popular in France.

3. Consumer Behaviour in Germany

The Germany of today is a united market, immersed in the democratic system. The cultural characteristics reflect the commonality between the east and west Germany of yester years. Evidence proves that it would be beneficial for the marketer to consider different strategies and operationalize in order to cater to the specific region in Germany than a homogenization.

4. Consumer Behaviour in Russia

A study of the Russian consumer conducted by D'Arcy Marius Bentons Bowles revealed, five psychological types, each representing a different market segment. The five psychological types are Kuptsi, Cossacks, Students, Business People and Russian souls

5. The Latin American Consumer Behaviour

The Latin American market, with its bustling cities like Caraces, Soa poulo, Mexico city, Rio de Janerio and Buenos Aires, represents a huge and dynamic consumer economy that is being reshaped by new technologies and media-just as in the united states. Like the United States, Latin America is struggling to integrate traditional values with new ideas and attitudes. Brand names mean less to Latin Americans, where finding the best price is all important.

6. American Consumer Behaviour

American consumers are classified in to four categories

Hispanic Consumers

Hispanics have long been a target from marketers of food, beverages and household care products. Hispanics are now emerging as an attractive market for prices products such as computers financial services, Photography equipment, large appliances, life insurance and automobiles.

African, American Consumers

The black population in the United States is growing in affluence and sophistification. They place more importance on brand names are more brand loyal and do less 'shopping around'.

Asian, American Consumers

They are largely family oriented highly industries and strongly driven to achieve a middle class lifestyle.

The 50 plus Market

Mature consumers are better of financially than younger consumer groups. Because seniors have more time and money. They are an ideal market for exotic travel, restaurants high- tech home entertainment products, leisure foods and services, designer furniture and fashion-financial.

7. Consumer Behaviour in Asia Pacific Region

The countries that comprise the Asia Pacific Region tend to be extremely diverse in terms of culture as well as market characterization. The difference in purchasing power and infrastructure are to be noted when trying to reach the entire Asia Pacific market. The newly industrialized economic of Taiwan, Singapore, and South Korea are markedly different from the South Asian economies, India, Pakistan and Bangladesh are as some of the association of south east. The economic volatility of these countries implies that companies should consider not only the demographic and psychographics characteristic prior to marketing, but look into the chief aspect of affordability.

Food and Eating Habits

- In China fish, shrimps, crabs poultry and pork are preferred.
- In Japan and Korea fish and beef are preferred.
- In Indian vegetation food is preferred but there is increasing meat consumption among new generation. Spices are considered important.
- In Malay and Indonesia halal meats are popular.
- Eating out is popular in Japan, China, Korea, South East Asia.
- Muslims don't eat Pork and consume only meats halal slaughtered.
- Hindus say no to beef.
- But, typical meal consists of staple and some side dishes, organic or chemical free fresh vegetables is considered more healthy all over the world.

8. Consumer Behaviour in India

- The Indian consumers are noted for the high degree of value orientation.
- Indian consumers have a high degree of family orientation.
- Indian consumers are also associated with values of nurturing, care and affection.
- Apart from psychology and economics, the role of history and tradition in shaping the Indian consumer behaviour is quiet unique.
- Most replacement buyers are seeking pleasures in newness and better choices, they are upgrading the product to go up in life. For them, price is not single most important factor.

Different Segments of Indian Consumers

1. The Socialites

Socialites belong to the upper class. They prefer to shop in specialty stores, go to clubs the weekends, and spend a good amount on luxury goods... They go for high value, exclusive products. Socialites are also very brand conscious and would go only for the best known in the market.

2. The Conservatives

The conservatives belong to the middle class. The conservative segment is the reflection of the true Indian culture. They are traditional in their outlook, cautions in their approach towards purchases; spend more time with family than in partying and focus more on savings than spending.

3. Women Consumer

'Indian women' are no more stereo typed household ones with a circumference being their family and their home. Today's women are "the women of substance". Together with her sharing and caring job, she displays the hidden ambition in her ambit to the world and her caliber comes to force.

3. Professional Consumer

Horizon 2003 a study by BBC world, BBC's 24 hour international news and informational channel, using the latest census as a base, gives some starting insight into the attitudes and activities of India's leading consumers and decision makers. The study reveals that in Indian men continue to dominate. The research was conducted by market research agency MFU-MBL across six top metros profiling 380,000 people. The results of the research tells that even today only 16 per cent of Indian professionals are women. Therefore consumer decision making in all areas ranging from what car to buy to which clothes manufacturer to patronize is dictated by men when it comes to the most upscale market segment in India .

5. Rural Consumer

About three quarters of the Indian population are in the rural areas and with the growing middle class, especially in the Indian cities; the spill over effect of the growing urban middle class is also felt in the rural areas. Low purchasing power, standard of living, per capita Income, economic and social positions are the traits of rural consumers.

6. Children in Family Purchase

Children constitute an important target market segment and merit attention from a marketing perspective. Children enjoy greater discretion not only in making routine consumption decisions for the family but also in pestering their parents to buy other products desired by them. Children constitute three different markets the primary, the influencer, and the future market.

7. Online Consumer

Research by Shun and Yanjie (2006) showed that are product types, which are more likely to be sold online such as software, books, electronics music. Reason for this is that when purchasing these type of products, one does not require personal inspection and most, if not all features, can be outlined in the product description and images.

According to the recent research on consumer behaviour on the internet users, there are four distinct consumer groups with different intentions and motivation. They use internet for

- Exploration
- Entertainment
- Shopping
- Information

Changing Trends in Indian Consumer Behaviour

- Urbanization is taking place in India at a dramatic pace and is influencing the life style and buying behaviour of the consumer.
- Indian consumer looking for quality choose expensive brands as they feel that price is an indicator of quality. Indian consumer buying behaviour is influenced by freebies.
- The environmental awareness in India has started affecting marketing of products based upon their eco-friendliness.
- ICE refers to Information, Communication and Entertainment. the dominant mental model of the ICE age consumer is drawn by the fact that they use the internet, cellphone and is entertainment-oriented.
- Awareness of info-tech opportunities and IT-enabled services, along with the communication revolution and the connectively leap have brought in an educational push. Education is now seen as a key to making life better.

Conclusion

To conclude one can say that it is not easy to solve the puzzle of consumer behaviour. The behaviour depends upon the consumer's decisions that cannot wait for the evaluation of all the alternatives available before him.

Consumer can not always, pause to find out the cause-effect relationships of his decisions. All that can be said is that he will normally take a decision, which he believes will meet his needs...And the marketer's job remains challenging, mainly because he has to predict the unpredictable the consumer.

So, The importance of consumer behaviour in marketing has been beautifully described in a journal titled Modern Management, Calcutta January '99 in the following words. "Consumer behaviour is a rapidly growing field of research and teaching which in addition to considerable value of marketing managers and others who are professionally concerned with buying activity".

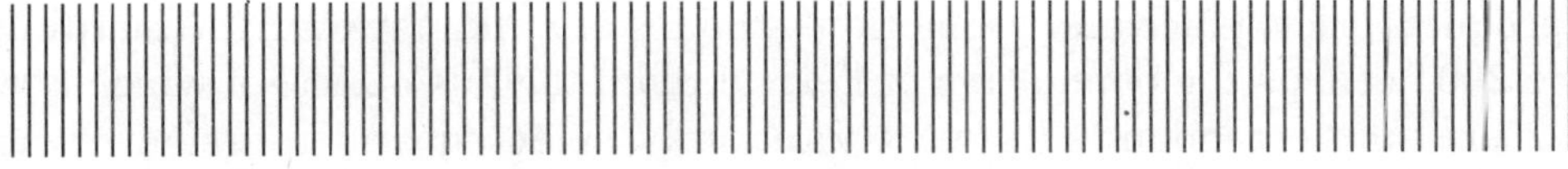

CHAPTER

30

A Study on Consumer Preference Towards Branded and Unbranded Milk

—Mrs. B. Sumathi

Introduction

Consumerism is a recent and universal phenomenon. Consumerism is all about protection of the interest of the consumers. In the new era of consumerism the concepts of 'comparative costs', 'consumer preference' and 'consumer choice' has been vital aspects of the economy. So, a study on consumer preference towards branded and unbranded milk in Periyakulam Town, Theni District was conducted to analyze the consumer preference.

Objectives of the Study

The study has been conducted to analyze the quality awareness of milk consumers and to identify the brand and packaging preference of consumers. Consumer's opinion about price and placement of the product milk has also been studied.

Milk has been used from time immemorial as the sole food for infants and as a supplement to the diets of children and adults. Milk is almost a complete food which has high nutritive value. It supplies body building proteins, bone-forming minerals and health giving vitamins and furnishes energy-giving lactose and milk fat. All these properties make milk an important food for pregnant mothers, growing children, adolescents, adults, convalescents and patients alike.

Methodology

The study makes an attempt to present the consumer preference towards product, price, place and promotion—the P's of milk marketing. According to 2001 census the population of Periyakulam town is 43,050 of which 800 (2%) sample respondents were randomly selected and interview was administered to elicit their opinion about branded and unbranded milk. Percentages were computed to analyze the data.

Consumer Preference Towards the Product Milk

Product is a bundle of attributes that satisfies the consumer. The attributes of product are its physical features namely the quality, branding and packaging.

Quality Awareness of Consumers

Quality is the attribute that brings consumer satisfaction. The milk with high nutritive value produced and marketed in hygienic manner can be considered as a quality product.

Table 30.1 : Purchase Motive of Milk

Sl. No.	Purchase motive	Branded milk	%	Un branded milk	%	Total	%
1.	Taste	-	-	-	-	-	-
2.	Neat package	-	-	-	-	-	-
3.	Easy availability	10	3	410	93	420	53
4.	Hygienic	-	-	-	-	-	-
5.	Thick contents	340	94	10	2	350	44
6.	Impact of advertisements	10	3	-	-	10	1
7.	Nutritious value	-	-	-	-	-	-
8.	Reasonable price	-	-	20	5	20	2
	Total	**360**	**100**	**440**	**100**	**800**	**100**

Table 30.1 reveals that out of 800 sample respondents only 360 (45%) respondents prefer branded milk and 340 (94%) of them had opined that they prefer branded milk for its thick contents. The remaining 440 respondents (55%) prefer to buy unbranded milk. The purchase motive of unbranded milk was easy availability according to 93 per cent of unbranded milk users. Hygienic and nutritive values have not been given consideration. This shows the lack of quality consciousness among great majority of consumers in the study area.

Adulteration impairs the quality value of milk.

Table 30.2 : Presence of Adulterants in Milk

Sl.No.	Presence of adulterants	Number of respondents	% of respondents
1	YES	310	39
2	NO	490	61

Of the 800 sample respondents only 310 (39%) respondents had identified adulteration in the milk they buy.

Table 30.3 : Type of Adulterant

Sl.No.	Type of Adulterant	No. of Respondents	%
1	Mixing of water	250	81
2	Removal of fat	—	—
3	Adding hydrogenated vegetable fat	—	—
4	Mixing skim milk powder	60	19
	TOTAL	**310**	**100**

According to Table 30.3 addition of water to milk was identified as the adulterant by majority of the respondents namely 81 per cent and mixing of skim milk powder with milk was identified as an adulterant by 60 (19%) sample respondents.

Brand Preference of Consumers

The brand image can do wonders to a product's marketing as is evident from the words of perfume princess- coco channel: In the factory we pack perfume; in market, we sell hope!

Table 43.4 : Brand Preference of Buyers

Sl.No.	Brand	No of Respondents	%
1	Aavin	63	19
2	Arokia	250	73
3	Amirtha	7	2
4	Imayam	20	6
5	Others (Specify)	—	—
	TOTAL	**340**	**100**

Table 30.4 shows that AROKIA is the popular brand among the branded milk buying respondents as 250 (73%) of them buy AROKIA brand. 63 respondents (19%) buy AAVIN brand followed by 20 (6%) respondents

buying IMAYAM brand and 7 (2%) respondents buying AMIRTHA brand. Though 440 (55%) respondents out of 800 respondents buy unbranded milk 210 (48%) of them had preferred to switch over to branded milk.

Consumers Pack Preference

Majority of the respondents namely 770 (96 percent) do not like sachet type of packaging of milk.

Table 43.5 : Reasons for Not Preferring Sachet Type of Packing

Sl.No.	Reasons	No Respondents	% of Respondents
1.	Spoilage	50	6
2.	Difficult to handle	170	23
3.	Wastage	550	71
	TOTAL	**770**	**100**

Table 30.5 reveals that 550 (71%) out of 770 sachet disliking respondents have opined that sachet type packing causes wastage. 170 (23%) respondents had felt that sachet type packing is difficult to handle. Sachet packing causes spoilage of milk was the pinion of 50 (6%) of respondents.

Getting direct milk in own container had been preferred against bottles and other plastic containers by all the 800 sample respondents.

Consumers Opinion about Price of Milk

Price determines the purchasing of milk. The unbranded milk is sold at Rs. 15 per litre and the price of branded milk varies between Rs 20 to 22 per litre in the study area. All the 800 respondents had felt that milk is available at affordable price and all of them have no intention to reduce the quantity of milk purchases even if price increases. This shows that milk is a price inelastic product.

Consumers Opinion about Point of Purchase-Place

Place here refers to the point of purchase of milk.

Table 30.6 : Purchasing Point of Milk

Sl.No.	Point of purchase	No. of respondents	%
1.	Door Delivery	410	51
2.	Milk Society	50	6
3.	Aavin Sales Depot	10	1
4.	Branded Milk Sales Depot	330	42
	TOTAL	**800**	**100**

Of the 800 respondents 410 (51%) respondents buy milk from milk vendor and the remaining 49 per cent respondents buy milk from sales depot. So, door delivery of milk is preferred by consumers. Convenience in buying dominates the purchase preference of milk.

Usually milk is purchased twice a day. The study confirms this as 750 (94%) respondents out of 800 respondents do buy milk both in the morning and in the evening. But round the clock supply is preferred by the consumers as 690 (86%) consumers out of 800 respondents have considered it essential to install automotive milk vending machines at convenient locations in Periyakulam.

Consumer Opinion about Promotion Strategy

Promotion refers to the strategy adopted to make the product acceptable. People in India love to drink milk and the study also confirms it, all the 800 respondents had opted milk as their favourite beverage when compared with fruit juice, cool drinks and others.

Hence, no efforts are needed to make milk acceptable. Because of this reason only few promotional strategies are adopted to sell milk. Advertisement is used only by branded milk sellers. Only 10 (1.25%) respondents out of 800 respondents have considered advertisement as a purchase motivator.

Conclusion

Indian dairying is endowed with the three A's of marketing–availability, acceptability and affordability. The study also confirms the same but as regards acceptability the consumers accept milk without any quality consciousness. Consumer's consciousness determines the effectiveness of consumerism. In this regard the following suggestions are offered:

The Government has to take pro-active role

- In increasing consumer awareness regarding importance of quality value of milk and educating the consumer in this regard.
- To encourage high levels of ethical conduct for those engaged in the production and distribution of milk.
- To undertake research to develop a packing material other than sachet, bottle and plastic containers.
- To develop cheaper testing equipments to check the quality of milk. The cost of testing should be affordable by individual consumer.

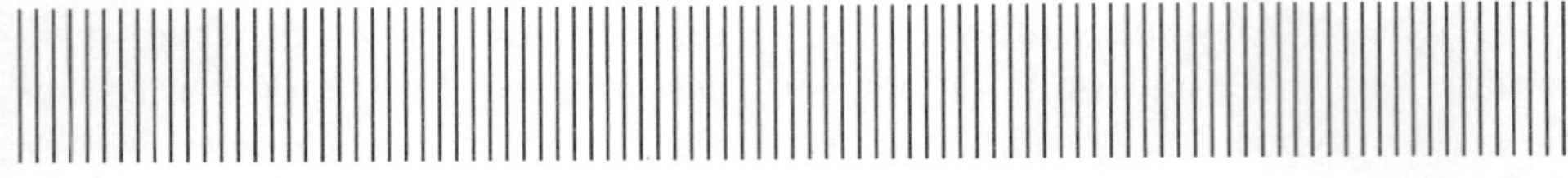

CHAPTER

31

Consumer Awareness and Protection

— M. Ganesh
— K. Soundarapandiyan

Introduction

Consumers must be aware of the sale and purchase of goods, the health and security aspects also. Ensuring the safety of food items sold in the market is essential these days. Legal measures for consumer safety and consumer awareness must be uniform, and transparent in terms of prices, quality of goods, and stocks. Consumers must have the tools to combat malpractices and protect their rights.

Anyone who consumes goods is a consumer. Consumers get exploited in the market. They respond to advertisements and buy goods. Generally advertisements do not give all the information that a consumer needs to know or wants to know about a product.

Consumer Awareness

Consumer awareness is about making the consumer aware of his/her rights. It is a marketing term which means that consumers are aware of products or services, its characteristics and the other marketing *P*'s (place to buy, price, and promotion).Though the first consumer movement began in England after the Second World War, a modern declaration about consumer's rights was first made in the United States of America in 1962, where four basic consumer rights (choice, information, safety and to be heard) were recognized. *Ralph Nadar,* a consumer activist, is considered as the father of '*consumer movement*'. March 15 is now celebrated as the World

Consumer Rights Day. The United Nations in 1985 adopted certain guidelines to achieve the objectives of maintaining protection for consumers and to establish high level ethical conduct for those engaged in production and distribution of goods and services.

High prices, duplicate articles, underweight and under-measurements, rough behaviour, undue conditions, artificial scarcity are some of the ways by which consumers are exploited by manufacturers and traders. Limited information, limited supplies and low literacy are factors causing exploitation of consumers.

In India, the concept of consumer protection is not new. However, an organized and systematic movement to safeguard the interest of consumers is a recent phenomenon. The consumers have to be aware not only of the commercial aspects of sale and purchase of goods, but also of the health and security aspects. Food safety has become an important element of consumer awareness these days. In case of food products, its quality depends not only on its nutritional value, but also on its safety for human consumption. Consumption of contaminated or adulterated food is a major cause of human illness and suffering.

This called for strong legal measures to ensure that the manufacturers and sellers observe uniformity and transparency in prices, stocks and quality of their goods. Enactment of Consumer Protection Act, 1986 was one of the most important steps taken to protect the interests of consumers. The provision of the Act came into force, with effect from July 1, 1987. The act recognizes consumer's right to seek redresses and right to consumer education.

The *salient features* of the Act are as follows:

- Applies to all goods and services unless specifically exempted by the Union Government;
- Covers all the sectors whether private, public or cooperative;
- Enshrines the consumer's rights related to safety, information, choice, representation and redress and consumer education.
- The act gives consumers an additional remedy besides those which may be available to them under the provisions of other existing laws and they are free to choose the remedy.
- Empower consumers seeking discontinuance of certain unfair and restrictive trade practices, defects or deficiencies in services and stopping in services or withdrawal of hazardous goods from the market.

There are no legal formalities for filing the complaint. Suppose, one is cheated by a trader or a manufacturer and wish to make a complaint to consumer court, one can write the details on a plain paper. Attach the supporting documents, that is, guarantee or warrantee card and cash memo with the complaint and submit it in the district consumer court. One need not have to go to any lawyer or professional for legal assistance and can plead the case in the consumer court. Since, the enactment of the Consumer Protection Act and even before that, newspapers and magazines have been responding to the needs of consumers. Apart from publishing articles, columns etc. newspapers have also tried to come to the rescue of harassed consumers. The Indian Express was one of the first newspapers to start a consumer complaint column.

The Consumers should undertake steps to create a facilitative mechanism with the following objectives:

1. Promote General Awareness of the rights of the consumer by encouraging consumer education and supplying information.
2. Publish periodical and product specific booklets, pamphlets, cassettes, CDs, slides, documentary films and other devices of mass communication for promoting consumer awareness in English and regional languages, highlighting the problem in specified areas like real estate, public utilities, non-banking financial agencies etc.
3. Enlighten the business community on its ethical and legal obligations to maintain quality of the products or services and to be transparent in dealing with consumers.
4. Encourage consumer activities to strengthen the existing institutional set up of consumer dispute redressal by acting as a facilitator between consumer and the institution.
5. Study the available legal remedies, analyze and suggest new measures for the effective and better consumer protection.
6. Bring together the consumer, traders and policy makers to exchange information of mutual interest for better coordination. Bring together the NGO's/Consumer activities operating in different areas and equip them with suitable and required information and knowledge to enable them to act as nodal agents of change in rural areas.
7. Organize and conduct seminars, workshops and group discussions and thus provide a platform for threadbare discussion of the issues and evolve suitable remedial action. Conduct motivational campaigns for groups of potential customers both in urban and rural areas.
8. Coordinate programmes organized by Central and State Governments, State Legal Aid Authorities, Academic Institutes, National and International Consumer Organizations.

9. Periodic interaction with electronic and print media on success stories of consumers.
10. Establish links with educational institutions like universities, colleges, high schools to emphasize the need for improving consumer education in the curriculum. Consumer clubs which were started recently by the A.P. Consumer affairs, Food and Civil Supplies Department would go a long way in achieving this.
11. Interact with national level organizations like NISIET, NIRD, and ASCI etc. to explore possible collaboration and organize awareness programmes for their clientele and undertake research projects.

Some of the *common methods of exploitation* are:

1. Under weight and under measurements –not measured or weighed correctly
2. Substandard Quality—defective home appliances and medicines beyond expiry date
3. High prices—charging above the retail price
4. Duplicate Articles—selling fake items in the name of the original
5. Adulteration and Impurity—is done to get higher profits
6. Lack of safety Devices—absence of inbuilt safeguards in appliances
7. Artificial Scarcity—hoarding and black marketing
8. False and Incomplete Information—misleading information on quality, durability, and safety.
9. Unsatisfactory after sales Service—high cost items like electronics and cars require constant and regular service.
10. Rough behaviour and Undue conditions—harassment in getting LPG connection or a telephone connection.

Factors Causing Exploitation of Consumers

1. Limited Information—providing full and correct information will help in the choice
2. Limited Supplies—when goods and services are in short supply then price shoots up
3. Limited Competition—single producer may manipulate the market in terms of price and stocks.
4. Low Literacy—illiteracy leads to exploitation. Hence Consumer Awareness is essential.

Rise of Consumer Awareness and Rights and Duties of Consumers

As codified under the Indian Laws the Consumers have the following:

Rights

1. Right to Safety—to protect against hazardous goods
2. Right to be Informed—about price, quality, purity
3. Right to choose—access to a variety of goods and services at competitive prices.
4. Right to be Heard—consumers interest and welfare must be taken care of
5. Right to seek Redressal—protection against unfair trade practices and settling genuine grievances.
6. Right to Consumer Education.—Knowledge about goods and issues related to consumers.

Duties

1. Get a bill for every important purchase and also the Warranty card
2. Check the ISI mark or AGMARK on the goods
3. Form consumer awareness groups
4. Make a complaint on genuine grievances
5. Consumers must know to exercise their rights

Consumer Protection Measure

1. Legislation Concerning Consumer Rights

The Consumer Protection Act 1986 provides for consumer disputes redressal at the state and national level. With the help of this law the agencies can solve grievances in a speedy, simple and inexpensive manner. A separate department of consumer affairs was set up at the state and Central Government. A three tier system of consumer courts at the National, State and District levels were set up. These agencies have done good work by handling lakhs of cases.

2. Public Distribution System

To protect the poor from price rise and black marketing the government food security to the poor by supplying essentials through the ration or Fair price shops.

3. Standardization of Products

These are done to assure the quality of products. The ISI stamp on goods is placed by the Bureau of Indian standards. This caters to industrial and consumer goods. These goods can be trusted to confirm to specific standards. Agmark is meant for Agricultural products.

At the International level the International Organization for Standardization (ISO) located in Geneva sets common standards. The FAO and WHO provide food standards.

Consumerism in India: Future Scenario

Through consumer movement in India is yet to gain its full momentum, growing consumerism may manifest its impact on trade and industry in the following ways.

As Indian customer is getting exposed to better quality products and services his expectations are also rising fast. The firms in future will be required to produce safer, effective and aesthetically designed user-friendly products to satisfy the needs of discerning consumers. The growing intolerance towards substandard and unsafe products is a healthy symptom in this regard. It should ring the warning-bell for those so for not concerned about the safety and quality of goods produced or marketed by them.

The public and the courts will probably more forcefully question unfair and arbitrary business performance causing damage to the environment. The growing awareness among the people would compel business houses to be more careful about pollution and adopt effective measures to prevent any damage to the environment. The social responsibility concept may also find its due place in business practices of Indian firms.

Despite liberalized economic policies, business in future will have to operate more under scrutiny of government, the press and public interest groups. Business units will be required to adopt necessary safety measures for the general public and also for their workers. Stringent punitive measures might be introduced to prevent child labour, not paying the minimum wages and violating other business norms. Public interest groups may come down heavily on the firms resorting to misleading advertising, and making unsubstantiated claims in business communications. Firms will also be required to provide the service necessary for making effective use of products marketed by them.

The creditability of existing business organizations and their ethical assumptions may come under public evaluation rather more forcefully. Meaning that, public opinion could question even the internal procedures and value systems of business firms as they affect the society and the individuals. This may probably damage the philosophy and practice of management in many ways.

Conclusion

A survey conducted by 'Consumer Action Group' revealed that due to higher media exposure and rise in literacy levels, public expectation from various products and services as well as peoples' perception of quality, service and corporate responsibility are changing fast. In future, this may call for a different marketing approach, especially for mass consumption goods, domestic appliances, utilities and personal services. Growing consumer awareness and the very concept of consumerism is bound to throw up several new challenges for the marketers in the next few years.

For business firms, gone are the days of arbitrary decisions, they will have to learn to live with consumerism. Business leaders accustomed to operating in sellers' market may find themselves in an uncomfortable situation in the new environment. Changes in the socio-cultural and the business environment that have largely been responsible for the advent of consumerism are here to stay and the bad news for such firms is that they are irreversible.

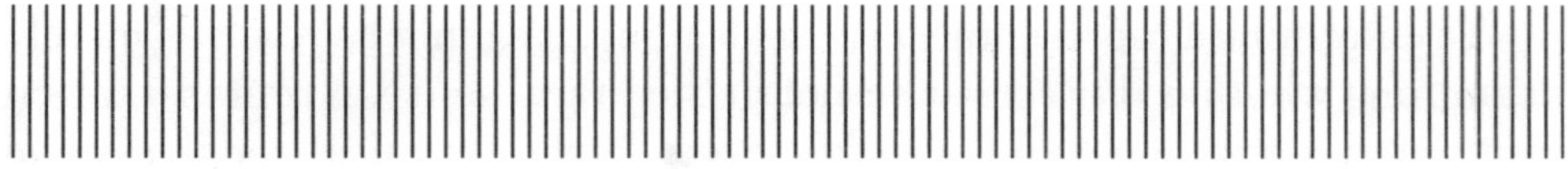

CHAPTER

32

Role of Media in Consumer Awareness and Promotion of Consumer Rights

— Ms. Deepa Viswam

Introduction

Comparative advertisement is correlatively recent development. This type of advertising might be called the don riches schools of advertising where nothing scores as well as a put down. The guiding principle don't tell consumers why they should buy your product. Try to persuade them not to buy your competitors. For example in USA struggling Seven Up co. brags that its lemon lime soda doesn't contain caffeine. The company doesn't explain what if anything is wrong with caffeine but not hat most other soft drinks have it.

When Proctor and Gamble introduced Ariel, it compares ariels cleaning and whitening qualities with those of archrival surf ultra of HLL. Similarly when IFB Bosche launched its sturdy washing machine, it compared it with Videocon washing machine instead of pointing out only its USPS. BPL compared its refrigerators with other bands claiming it as a refrigerating system.

The informative content of advertisement has raised many problems for interpretation. although there is consensus that the false and misleading advertisement are bad, few however agree about how best to tell whether an advertisement is misleading. In the course of interpretation of advertisement rules were formulated by various courts, an over view of the rules are follows:

To determine a representation is misleading, it cannot be resolved merely examining whether it is correct or not in the literal sense. A representation containing a statement apparently correct in the technical sense may be have the effect of misleading the buyer by using tricky language. Similarly a statement which may be inaccurate in the technical literal sense can covey the truth and sometimes more effectively than literally correct statement. It is therefore necessary to examine that does a consumer on reading the advertise form a belief different from what the truth is?

This consumer belief can be determined by two methods:

To ascertain the effects of the advertisement, which places a handiwork on the eye and mind of the reader. For example an advertisement might be deemed to be deceptive if deceives some consumers by causing them to hold false belief about the product.

2. To ascertain the character of the advertisement, without explicit reference to the advertisements effect on consumers. For example an advertisement is deceptive if I make factual claim and that claim is false. The federal trade commission in United States and MRTP commission in India has been made in the advertisement. It is easy then decide whether that claim is true or false. However it is difficult to determine which claims an advertisement can fairly be read as making.

Where statement is capable of bearing two meanings—one of which is true and other is false. The mere fact that one possible meaning is true will not necessarily prevent finding of deceptiveness. However where a statement can convey a secondary meaning it may be allowed even though the primary original meaning could not be truthfully asserted, if it shown that the word in fact has secondary meaning to the general public.

The advertisement may be misleading because things are composed or purposefully printed in such a way as to mislead. In case of advertisements common law principle will apply to the extent that seller is not generally bound to disclose information which may be relevant to prospective purchaser's decision but if he does speak on any given matter he is bound not to distort the information he gives by revealing only part of the truth.

Consumer is considered to have been wronged when he does not get goods or service of the stated quality made in the advertisement. It is no defensing that although the product was of lower quality than claimed it was still worth the price charged.

Where an advertiser is making a claim which is not susceptible of objective proof for example a claim that the product will produce a subjective sensation which is matter of taste or emotion and will greatly very from person to person. In such cases physical factors which produce the sensation can be examined objectively.

When an advertiser is making a false or misleading claim, it has to be scanned in order to ascertain whether that claim is a promise, prediction or opinion. If it falls in the category of promise it should be declared false or misleading and not otherwise irrespective of the fact whether the promise was made which relate to present, past or future.

REFERENCES

- Dr. Atul Dhyani *'Indian Journal of Marketing'* (Consumerism: Gobal *vs.* Indian Perspectives)
- Dr. S.B. Sadar *'Indian Journal of Marketing'* (Consumerism)
- V. Seshadri *'Consumerism'* Mittal Publications
- P. Sivapradlism and S. Rajamohan *'Consumer Empavement'* Kanishka Publishers and Distributors
- David L. Lowdon and Albert and T. Della Bitta *'Consumer Behaviour'*

  Tata McGraw-Hill Publishing Company Ltd., New Delhi

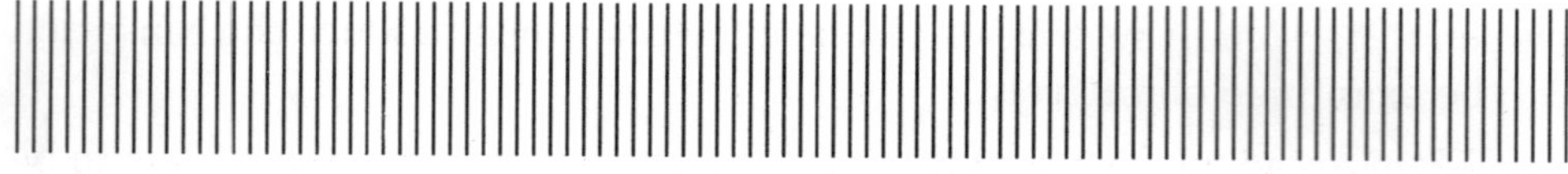

CHAPTER

33

E-commerce and Consumer Behaviour

—Dr. K.M. Murugesan and Mr. K. Alagar

Introduction

The Fast and dramatic changes in information technology specially in last one decade has given new concept of marketing in which buyer and seller do not see each other face to face nor see the goods physically; the whole transaction is carried out with the help of 'on line' communication. The entire deal is carried out with the help of Computer-Telecommunication and Networking with associated Hardware.

Meaning

It is "a way of conducting imagines and executive business transactions and services through electronic media and networking is computer and communication network, website, email or resorted.

Types of Internet

The types of selling through the uses of internet and other electronic devices can be of following types:

1. Business to Business

This implies selling by one business manufacture to other business manufactures, trade, wholeseller or retailer. The number of companies like TELCO, IBM, CITI BANK, ESSAR, TVS, MARUTI, BAJAJ, and many other are doing B2B. In 1998 out of total E-Commerce of US $ 210 billions US $100 billions was accounted for B2B.

2. Business to Consumer

When business sells to consumer it is called B2C and is most important for over point of view. The products included item sold Departmental Stores, Chemist shops, grocery stores, books, stationery, clothes, vegetables and fruits. As yet in India such sales are only of US $ 100 billion but are expected to go up to US $900 billion by 2005. Many service sectors are adopting this mode.

3. Consumer to Consumer

Under this system when some consumers want to dispose of his old items, he can take the help are selling through Internet. But this type of E-Commerce is not very common at least in India and the business is negligible.

4. Business to Government

Business House or on individual business has to file Income Tax and Sales Tax of various types of other returns. As yet this requires filing of return in respective of office and apply for approval in concerned office. But now many countries allow this type of activity through email/E-commerce.

5. Government to Consumer

In order to provide facilities to public speed up information and records government in many case provided record of information through this system; sale of documents, passport forms, copies of returns etc..

Main features of E-Commerce are that one does not physically feel an item on basic information supplied through website or in response to consumer inquiry. It is largely limited to durable goods like computers, TV's, Automobiles, Books travel reservation in case of service it is popular for banking and share purchases.

E-mail Network

E-Commerce requires visit of website, selection of products, select a payment mode, realization of money and dispatch of goods. This process may be depicted as under.

A. Visit of Website

Selection of products

Selection of payment

1. Credit card
2. E-Banking
3. VP-Courier

4. Placement of Order through e-mail
5. Realization of money

Dispatch to the customer can be online or through courier.

Advantage to Consumer

Consumers have number of advantages and convenience and therefore the system is becoming popular.

1. Consumer has wider choice not from his town or country but also round the globe unless there are import restrictions.
2. Customerized or personalized product and service. For instance of if some lady wants bra of exact size, her size can be measured through internet and stored and she will be supplied bra of her requirement.
3. It helps to globalize retail trading. One can buy things without geographical boundaries.

Disadvantages to Consumer

1. Biggest disadvantage of e-commerce is that one is not able to see and feel the product;
2. The market is restricted to high income and educated population own and knows the use of Internet;
3. There is the big problem in online payment it is with regard to time and legality of order to complete the transaction.

Operation of E-Commerce

The goods or services are selected by opening up websites, and orders or placed through e-mail without use of paper.

The seller asks the buyer through e-mail mode of payment which is generally through credit card.

The seller makes bill on e-mail confirms the order subject to satisfactory arrangement for payment which are generally through credit card or e-banking but some time value payable parcels are also supplied.

Government Regulation Act

In addition procedure for Government procurement on Internet has been laid down. In order to facilitate E-Commerce India has also allowed digital signatures and passed IT act to protect all its players and promote e-commerce. In India e-commerce started in November, 1998. After the Monopoly of Government on Internet Service private sector was allowed to provide Internet service. Thereafter digital signature have been recognized and rules framed for it. India's first E-commerce was started on August 13, 1998 by Rediff.com. Now it has been estimated by market research that by 2003 in India there will be 27 million household with Internet it is expected that Internet through cable bill start in India like other country's which will make operations popular; already there are a number of *dot.coms* like *Rediff.HLL, Amul, Baba bazar.com buy everything.com, hids club of India.com, emedlife.com, jobmart.com* etc. It should be understood that registration of dot.com with international organization is must for e-commerce. In order to promote e-commerce the Indian Electronic Commerce Act was enacted in 1998 which provides that electronic records and signatures (with certain exemption) should be accorded the same treatment as paper records and signatures for the purpose complying with statutory writing signature evidence and record keeping requirements. This has helped development of e-commerce in India.

CPA Website

CPA Webtrust is a comprehensive e-commerce seal of assurance has been developed to build trust and confidence among consumers. Any CPA and CPA equivalent who have completed 3 years and have been permitted by the AL CPA are allowed to issue CPA webtrust seal of assurance. The CPA webtrust seal assurance to consumer and business purchasing goods through e-commerce that the quality and other description of goods are as advertise on website.

Advertisement Methods in E-Commerce Sales

Most important roll of advertisement in e-commerce is to get to consumer made interested to surface the particular website for which it is not enough to advertise and Internet but in Print Media and on Audio Video also. For the Instance Bababazar.com operating form NOIDA near Delhi delivers goods for as low amount Rs. 150 and claims that "one can buy most of vegetable and fruits that are not available at local market".

Conclusion

In order to promote sales through e-commerce one is required to target right customers, provide him the information asked, for develop accepted brands, develop confidence by supplying the products as per specification and details provided and fast delivery. In order to get grater market access one should not sell what everyone else is operating. Products must be consumer specific. The system of advertisement on net is different must be properly understood and followed to make them more fruitful. There are certain problems are globalization regarding traffic, trade and exchange restriction which will have to be tackled by WTO and international code will to be developed.

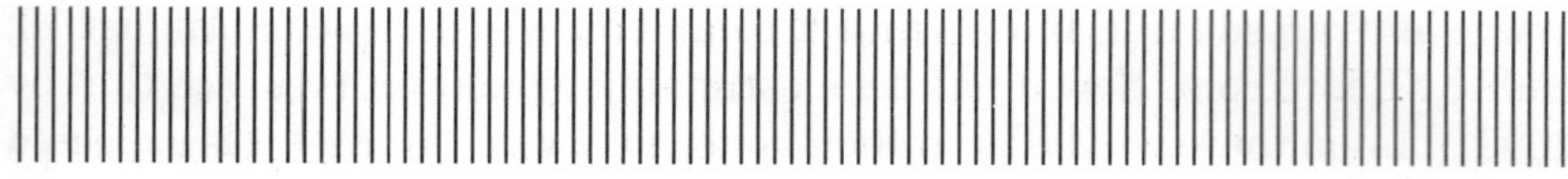

CHAPTER

34

Psychological Aspects of Consumerism

— Mrs. M. Fowzia Sultana

Introduction

Psychological aspects play a significant and most enduring role in influencing the buyer behaviour of the customer. They have contributed much to the markets to understand the buyer and explain how consumer learns regarding a product and how they improve their buying styles. A set of psychological processes join with certain consumer features and ends with the purchase decision finally. The markets aim is to understand what happens in consumer consciousness between the outside marketing stimuli and the purchase decisions. The buying decisions of the customer are influenced by four major Psychological factors—motivation, perception, learning and belief and attitudes.

It is obvious that the psychological factors like, motivation perception, learning and belief and attitudes it makes a person to take a buying decision.

Motivation

What is motivation? Like tension, discomfort, motive is needs that are sufficiently pruning to alive the person to act.

For example,

When a person is in need to travel a long distance frequently regarding his work he is feel to buy a car (or) scooter. From this example we understood discomfort and expectation lead to motivation.

Perception

A motivated person is ready to act. It is the processes by which an individual select to organize and interprets information input to create a meaningful perform of the work.

Perception is the process which makes aware of and gives meaning to their environment. Some of the technical factors affect the way a product is perceived. It does not refer to the product technology but rather to how the person looks at the product.

Example

People's perception towards colour set mobiles is more when compared to people preferring block and white mobiles.

Consumer's mental readiness to buy a product is also an important factor in perception.

Example

Consumers who are satisfied with the features of Sony TV may continue to purchase the same company television knowing that better televisions can be bought at a lower price.

Previous or past experience also influences perception. Though past experiences makes a consumer to buy the same product on the other side, if the same person is mentally disturbed or depressed he may feel of difficult to see the benefits or advantages of the product.

Characteristics of Perception

1. Subjective—no two individuals perceive the same product in the same way.
2. Selective—a few of the advertisement that people receive a day are converted to message.
3. Summative—the frequent note of the advertisements leads to better understanding of the object

Learning

Learning is the changes in ideas and views that an individual's behaviour arising from experience. Learning is created through the interplay of drives stimuli, cues, responses and reinforcement. Example—Marketers.

Belief

A belief is a descriptive thought that a person holds about something. These beliefs may be based on knowledge, opinion or faith. Marketers are very much interested in the beliefs of people about their products and services because they influence their buying behaviour. It some of the beliefs are wrong and inhibit purchase; the marketer should launch a campaign to correct these beliefs.

Example:

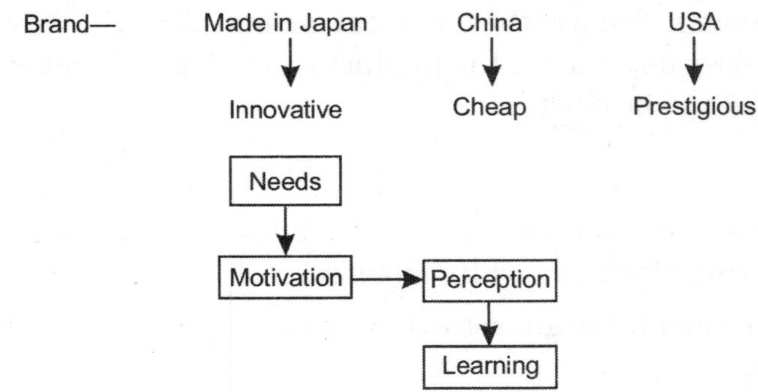

Attitudes

An attitude is a person's enduring favourable or unfavourable evaluation emotional feeling and action tendencies towards some object or idea.

Conclusion

A psychological aspect that is motivation, perception, learning belief and attitudes tend to react correspondingly and influence the buyer's choice. It is the company which would formulate the appropriate marketing programmed depending in the nature and intensity.

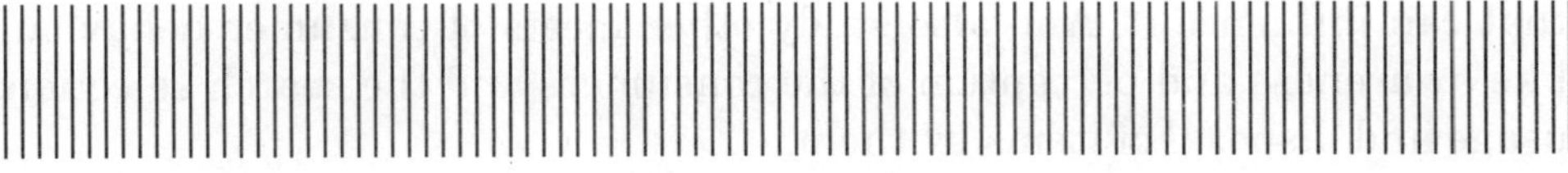

CHAPTER

35

Consumer Behaviour

Gender-wise

—Ms. S. Sowdeeswari

Consumer behaviour can be defined as the sum total of how individuals and groups recognize and determine their needs and how they purchase and experience goods and services to meet those needs. The study of consumer behaviour investigates and develops methods to quantify forecast and influence the behavior of consumers. The applicability of consumer behaviour science is indeed universal at present. Consumer behaviour is a science that serves Marketer, Entrepreneur, Economist, and Consumer. Woman as a special object of study required some courage. Some experts, men as well as women, whom we consulted, felt that making gender as a base for studying consumer behaviour and treating woman as an exception rather than as normal average is a retrograde step. Apart from their nature, we have to admit and recognize that every society impose certain gender—based behaviour on women. Studying consumer behaviour is an essential part of doing business with consumers.

Introduction

Every human being by his behaviour throws up a picture about himself over a period of time. This picture shows his values, habits, preferences, activities, exposures and attitudes. Such information would be useful for a variety of people and purpose. The profile also should indicate what motivates the consumer, what his preferences are and the why of it. This study focus on the purchase behaviour of the consumer and the factors that can influence it. And also study other facets of consumer behaviour like awareness and perception of the consumers and the search selection, usage and disposal of items by them.

Consumer

Consumer is a broad term and any person who uses a product are services or deals with it can be called a consumer. It is not necessary person should be a buyer of the product or service. The term consumer should not be confused with the word 'customer' which has the limited meaning of usually denoting a person who contracts to buy the product. For example, if you are selling tea-dust, you may have just one customer in the manager of a cafeteria. On the other hand all the persons who drink tea of cafeteria are your consumers.

The *two* broad categories of consumers, which are personal consumers and industrial consumers.

Personal consumers are those individuals and households who themselves consume goods are services.

Institutional consumers on the other hand are businesses, organizations and groups that buy and consume goods and services during the course of their operations.

Consumer Behaviour

Consumer can be defined as the sum total of how individuals and groups recognize and determine their needs and how they purchase and experience goods and services to meet those needs.

Application of Consumer Behaviour Science

The study of consumer behaviour certainly is an off-shoot of marketing. Marketing and consumer behaviour are so closely related that the study of consumer behaviour can be said to be the first step in refined marketing. Consumer behaviour studies helps marketer understand the rational for the behaviour of consumer and their real needs. Products and services are designed by marketers to meet those real needs.

Consumer research studies help research and forecast the behaviour and response of consumers to existing as well as proposed new products. They help to build profile of consumers who are likely to use the product.

Consumer behaviour studies help to segment the market so that marketers can address different consumer segments with different products and formulate suitable strategies.

Changing Roles of Producer, Marketer and Consumer

Over a period of time it has been realized that the production and marketing of goods and services exist after all for the consumer. The economics are trading towards consumer driven and the diagram – 1 illustrates the steady shift and the changing roles of producer, marketer and consumer.

Consumer Behaviour—Who Else It Helps

Consumer Behaviour is a science that serves not only the marketer but also a variety of others:

Marketer

The marketer, as already explained, depends heavily on a study of consumer behaviour for achieving the objectives of marketing.

Entrepreneur

The entrepreneur, who is essentially a future marketer, is helped to take correct and timely investment decisions and improve the chances of success of operation by a study of consumer behaviour.

Economist

The economist and planner takes note of consumer behaviour forecasts while planning for communities and countries and while making cost-benefit projections.

Consumer

It may sound strange to emphasize but it is the consumer who benefits most by a better dissemination of the science of consumer behaviour. Firstly they can get an insight and understanding of the rational behind their own behaviours. Once this behaviour is understood, any wrong attitudes, misconceptions or illogical loyalties can be scientifically viewed and corrected. It is said the consumers become more value-oriented and emerge as wiser users, after an exposure to the science of consumer behaviour.

A Woman as a Consumer and Dicision-maker

Treating woman as a special object of study required some courage. Some expert's men as well as women, whom we consulted felt that making gender as a base for studying consumer behaviour and treating woman as an exception rather than as normal average is a retrograde step. On the other hand a lager number of these experts felt that it is a fact of life that woman consumers exhibit special traits and behaviour.

Earlier Roles

Product

The most important person in the economy, he produced what he found possible

Trader

As the next important person, he distributed efficiently what was produced. He faced competition but managed it mostly by price—financial management.

Consumer

Bought what was made available and what he could afford within means and tailored his lifestyle accordingly. Consumer behaviour was somewhat inhibited.

Current Roles

Consumer

The most important person in the economy. Constantly tries to achieve a better standard of living by acquisition of goods and services. Strives to increase income to meet growing needs. Realizes that needs can be ever-growing and yesterday's luxuries are today's necessities. Exercises options, dictates certain on goods and services. All these constitute uninhibited consumer behaviour.

Marketer

Constantly helps and leads the consumer in determining what he wants. Investigates wheat improvement innovations and changes are possible. Realizes that the quest in unending and that actions are greatly propelled by competition and consumer behaviour.

Producer

Takes direction from the marketer and consumer. Tries to produce anything the consumer wants and strives to make things as they are wanted and employs technology towards this end. Innovation, service and relationship management are on the prime agenda of producer.

Fig. 35.1: The Changing Roles

Madam Buyer

The concerns visualized and addressed by a woman buyer are same while purchasing for herself or for others (like her family). The concerns are not superficial but hover round the basic theme of economy in purchase by Need-based Acquisition and Value for Money. The seemingly simple process of "shopping" is not all fun.

Optimizes on quantity to buy now (to last till next shopping visit)
Considers bigger unit package for economy. Weights hidden costs of wastage/storage/abuse/spoilage.
Select right package to go for ...
For the right package, compares brands
For the brand checks for familiarity (TV, Ads, peeress' Word of mouth)
Checks Warranties / returnability etc.
Compares prices, makes the shortlist zeroes on to a package
Scans the stores for 'sale' offers. Evaluate 'freebie' offers for their real worth and utility.
Considers reusability of packing
Consults retailer if there is a close run of the choices, for reassurances.
Absorbs label information on price, nutrition values / tech details, dates of expires special warranties etc.

Fig. 35.2 : Madam Buyers

Rural Buyers

Rural consumers as a segment have several distinctive characteristics. The value, aspirations, and needs of this vast heterogeneous culture of rural consumers are quit different from their urban counterparts. For instance, in spite of the fact that literacy has increased awareness at the level of actual consumers, often, the purchase decisions are made by outsiders.

Conclusion

In early stage consumers consume only which goods or services available in market, but now the trend is moderate the consumers have the deciding authority. The market research will help for identifying the consumer's interest. The consumer behaviour which is mainly helps the marketers but my thought every consumer known them behaviour are rightly help select the good products and service. Every human being throws his/her behaviour for a period of time. Slogan says 'Consumers Beware' based that slogan consumer behaviour give root for studying himself. Consumers who know their interest, need, potentiality and etc. will not suffered of forgery goods and services. Every consumer follows the women buyer approach means we avoid many problems against consumer.

REFERENCES

- Panta, Murali Prasad. *Business, Consumer and the Government*. New Delhi: Mitten Publications, 2001.
- Meenu Agrawal (2006), *Consumer Behaviour and Consumer Protection in India,* (New Delhi: New Century Publication.)
- Pardeep S Mehta and Dr Anant Sharma (1989), *The Consumer—What to Do? How to Do?,* (Jaipur, Consumer Unity and Trust Society 'CUTS').
- Prof. Praful Chandra (1994), *Servants Not Master*, (Udupi Consumer Forum).
- David Harland (1987) *"Global Concerns for Consumers"*, United Nations Guidelines for Consumer Protection, (10): 245-266.
- Avtar Singh (1994), *Law of Consumer Protection—Principle and Practices*, (Delhi: Eastern Book Co). Mark V Nadel, (1971), The Politics of Consumer Protection, (Indianapolis and New York, Bobbs-Merrill).
- P Hirst and G Thompson (1995), *Globalization and the Future of the Nation-state,* 24 Economy and Society.
- S.H.Venkatramani: *"Wretched of the Earth",* The Times of India, 22.8.1995
- Jocelyn Kellam (1995), *Product Liability in the Asia-Pacific,* (Sydney, Legal Books).
- J Goldring, (1990), *Consumer Law and Legal Theory: Reflections of a Common Lawyer,* 13 J Consumer Policy 1.

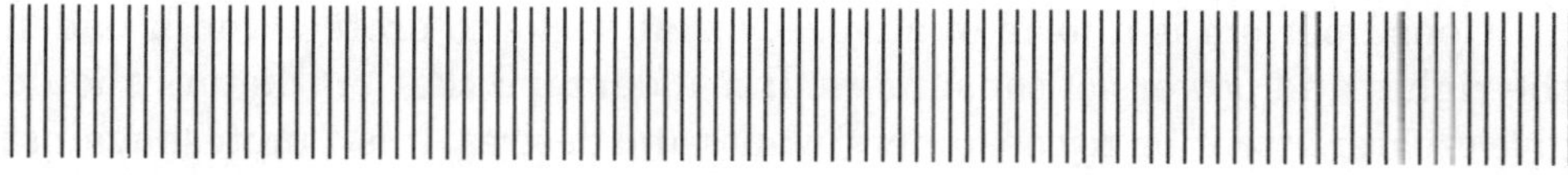

CHAPTER

36

Need and Scope of Consumerism

— N. Jayaveeran
— A. Shaik Abdul Khadir

Everyone is a born consumer, whether he is an industrialist, a producer, a trader engaged in any profession or service or belonging to any other class. Whether one is a producer or whether he renders a service, the ultimate object of all production is to ensure consumption of goods and services to the satisfaction of the consumers. This could be achieved only when the products are of acceptable standard quality and are not produced and distributed with the only motive of making profit.

There are three types of consumers:

— who makes enough money by earning, which enables him to buy anything he wishes to use at any price;

— who mainly represents the salaried class with limited resource available for consumer goods and services. This class also includes a very large segment of non-literate consumers who are ignorant of the products they are surrounded by and feel frustrated by their inability to receive even essential services in time for survival;

— who is in rural area and completely unaware of the trade practices around him and he tries to survive with whatever he is getting and unable to afford even the bare necessities of life.

Consumerism is the policy or programme of protecting the rights and interests of the consumer.

Consumerism is a form of advocacy that seeks to protect and broaden the rights and powers of consumers. It is a demand that marketers should give greater attention to consumers' wants and desires. It is a protest against abuses and malpractices in the marketing system.

Consumer orientation is an essential ingredient of marketing. Satisfying the consumer interest should be the objective of all business units, as it will create a sense of loyalty in the minds of the consumers to business organisations and their products.

Need for Consumerism

The need for consumerism has been primarily due to the indifference of the business community. The main aim of all business is to maximize profit. Consumers have not only been called upon to pay higher prices but also have to settle at lower quality, spurious, duplicate and adulterated products that are being sold through misleading and powerful advertisement media. Hence, consumerism is required to protect consumer interest.

The producer has the power to design the product, distribute, advertise and price it, but the consumer has only the power of not buying it. One may argue that the producer runs his business with greater risks in spite of having several rights, because the veto power remains with the consumer. However the consumer often feels that while he has the power of veto, he is not always fully equipped to exercise that power. This situation may be the effect of lack of information, too much indigestible information or even misinformation from one or several competing producers.

Scope of Consumerism

Basically, Consumerism involves discontent with direct buyer-seller exchange relationships, and between the consumer and the business firm. Marketing is the main target of consumer discontent with business. This is because marketing is the most viable part of a company's total programme and the easiest for consumers to reach.

Secondly, consumer discontent extends beyond mere business. Consumerism extends to all organisations with which there is an exchange relationship. Consumerism therefore involves such diverse organisations as hospitals, schools and government agencies.

Thirdly, consumer discontent involves the indirect impact that an exchange relationship between two social units. In other words, an exchange between two people or groups can create a problem for the third group.

People should start knowing their rights as consumers. They must assert their rights against defective products and deficiency in services. "*Consumers and rights*? Indian manufactures would have laughed at you if you had asked that question as late as a decade ago. Actually, many will hold their sides even today. But the laughter is fading. Aggressive consumers, proactive Consumer Courts and cut throat competition are ensuring a new age".

In the first decade of real consumerism, the 1990s, the Indian consumer was like a child running around amidst a playground—full of noise, colour and choice—wanting everything in the shop window. Today, the consumer is like an awkward teenager, in the process of making the transition to a more restrained, more mature future, taking a long hard look at what lies outside the window.

REFERENCES

- Dr. Atul Dhyani *'Indian Journal of Marketing'* (Consumerism: Gobal *vs.* Indian Perspectives)
- Dr. S.B. Sadar *'Indian Journal of Marketing'* (Consumerism)
- V. Seshadri *'Consumerism',* Mittal Publications.
- P. Sivapradlism and S. Rajamohan *'Consumer Empavement',* Kanishka Publishers Distributors.
- David L. Lowdon & Albert and T. Della Bitta *'Consumer Behaviour'* Tata McGraw-Hill Publishing Company Ltd., New Delhi.

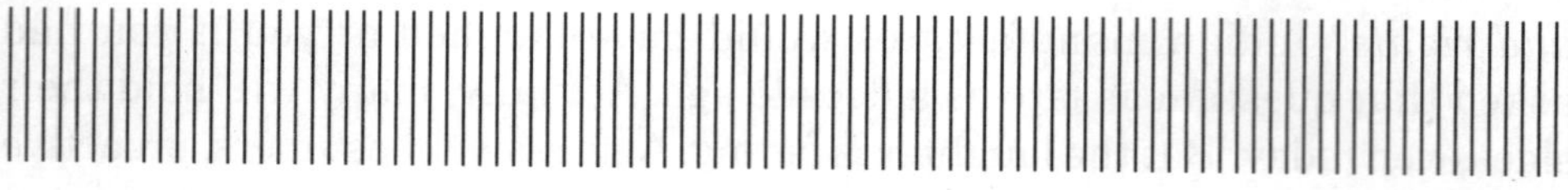

CHAPTER

37

Cultural Aspects of Indian Consumer Market

—Ms. S. Srimathi

Definition

The culture is one of the most important environmental factor influencing consumer behaviour. The culture affects the consumer behaviour to purchase or not to purchase any product based on his values, norms, ideas, facts and meaningful communication, symbols, habits, language, beliefs and attitudes, and other factors. It becomes more important in a country like India which has number of subcultures and some believe it is multicultural country.

Attitude and Behaviour Influenced by ones Culture:

1. Personality *i.e.* sense of self and society;
2. Language *i.e.* communication;
3. Dress;
4. Food habits;
5. Religion and religious faiths that is beliefs;
6. Customs as marriages and religions and special social customs;
7. Social relationship (system of marriage, family structure and relations, social and religious organisations, government);
8. System of education, role of churches, temples, mosques etc. on education system) *i.e.* mental process of behaviour (formal and religious symbols, colleges, technical institutes universities etc.).

9. Work habits and products. They differ widely from country to country. and region to region;
10. Time value (punctuality, late coming working hours, rest hours and so on;
11. Values and norms (discussed later);
12. Beliefs and faiths (religion, vegetarianism—meat eating, non-violence—rebirth, fate and 6:1, and so on;
13. Festivals;
14. Art, music, pictures, TV radio, movies, theatres etc.;
15. Technology and innovation;
16. Products and services;
17. Knowledge;
18. Laws of the Government and social traditions and laws laid down by religion.

Characteristics of Different Indian Cultures

India is said to be country of multicultures. It is because of long history of thousands of years. At different times different rulers ruled over the country. Further, at the same time there had been different rulers in different parts of India. Then there was invasion from outside especially from Arab countries and then over 200 years long British rule. In part of the country for sometime there had been French and Portuguese rule. The different rulers had different systems of governance and social practices. All these factors left a deep imprint on culture. As in olden days means of transport and communication were very poor; large number of languages, systems, habits, values developed which continue even today. These facts of history made India a multicultural nation but as will be evident from later discussion the core values are same throughout the country. Thus there is unity in diversity which is an important land mark to remember by any marketer in framing strategy for marketing. But the diversity gave birth to ever increasing number of states.

Geographical Factors

For instance in U.P. even after division of the state there are different cultures in Bundelk Ruhelkhand, East U.P. and West U.P. In Madhya Pradesh Vidhrabha has lot of cultural different compared to rest of M.P. Rajasthan is one state but culture of Jaipur, Jodhpur, Udaipur, Bihar, Jaislmer etc. have different distinct features. Culture of Assam, Bengal, Gujarat, Goa, Karnatka, Kashmir, Punjab, Haryana, Pondichery Mizoram, Nagaland etc. differs widely from each other.

Language

India is a multi language country. There are 18 languages officially recognized in the Constitution which are spoken or used in different parts of the country.

The languages and their area of operation usage are as given below:

Language	State/Area /Spoken
Assamese	Assam
Hindi	Bihar, Delhi, Haryana, Himachal Pradesh, M.P., U.P, Rajasthan, Uttaranchal
Tamil	Tamil Nadu
Telgu	Andhra Pradesh
Urdu	Delhi, Bihar, U.P., part of Hyderabad.and muslims in other parts of the country.

Religion

- Hindus
- Muslims
- Sikhs
- Christians
- Jainism, Buddhism

Every religion has its own values, faith, beliefs and greatly affect consumer behaviour. For intance Hindus by and large are vegetarians and those who are non-vegetarians generally do not take meat on Tuesday and in Navratas and days of fast. Cow in considered Mata by Hindus and so they do not take cow meat. Muslims do not take pig meat. Sikhs do not consume tobacco in any form. Stunch Jains do not take even many vegetables and believe in Ahinsa (non-violence) and they do not take food at night Hindus and Jain believe in sacrifice and therefore sadhus use minimum of clothes, eat minimum and some sadhus remain nude. Actually the impact of religion on culture and consumer behaviour is so strong that it is not possible fully describing its impact.

Education

It also affects values, faiths and beliefs. A poor educated country has greater faith in superstitions and traditions, he believed more on luck, fate, stunch believer in God. As India is poor educated these tributes should be properly studied and researched to find out consumer behaviour and about preferences for their products and services. According to 2001 census India has a population of 102.7 crore on March, 2001 out of which 65.38 per cent were literate. The literacy is the highest in Kerala which has reduced its birth rate to lowest and helped migration of persons to other states in India and abroad.

Conclusion

The culture is most important environmental factor influencing consumer behaviour to purchase or not to purchase any good or service. Though there is no one definition of culture it can be defined as "complex of values, ideas, attitudes and other meaningful symbols created by a man to shape human behaviour and the artifacts of that behaviour as they are transmitted from one generation to the next. The behaviour and attitudes which are influenced by culture are personality, language, dress, food, habits, religion and religious faiths and beliefs, customs, social relationships, system of education, work habits time value, values and norms, festivals, arts, technology products and services knowledge and laws.

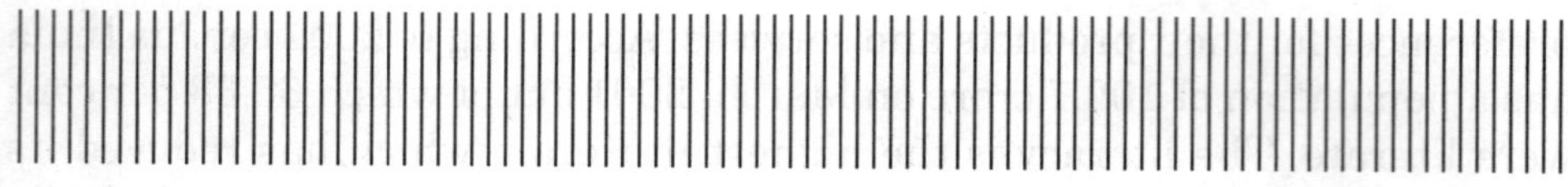

CHAPTER

38
Consumer Protection in India

—Ms. P. Jayanthi

Definition

The consumer is an important part of economic system in any country and every individual is a consumer. Thus on Ist March 2001 in India there were 102 crore consumers which are cared by the government through various acts, regulatory authorities and administrative actions and Central and State governments have been very thoughtful to safeguard the interest of consumers even before independence but the level of protection and their rights awareness has been evolved over a long period.

Consumer Protection Before 1986 Act

Before Consumer Protection Act was enacted in 1986 there were following main laws to protect the consumers:

- Defence of India Rules;
- Trade Marks Act, 1969;
- Essential Commodities Act, 1955;
- Monopoly and Restrictive Trade Practices Act 1969 which was thoroughly amended after 1991 and unfair trade practices were included in it;
- Standards of Weights and Measures Act, 1951;
- AG Mark Act;
- Food Adulteration Act.

Standards of Weights and Measures Act 1976

Establish standards of weights and measures to regulate inter-state trade or commerce in weights, measures and other goods which are sold or distributed by weights, measure or number". The basic objective of the Act is that consumer gets the quantity as agreed and is not cheated in this regard but the Act has tried to achieve other objectives too which will be clear from the following description.

Trade and Merchandise Marks Act

To provide for the registration and better protection of trademarks and for the preventation of the use of fradulent marks on merchandise". After valid registration of a trade mark the registration" gives to the registered proprietor of the trade mark the exclusive right to the use of the trade mark in relation to goods in respect of which the trade mark is registered".

Trade Mark Act 1999

To amend and consolidate the law relating to trade marks to provide for registration and better protection of the trade marks for goods and services and for the prevention of the use of fraudulent marks".

ISI Marks

Bureau of Indian Standards has prescribed standards for large number of products with regard to specifications of materials to be used, processes to be applied. Standards have been fixed for strength, finish, safety etc. In some cases like electrical appliances use of ISI standards has been made compulsory for the protection of user. Thus ISI marks assure that the goods are having the quality as prescribed in the standards of Bureau of Indian Standards.

AG Mark

AG MARK for agricultural products which is mark that goods are as per standards laid down. These standard have been fixed for almost all the agricultural products including wheat, rice, spices, ghee etc.

Food Adulteration Act

This Act has been passed to ensure that consumer gets unadultered products be it wheat, rice, pulses, spices, milk, vegetable oils or other food products etc. If some one is found guilty there is severe punishment which is vehemently opposed by trade and industry and their associations. First they object to the standards fixed and secondly to severe punishment even when one, is selling packed goods.

Laws to Control Price and Distribution

The government controls prices and distribution system through various laws amongst which following are most important.

Industrial (Development and Regulation) Act 1951

To provide for the development and regulation of certain industries" as specified in the first schedule which includes almost all industries metallurgical, fuels, boilers and steam generating plants, prime mover, electrical equipment, telecommunications, transportation, industrial machinery processing industries, vegetable oils and vanaspati, soaps, cosmetics and toilet preparations, rubber goods, leather goods, glue and gelatine, glass, ceramics, cement and gypsum products, timber products, defence industries and miscellaneous industries.

Essential Commodities Act

Essential Commodities Act 1955 was enacted in 1955 "to provide in the interests of the general public for the control of the production, supply and distribution, of and trade and commerce in certain commodities" as per preamble of the Act. The Act has been amended from time to time specially in 1986. The essential commodities have been defined in the act which means cattle fodder, including oil cakes and other concentrates. coal including coke and other derivatives, component parts and accessories of automobiles, cotton and woollen textiles, drugs, foodstuffs, including edible oils seeds and oils, iron and steel, including manufactured products of iron and steel paper including newsprint, raw cotton, whether ginned or unginned and cotton seed and raw jute.

Monopolies and Restrictive Trade Practices Commission

Monopolistic trade practice is which has or likely to have the effect of:

1. Maintaining prices at an unreasonable level by limiting, reducing or otherwise controlling the production, supply or distribution of goods of any description or the supply of any services or in any other manner;
2. Unreasonably preventing or lessen competition in the production, supply or distribution of any goods or in the supply of any services;
3. Limiting technical development or capital investment to the common detriment or allowing the quality of any good produced, supplied or distributed, or any service rendered, in India to deteriorate".

Restrictive trade practice means a trade practice which has, or may have the effect of preventing or distorting or restricting competition in any manner and in particular:

I. Which tends to obstruct the flow of capital or resources into the stream of production; or

II. Which tends to bring about manipulation of prices, or conditions of delivery or to effect the flow of supplies in the market relating to goods or services in such manner as to impose on the consumer unjustified costs or restrictions".

Consumer Protection Act

1986 the Consumer Protection Act was passed "to provide for the better protection of the interest of consumers and for that purpose to make provisions for the establishment of consumers councils and other authorities for the settlement of the consumers dis-putes and for matters connected therewith.

Conclusion

The objectives of state policy are to ensure that transaction are fair and consumer must be provided full information and nothing should be concealed. Secondly, there should be discrimination against any class based on sex, race, colour, region, income level, religion, culture, cost or for any other reason. Similarly various regulatory authorities have taken greater interest to protect consumers; still the level of protection in India is much lower than in developed countries because of lack of consumer movement.

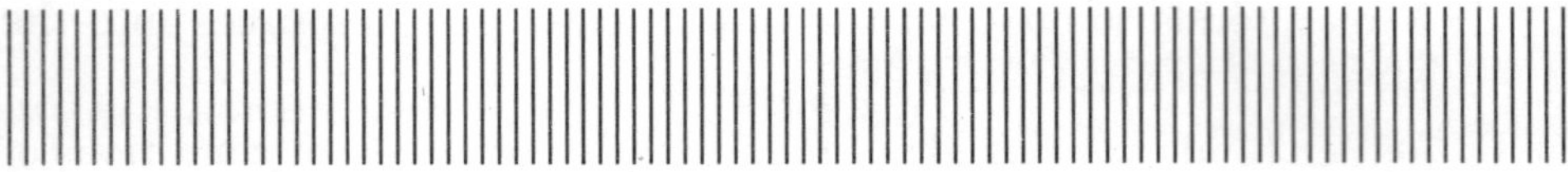

CHAPTER

39

Reduced Urban Consumerism and Enhanced Rural Bio-enterprises for Food, Water and Climatic Security

— V. Maheswaran

Rampant urbanization covers 28 per cent of the Indian population. Growing urbanization and consumerism in South Asia are already feared to soon surpass greenhouse gas (GHG) emissions of many developed nations due to high population, though low on per capita basis. About 3–4 years ago it was argued by developed countries that the Asian brown cloud resulted from increased Indian industrial emissions, though Indian scientists contested it by showing that such haze occurred regularly elsewhere also. As carbon emissions are responsible for about 80 per cent of the global warming and climate change, carbon sequestration is promoted as a mitigation measure, including afforestation, even in urban and semi-urban areas. We attempt here to depict trends of urban carbon emissions, their driving factors and consequences. Besides data from literature, stakeholder consultations at Madurai city have also been used to identify various response options and sketch future scenarios. Madurai city is one of the largest market amongst 745 towns in the country with population exceeding 50,000 each.

Madurai city with its more than 2.75 million population and 1.2 million vehicles, emits an estimated over 100 tons of air pollutants per day. Among the three largest cities in the country with over 10 million population, Kolkata and Mumbai have efficient public transport in the form of metro railway and emit 300 and 600 tons each respectively. New Delhi, the metropolis emitted 1300 tons pollutants per day, before the metro rail service commenced recently. Vehicular pollution constitutes 30, 52 and 64 per cent of the total pollution in these cities. Among the vehicular fleet, 80 per cent vehicles are private, 65 per cent being petrol-driven two-wheelers and 15 per cent being four-wheelers, often petrol-driven, which contribute to over 50 per cent of the urban carbon emissions. The number of two-wheelers has grown by nearly six times and that of four-wheelers by three times during the last 10 years, due to government sops to industry such as tax concessions, besides easy consumer loans from manufacturers and banks, and the false cultural prestige infused by publicity.

Fuel efficiency can be enhanced by 10–30 per cent, including techniques such as catalytic converter and cleaner fuels such as gas, alcohol and biodiesel, while per capita emissions can be reduced by 85–90 per cent using public transport. Electric cars are touted as 'emission-free' by neglecting the carbon emissions at the thermal power plants and 40 per cent transmission and distribution losses. Solar or hybrid vehicles may be cleaner during operation, if not during production and disposal. However, both solar and the much hyped hydrogen fuel mode may not be significant before 2025. Multimodal Metro Transport System that involves combination of railway and bus vehicles is planned to develop in most cities by 2015, which may reduce some emissions, if found widely accessible and fast. Altogether, carbon emissions (50% of total pollution) may more than double from 50 tons at present to 100 tons by 2015, largely due to growth in fossil-fuel-driven private vehicles. Sequestration of about 35,000 tons of carbon would require 14,000 ha, i.e. 140 km^2 of tree plantation, as 5–10 year-old tree plantations grow about 5 tons per year, of which about 50 per cent is atmospheric carbon sequestration. However, this amounts to almost 22 per cent of the present urban area of 700 km^2, which is untenable since so much vacant land does not exist. Tree plantation areas such as avenues and gardens with fully grown tree canopy comprise about 10 per cent in Madurai city, but are not net carbon sequesters as they emit carbon through litter fall and decomposition. Urbanization has wiped out 50 per cent of tree canopy in the last 50 years.

India emits about 700 metric tons of carbon annually, given its consumption of 500 metric tons of oil equivalent of fossil fuels as commercial energy and 200 mt of biomass energy. Sequestering this emission would need 300 m ha of afforestation, which is almost 90 per cent of the Indian land area, and clearly untenable. Thus reducing emissions at source is inevitable. About 50 per cent of the commercial energy is used by the industry, 24 per cent for transport, and 12 per cent for commercial purpose, irrigation being less than 10 per cent. Over 80 per cent of the energy is consumed by 10 per cent of the population that is rich and resides in cities. This includes direct consumption through luxury appliances such as commuting vehicles, refrigerator, television, fan, air cooler, computer, etc. which is hardly 10 per cent. Indirect emissions are ten times or more, for example, cement and steel manufacture accounts for 50 per cent of the emissions and another 25 per cent is through transport, say of minerals to factories or transport of rice from Andhra Pradesh to Kerala, as Kerala has converted its paddy fields to commercial crops such as betelnut. Thus, of the 500 metric tons of annual carbon emissions, at least 50 per cent could be attributed to ten mega-cities, who consume or even export much of these commercial commodities. Nearly 56 per cent of national travel demand in the country is concentrated in just four metropolises! This implies 550 metric tons per 50 million citizens, and a staggering 5 tons per capita annually, seven times the national average of 0.7 metric tons! The urban rich emit much more per capita for luxury. The indirect annual carbon emissions of 10–100 mt per city (in the rural catchment) are 100 times the visible urban emissions of 0.1–1 metric tons.

Climate change could reduce food production up to 15–42 per cent by 2050, which may compel food imports, under the 'virtual water' economic policy, leading to economic slavery, even if not political, as is happening with the poor South American and African nations. Non-productive urban fancies of IT, BT and outsourcing are highways for globalized monoculture and epidemics. Food-production growth has retarded as soil nutrients are washed down the urban drainage to sea, but not returned to the farms. Already, 20–30 per cent of irrigated farmlands has been sold to the industries for commercial floriculture, etc. or are eroded and saline. Canal water is wasted and groundwater is mostly exhausted due to overuse of bore wells. Thus, any climate change would spell disaster, as evident from the drought during the last four years, which triggered the industry and the government to attempt 'cloud seeding' for artificial rains, ignoring the 'precautionary' principle, and with potential climatic disturbance. As the irrigation and drainage system remained wasteful, the techno-commercial experiment failed. The last two years were the warmest in 100 years, Himalayan apple production declined massively due to unprecedented cold wave, with Himalayan glaciers receding and coastal villages sinking.

Climate change is a global process and reducing Indian emissions alone will not suffice. However, India can be proactive in reducing urban consumerism, with the help of supportive developed country initiatives. India has led the world in legislating to share commercial benefits with traditional resource and knowledge providers, with the Biological Diversity Act, 2002. Local biodiversity registers and funds therein can be used to promote biodiversity-based handicraft enterprises of organic food, herbal healthcare, handloom textiles, biogas and biodiesel. This can productively revolve around micro-finance of the women self-help groups, using eco-technology (local resources and traditional skills) as a tool of supply-side management. Besides meeting the subsistence village needs, excess produce can be sold to nearby cities, to avoid bio-cultural pollution from both centralized industrial production and faraway transport. Such near-surface recycling of carbon will maintain village stake and control over eco-culture. India's plant production is annually about 2000 metric tons, 50 per cent of it being carbon recycling. India's culturable wastelands measure over 50 mha, which can absorb about 125 metric tons of carbon annually, *i.e.* 20 per cent of the present emissions, permissible for sustainable development.

Such a 'bio-regional' approach is recommended by the International Convention on Biological Diversity, 1992. The recent electoral defeat of the techno-commercialized National Democratic Alliance reflects public refusal of the export-oriented economic growth statistics using manipulated and misleading Western indices such as Gross Domestic Product and forex reserves that hide failures on the social equity and well being, evident from the growing hunger, water scarcity and unemployment. In an increasingly uncertain climate, safety and stability lie in diversifying each state or even taluk or panchayat to be self-sufficient in food, water and healthcare. This will enhance long-term savings sustainably rather than short-term and inequitable economic growth ('earn and spend' more) mania. The Government can earn from luxury, energy-intensive goods and industries through heavy 'carbon tax' as wise demand-side management. Further, agro-based jobs need to be created both by replacing mechanization of farming and creating local value-addition opportunities, as proposed in the recent 'Common Minimum Programme' of the United Progressive Alliance government. This can also decongest the swelling cities by retrenching much of the stagnant industrial and service sector labour that comprises 40 per cent of the urban population. Cities are already bogged down with crime, violence and suicides, besides an unhealthy society with 20 per cent obese over-consumers, and 23 per cent people who go to bed hungry. Cities cannot infinitely grow parasitising on villages, encroaching on their land, food, water and ploughing back only toxic wastes in to the air, water and soil. Such rural bio-cultural poisoning may only enhance unsustainably by reducing rural self-reliance under the proposed 'Providing Urban Amenities to Rural Areas' plan. Urbanized Greek or Indus valley Civilization did not last long, after agrarian failure due to soil degradation and climate change.

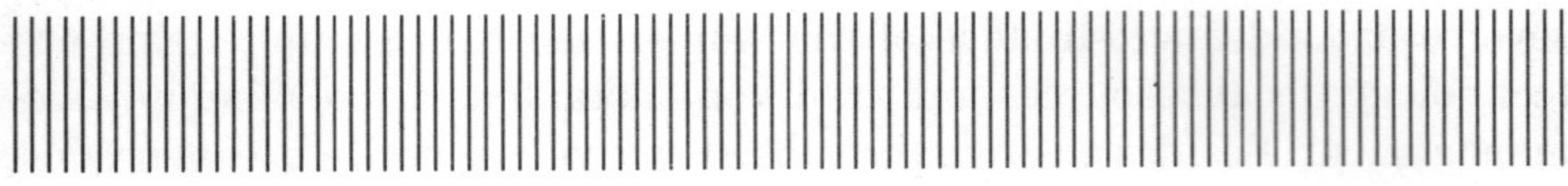

CHAPTER

40

Impact of Television on the Indian Consumers

— S. Aravind Krishnan

Ever since the advent of modern communication technology that has allowed people around the world to communicate ever so easily, the world itself seems like a smaller space. Broadcasting is an especially effective manner through which millions of people are able to become unified on the basis that they are common recipients of a particular message. One of the most powerful transmitters of these messages is of course the television programmes of which can be seen around the world to serve many purposes. In most contemporary societies, television is a highly influential medium of popular culture and plays an important role in the social construction of reality. The effects of television should therefore be recognized as having the ability to alter social, economic and political situations in its places of propagation and beyond. This chapter will be exploring these cultural shifts in detail pertaining to India, a developing nation undergoing a grand cultural shift in part due to the rapid growth of satellite television in the 1990's and its programming.

Television is unlike any other medium of mass communication in that its social effects are prominent and able to prompt substantial change. The strong cultural influence of television on developing nations can therefore be linked to the following factors as outlined in the book "Media and Social Changes: the modernizing influences of television in rural India." First, television programming is easily accessible and inexpensive, which is mainly due to the fact that American television is sold inexpensively around the world after profits in its home market have already been made. Television's potency is also a result of its broad scope and diversity of programmes which therefore makes it appealing to almost anybody. Yet another reason for television's mass appeal is its benign presence, which allows viewers to be in control of what they watch, how much they watch and when to watch it. Ultimately, it is these factors that propel the reliance on the medium which has the power to inflict many societal changes in developing nations such as India. Through the examination of diverse groups in India such as rural villagers, youth, women and the middle class, I intend to illustrate the vast social and cultural changes taking place in a culturally rich country, in large part due to the relatively recent popularity of television throughout the country.

According to statistics the population in India was:

In 2000, it was 1,003 million people.

In 2001, it was 1,019 million people.

In 2002, it was 1,050 million people.

In 2003, it was 1,060 million people.

In 2004, it was 1,080 million people.

In 2005, it was 1,094 million people.

In 2006, it was 1,110 million people and it is going up and up.

While almost 75 per cent of India's one billion people live in villages, their thoughts and actions consequently have a large influence on the country's social, political and economic state. One of the most prolific changes in village life which can be linked directly to the influence of television is rise of consumerism in rural India. Just as we are enveloped with advertisements and endorsements which propel us to purchase that which we deem necessary, the same is true in rural India in which such things as blue jeans and hand cream have become necessities. Villagers themselves acknowledge this growing need:

> "I want many things that my parents never had. I want a motorcycle and a nice colour TV, I want to eat mutton once a week instead of three times a year".

Through this illustration, it is evident that needs are certainly growing and it is due to television and advertisements that the economically dependent third world is now being internally pressured to make shifts that may not be financially possible yet incredibly desirable.

Another growing desire of the rural Indian population is to become urbanized, leading to a shift in behaviour and relationships. Not only do these villagers want to mimic the representations of their urban counterparts by changing their attire and consumer goods, their attitudes are also altered as a result. Such phenomenon can be seen as a positive shift which allows modern attitudes to flourish, through which more sensitivity and emotion are finding their ways into the rigid caste system and competition, therefore adding sentimental value to various relationships. In the case of rural parts of developing nations, mediation may also be useful as a way of educating villagers about their own country. The programmes that are seen by the villagers are those which are produced in India yet reflect a Western undercurrent of values and lifestyles. The rural audience is therefore able to learn about other parts of their own country, which is useful due to the fact that many do not venture far from their village for touring purposes.

Although the middle class in India is generally more urbanized and therefore more in touch with the globalizing effects of media, they resemble the villagers in terms of the effects of television on their daily lives. While villagers are enticed with what is outside their village, the urban middle class is able to see the correlation between the foreign and national trademarks.

"Multinational companies consistently attempt to associate their products with signifiers of the Indian nation, for instance through sponsorship of the Indian Olympic team in the 1996 Olympics or through more subtle references to specifically Indian conditions such as the monsoon season".

While conglomerates such as Pepsi and Coke are striving to merge the Indian identity with their brands by sponsoring sporting events and relying on Indian celebrity endorsements, the Indian audience fails to see that what they see as sponsorship for India's pride is actually a mere scheme to boost consumerism. It is therefore evident that just as the rural class is becoming increasingly commoditized, the middle class urban population is no different. Although many televised advertisements tug on the nationalized heartstrings, many direct correlations are also made between Indian cities and North American or European ones. In this sense, the existence of the Indian city dwellers is being justified on the basis of their city's comparison to Western cities. It is through these processes that Indian's are made to feel that they are being recognized, but the concern is whether this recognition is strong if it is formulated through comparison. While many of these discrete messages are being transmitted through television and advertisements, they are transforming into ideals; and, just as the rural population is in search for an urban setting, the urban dwellers are looking towards Western societies for opportunity.

The effects of commercialism cannot be underestimated. Today's children are besieged by manipulative commercial messages day in and day out, on TV, and even at school. Companies hire psychologists to help them target children and manipulate them; this is called the 'art of whine-making.' The bombardment of commercial messages has created a sense of chronic dissatisfaction in children and, many psychologists think that is has contributed to the increase in teen depression.

In terms of programming, television shows are either American, or Indian imitations of them.

> "Programmes targeted specifically at the middle class are often characterized by a hybridized language which combines Hindi and English. This mixture, termed 'Hinglish' by the popular media, combines Hindi and English in different television shows".

Through this very example it is evident that Westernized ideals are seeping into Indian mainstream media through the use of television. Moreover, an important shift to consider is that while English is becoming increasingly predominant, the non-English speakers are being marginalized and degraded in their own home country. Secondly, the predominance of Hindi as the main language on television weakens the diverse languages spoken in India which have contributed to its cultural heritage for centuries.

One of the most prominent examples of the hybrid of Indian and American culture is through the phenomenon of MTV and youth culture in India.

> "The two main foreign-owned music television channels operating in India, News Corporation's Channel [V] and Viacom's MTV, have followed a market strategy of aggressive 'Indianization.' This has taken the form of programmes featuring Indian film songs and music videos..."

Although it may hold true that television which is geared towards youth may support Indian entertainment, these channels directly model the American versions of them; therefore, enforcing a global Americanized culture upon middle-class Indian youth.

Consumerism is extremely prominent among this group due to the cultural icons represented through music videos and advertisements, along with their parent's willingness to support such spending. This seems to hold true as a characteristic of youth culture across the globe, which raises the question of whether this global identity was created to homogenize this particular group.

Yet another concern that satellite television and its growing Western influence has brought about is the generational reformation of these viewers.

> "... graduate students of classical dance and mainly Telugu Channel [V] viewers and say that they have frequently experienced discomfort (and so have their parents) because of the growing trend of obscenity in Telugu film songs (including nudity, suggestive body movements, and 'double-meaning' lyrics)."

Families were once able to enjoy programmes without any discrepancy among parents and children, the ever growing influence of Western ideology that 'sex sells' in the media has transgressed into the Indian market, and led to reformation of the family unit, creating obvious distinctions between tastes. The new trends in television broadcasting may therefore effectively deconstruct the family unit as the Western ideals transgressing through Indian television are slowly creating gaps within the home.

Some young viewers of these provocative music videos seem to think that due to their promiscuous nature, that these television programmes are also being aired in the West; however, it is this misconception that demonstrates the young Indian's desire to be recognized by its American counterparts. This ideal requires placing cultural regulations on the backburner, meeting and enjoying Westernized standards and masking them with an overarching Indian identity, all in a subconscious attempt to escape that very identity.

Study has shown Television viewing occupied 10.9 per cent of an adolescent time that is about 12 hours per week. 90 per cent of this viewing occurred at home, 73 per cent was done with other family members including 7 per cent with grandparents, uncles, or aunts. This indicates that TV viewing is a typical family activity.

Adolescents' rates of viewing were correlated with mothers' rates of viewing, with rates for both higher when mothers were unemployed. Adolescents' TV rates were also correlated with fathers' rates and with fathers' type of unemployment. Study has prove, during TV viewing adolescents reported lower than average challenge, worry, and paying attention and higher than average choice, clam and relaxation. In short TV viewing of the middle class Indian youth is a relaxed antidote to the stress of the day that they share with their families.

Television has a major impact on toddlers it influences their viewing habits throughout their lives. Since toddlers have a strong preference for cartoons and other programs that have characters that move fast, there is considerable likelihood that they will be exposed to large amounts of violence. Children do not become full-fledged 'viewers' until around the age of two-and-a-half. As toddlers, they begin to pay more attention to the television set when it is on. They develop a limited ability to extract meaning from television content.

At the age of eight, children are more likely to be sensitive to important moderating influences of television content, and will not become more aggressive themselves if the violence they see is portrayed as evil, as causing human suffering, or as resulting in punishment or disapproval. However, they are especially likely to show increased aggression from watching violent television if they believe the violence reflects real life, if they identify with a violent hero, or if they engage in aggressive fantasies.

One major group which television watching has effected is the age group between 5-13 years of age. Television violence is accompanied by vivid production features; preschoolers are predisposed to seek out and pay attention to violence—particularly cartoon violence. It is not the violence itself that makes the cartoons attractive to preschoolers, but the accompanying vivid production features. With this preference for cartoons, preschoolers are being exposed to a large number of violent acts in their viewing day. Moreover, they are unlikely to be able to put the violence in context, since they are likely to miss any subtlety conveyed mitigating information concerning motivation and consequences. Preschoolers behave more aggressively than usual in their play after watching any high-action exciting television content, but mostly after watching violent television.

Another important group that has faced major identity transformations, sparked by the engagement in television is women. In recent years, viewers of Indian film and television have witnessed a shift from portrayals of females as innocent and subordinate in nature, into independent sexual beings. While India's strong traditional heritage has always been significantly characterized by the traditional roles of women as homemakers and mothers, the portrayal of women on television has challenged this ideal, and therefore cultivated a new perception of womanhood for the Indian woman.

> "In the 1990s, the Indian ideal of female beauty changed to become more aligned with the Western concept of 'thin is beautiful'. This change can be unhealthy because the average female Indian body type generally includes large hips."

It is therefore evident that the increasing popularity of Western norms through television can be equated with the changing attitudes of Indian females and their bodies. The concern here is obviously the potential damage these ideals may inflict upon the health and self esteem of women exposed to such figures.

One particular article which examined the portrayal of women in Indian television states, "Although many of the programmes continued to relegate women to the role of either the glamorous host or the traditional housewife, there were many examples of non-traditional roles for women."

The very concept of woman has been revolutionized by the integration of Western ideals and practices that are seeping into Indian-produced television. Conflicts are therefore surfacing which pertain to the issues of female identity. Similarly, with the recent uproar of music-based television, Indian youth culture is flourishing into an 'Indianized' group which depends on Western ideals to propel their tastes. This consequently, is creating drifts within the nuclear family structure, and producing a generation gap. The urban middle class, as well as rural villagers are also affected in that they now utilize commodities as a signifier of rank, and these commodities are determined by conglomerate advertising through mainstream Indian television.

Television watching and physical activity both are related to obesity. However this has been investigated mainly in children. Television viewing takes up 10.9 per cent of an adolescent's time (about 12 hours per week) study proves. Children get glued to the television and do not exercise. They watch one programme after another without giving them self's a break. They do not even have half an hour to do any kind of physical activities. This finally results in obesity.

Socially, one of the greatest problems plaguing India today is the consequences of Americanization. Indian's have eroticized the culture of America to such a degree where they do not realize that they are constantly consuming high priced merchandise at the expense of their own enriched diverse culture. The Indian economy is so motivated by the capital gain from multinationals that they often try to counterbalance the impact of the western images by enforcing radical Nationalistic themes. The growing popularity of television in all parts of India is therefore making way for a homogenized Indian culture whose cultural identity is becoming ever so fragile.

REFERENCES

- Fernandes, Leela. *"Nationalizing 'the Global': Media Images, Cultural Politics and the Middle Class in India"* Media Culture Society, 22 (2000): 611-628.
- Johnson, Kirk. *"Media and Social Change: the Modernizing Influences of Television in Rural India"* Media Culture Society. 23 (2001): 147-169.
- Juluri, Vamsee. *"Music Television and the Invention of Youth Culture in India"* Television and New Media, 3 (2002): 367-386.
- Morgan, M. and N. Signorielli (1990) *'Cultivation Analysis: Conceptualization and Methodology'*, pp. 13–34 in N. Signorielli and M. Morgan (eds) Cultivation Analysis: New Directions in Media Effects Research. Newbury Park, CA: Sage.
- Malhotra, S and E. Rogers. *"Satellite Television and the New Indian Woman"* Gazette, 62 (2000): 407-430.
- *"Brand Equity—TV Rating."* Retrieved June 23, 2007 from http://www.brandequity.com.my/Charts/AsiaPacific/asiapacific_tv_advertising.html.
- *"Impact of Television"* Retrieved June 25, 2007 from http://world.std.com/~jlr/comment/tv_impact.htm.

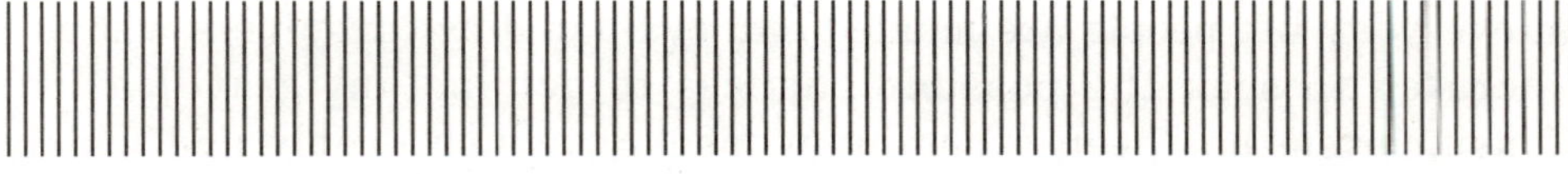

CHAPTER

41

Consumerism and the Predicament of Moral Education

— Dr. P. Chilar Mohamed
— Dr. N. Mohamed Mohideen

Introduction

Today as consumer society has risen and formed throughout the world after World War II, consumerism has become a topic of increasing interest throughout many academic disciplines, from sociology to anthropology, psychoanalysis to political philosophy. In education, there are some theorists such as Henry Giroux, Trevor Norris as so on discussing the influence of consumerism on education and schooling. In this chapter, I intend to discuss consumerism as a new cultural ideology and its influences on moral education.

In the pursuit of modernization or development, many societies set up the economical growth as the target and market economy is treated as the main instrument to realize the target. The development of the market depends on the liberation and production of people's consuming desires. Raising the level of consumption has become the goal of the society and it is regarded as the only way to bring the society into the economic progress and even political thriving.

Both western prosperous societies and other underdeveloped and developing societies are increasingly oriented around consumption: "the act of consumption, the desire to consume, and the extensive communicative apparatus designed to celebrate consumption and elaborate its signification". We have come into a consumption era. The commercialization of culture and society and the impact of mass media drive people to become consumers.

In everyday life people are molded and evaluated as consumers who are liberated to seek the possible chances to get instant gratification. Consumerism has been a dominant ideology which deeply and widely penetrates into every corner of different societies and different cultures. People are being controlled by consuming structure and are bound up to the process of desire production and reproduction. The public sphere has been inundated by an unending parade of commodities and fabricated television spectacles that keep it preoccupied with the values of consumerism.

For the public at large, the integrating and transformative experiences of culture have been replaced by participation in consuming trends. Consumerism leads to a new kind of social control and it is techniques of social power that refashion mind and body.

Consumerism has very serious influences on moral life, because people are tempted only to concern about their own consuming desires and to throw themselves into the chase of pleasures of being consuming. Mass consumer culture becomes the ground of a pleasure-seeking morality and hedonist lifestyle, that is, a morality which concentrates individuals' selfish short-term ego-gratification. It causes the decadence, apathy to the public life, social alienation and egoism.

Consumerism is the myth, which believes that individuals will be integrated by consuming. It degrades the need for morally fulfillment to satisfaction of owning commodities, and it substitutes the requirement of capacity to do more consumption for the pursuit of virtues in the public and spiritual rebirth. In the myth of consumerism, there is no rebirth or renewal of moral personality. And there are no symbols to evoke transcendent truths and ultimate values.

Because consumption is related with capital and money is the necessary condition of the consumption. Consumer society is giving rise of mammonism as well as fetishism.

In the midst of a major identity crisis and the loss of moral consensus, have we realized the lack of morality and humanism in our society, which is now supported by the transient satisfaction of ownership rather than the ontological value of the meaningful cultural and moral experience? Is consumerism a kind of social oppression that distorts moral freedom?

Has it made education demoralizing? Have we realized the confliction between the pursuits of consumption and moral excellence? Have we really acknowledged the crisis which consumerism causes in our school moral education? What does education in a consumer society offer to the youth by the way of moral guidance? The challenge that Chinese society has confronted is somehow a predicament that the western world has involved since a long time before. So those questions can be raised globally.

Consumerism and Egocentrism

In consumer society, the commoditization of everyday life made its reconstruction of values orientations and aims to depend on the desires production and consumption. Human values are only evaluated by the market and individuals' capacity of consumption. Therefore individuals only have commercial values that can be calculated and exchanged in the market.

Consumer culture drives people to worry about their personal abilities of consumption. Everyday life is a kind of practice to seek consumption targets that can satisfy the desires. As desires belong to private affaires and only can be satisfied individually, the consuming life is located in the pursuit of self-interest and it is competitive between people. Consumers don't care about the common well-being in case his own consumption interests and pleasure relates.

They don't concern the universal values but the improvement of their instrumental functions in the consumption. Therefore in the consumer society individuals are atomically egocentric.

In the consumer culture people's preferences of desires determine their lives and sensual pleasure turns to be the central end of life. Consumption authorizes pleasure to be the particular forms of meaning and value of life. Commodities of consumption are not only the objects to meet the needs, but there are symbols of social identity and personality. Consuming desires and the tastes define the consumers and rank the social status and personal qualities.

People are differentiated by their capacity of consumption and their particular tastes. From the consumption people define their lives and choose their life goals and social roles. Consumer culture forms an illusion that the realization of pleasure is the very kind of self-fulfillment.

The meaning of consumption is substituted for the meaning of life, and an individual is evaluated by the owning of consumables. So consumption shapes and refashions the self-identities of people and their self-expectations, and provides them the fundamental values of lives. In the consumer culture, tastes and styles mark and reshape personalities. Everyone shows his or her characteristics by the idea of consumption and the way of consuming. The differences of personalities are produced by the differences of desires and tastes. In this way experiences of people become commercialized and personalities turn into unification, that is, people are characterized by unified pleasures. People have to seek out their differences of characters in the consumption because they aren't able to find who he or she is in the consumer culture. Pleasure satisfaction cannot give a real self-identity other than an illusion of self because materialized pleasure naturally is the same though it has the different degrees.

Thus the egocentric pursuit of pleasure is the only thing that an individual feels real. Lives lose its spiritual and moral contour altogether.

For consumers, self-worth is gauged by buying power. The acts of buying and owning reinforce self-worth and construct their selves as well as the social relations. Personal well-being is evaluated and marked by the amount of consumables that he or she is able to have. In the temptation of the consumption and competition for personal interests, people as consumers pursue the satisfaction of personal pleasures without any concerns about the social well-being. Things worth doing are only those related with their own consumption.

Consumerism delivers the society into a state of social coldness and alienation from each other. Consumerism produces egocentrism and undermines the sense of morality. People reject moral reflection on their lives that are now only based on personal preference of pleasure.

There are no value criteria to make judgement of the right and wrong. Consumption made lives devalued. What we teach in schools are not moral reason and virtues, on the contrary, we teach our children how to realize themselves in the pursuit of the success of appetite satisfaction. Consumer culture forms a new kind of individualism, narcissist individualism, which would cause fragments of social identity and collapse of morality. Except shared preference to certain tastes, no moral consensus and shared values can be identified in the society.

Consumerism and Deconstruction of Moral Agency

Moral agency is located in reflective moral practice in the wholeness of life, that is, life itself is essentially a matter of morality and individuals are moral agents in the life-world. But in the consumer culture, individuals are not moral agents. They lost their characteristic as moral agents because they don't think their lives matter morally. Consuming culture is guiding and training people to be consumers and the ethical essence of the personal lives are undermined by the consumerization and reification of life-world. Individuals are only consumption agents.

Consumer personhood is being reproduced by consumerism and new kind of social integration and conformity are molded in consumer culture. Consumption is a structural mechanism that people are placed in to be after the passing fads that might give pleasure and a concordant identity with the consumption trends.

Consumer society produces an apparatus of social control which is different from totalitarian's whose tricks are depriving people's freedom from them, that is, to destroy their agency. In consuming culture people act as if they are free agents because everyone is liberated to make his or her own choice in consumption. Consumer structure provides freedom for people to get what they want in the process of production of the desires and catering for the tastes. Consumers seem self-determined, that is, they have positive freedom to meet desires and tastes. It seems that they have autonomy to decide their consuming behaviours and make their own choices. Can people really have personal autonomy in consumer society? People only have freedom to meet the desires that are produced by the market. This is a mutual-advantage process in which the market gets profits through the production and stimulation of desires and people gain pleasures from satisfaction through catering for the market. Consumers are enchanted by the consuming market's surface freedom.

Individuals are placed in the consuming structural chains of desires and pleasure seeking. The temptations permeate minds and bodies and refashion them in a very delicate way and weaken the people's value reflection of lives as reflective agents. Thus consumer culture puts the consumption market in a supreme status and enlarges and expands its capacity of manipulation. People are compelled into and are bounded up onto the chains of desire and pleasure. Consumerism eliminates personal autonomy and freedom to pursue the excellence and moral virtues and the consumption pleasure substitutes personal well-being.

In consumer society the primacy condition to be a consumer is that one must firstly be consumed by the social-economic system rather than to be an autonomous moral agent. Individuals must adapt themselves to the commercialized society and cater for requirements of consumption. They are commercialized and only have instrumental values. Desire-pleasure domination saturates life process and forms the homogeneity through the consumerization of individuals who turn into consuming objects selected by the social and economical systems.

In a consumer society the different levels of personal consumption are even regarded as the differences of personal qualities and merits. The values of lives seem to be located in what and how one can consume. Successful consumers' life style is set as the model of social striving. Schooling sets it as the image that the future consumers must have and education must shape for the consume agents. School education emphasizes the individual's competences of consumption more and more. This means that public school is a market where knowledge and education is commercialized. Education produces the commodities for the systems and primarily expects the students to be consuming agents. The relation between school and students is like the relation between the market and customers. Schools intend to cater for the consuming interests of families and students and they design the curricula according to the consumer society and distribute them to the student consumers. They foresee the consumption trends of future social market and allure the students in definite ways of catering for their tastes and promise them for the satisfaction. This is the new characteristic of modern education.

The commercialization of school education changes personal spiritual communication in whole range into consumption. The school market service and the educational consumption change education and cultivation into a consumption style. The communication between education and people becomes relationship of the exchange. Education abandons its intrinsic values in the cultivation of moral person. Commercialized schooling debases moral education.

Morality seems only to be a kind of adjustment to the social order and conventions to define peoples' activities.

In a consumption era children are exploited and socialized by commercial consumer culture and there are fewer public spaces and chances to develop agency and learn democratic and cooperative social relations and values in an increasingly commercialized and privatized culture and society. Individuals in the consumption culture do not represent the privileged terrain of moral agency, but rather serves as objectified bodies, whose values and lives are marketed and consumed by the consuming system that indulges stylized narcissism and forms simulacrums of selves. The consumer culture presents the fragmented individuals as actors of seeking of desire and pleasure in a commercialized life. The moral agents are dead because no moral autonomous persons are educated. Individuals are indulged to pursue the success of capturing more capitals and objects in consumption life and they lost themselves as reified bodies. The moral person no longer exists because the dominant consumer culture can only bring up consumers who are only intersecting concourse of needs, desires and pleasure.

The oblivion of moral agency occurs in the relation between needs and social structures, the relation between freedom of choice and the power of commercial systems. The reproduction of social order, prosperity and progress commercially decide the modern fate of individuals.

In the intimate, private everyday world, questions of identity and ethics remain unanswered:

What kind of social actors can individuals be?

What form can we take as moral agents?

How do we understand the very relation between the everyday world and moral autonomy, between our moral value and the ability of consuming?

Do we think reflectively about the consumerist power which is the disposal over our lives?

We see ourselves as people who are inescapably 'free' and self-managing, who make decisions about who we are, but consuming activities drive us to carry out a social identity of the consumer. Consumer culture endows a new identity for us instead of the nature of moral agency.

Consumerism and the New Social Responsibility

In the rise of commercial society, the production and reproduction of desires and the objects of consumption form a new relation between individuals and society. People form the social conformity as consumers who are involved in the circle of desires and pleasure satisfaction.

Choices of the multifarious commodities and their symbolization of meaning become the ultimate end of life, but the choices of moral values turn to be like 'Supermarket Choice'.

Moral values are determined by personal tastes and personal preferences. Values relevant to self and others do not matter morally, which become neutral and everybody can freely determine how to dispose his own mind and body according to his desires and needs. Values have no relations with the flourishing of personal and social well-being. So there are no moral duties and responsibilities to self and communities in the values preferences. What is more, in the dominant consumerism era, the difference of desires and the multifarious preferences bring the situation of lack of shared values and public spiritedness. To be apathetic to others' well-being and alienated from the community is regarded as the justified private morality. No common and shared social values hold the modern individuals together except the consumption mutual advantages. The social solidarity and social trust are degenerated and we are related each other not morally but in the consumerist way. Consumerism reduces the social life to a trivial materialism. It makes social responsibility lapsed and constructs lives in relation to a future devoid of moral obligations and social responsibility of citizenship.

The definition of an individual as a consumer has a reduced sense of social responsibility for the common well-being. In this sense modern man—the consumer has no moral commitment for the society because a life of consumption is not relevant to social responsibility.

Individuals become the means of the consumer society. This disavows the dignity of man as the ultimate end of society. Consumerism is detrimental to the commitment to the public life and common well-being and to the production of citizenship in democratic sense.

In consumer society social distinction and cultural discrimination made by consumption bring crisis to the social trust and concordance. Everyone cares about his self-interest and the ligament of social solidarity is at risk. Nothing can form the social coherence except the conformity of seeking and enjoying consumption. The fragments of society make the consumer culture to be new kind of social denotation and code to signify the social coherence and to endow the members new value commitment. Consumer culture produces the identification of the social conformity and provides the basis for morality. It firstly produces divisions of society and separates the individual members by the process of consumption and pleasure, and then it controls individuals by placing them into the desires and consumption circle.

Consumption is not simple based on meeting life needs. There are social influences or social pressures or processes of socialization in consumption through which society molds the individual. This molding force contradicts moral education in school, and causes great confliction in society. In the conditions of consumer culture, we desperately need shared values to underpin the social solidarity and to support the flourishing both of personal and social well-being, but we cannot have a shared basis of value commitment.

Consumerism and the Displacement of Virtues

In consumer culture, personal well-being or happiness is evaluated by the possession of objects. The pursuit of the good life means seeking for instant gratification. The end of life is limited within possession and pleasure. This hedonistic life style drives away the virtues. Life is no longer the process in which man can realize good values and pursue virtues. It turns to be after the pleasure of possession and not to be a process of 'eudemonia' with the involvement of virtues. Both life and life agents become means of possession in the consumption.

Everyone thinks competition for self-interest is justifiable and will take rivalry of abilities and pleasures and gratification for granted. Consumerism supports those who are successful at this rivalry. This is the Social-Darwinism and consumerism obeys something like 'jungle law'. In this rivalry structure consumers stress and place the competences and skills more than the moral virtues and characters.

Conclusion: What Can Moral Education Offer to the Students?

Consumerism is a justified myth in our society and it is the malaise for moral education. Up to now we have not been acknowledgeable about the challenges that consumerism put forward to moral values and moral education. In the confliction and contradictory between consumerism and moral values, what does moral education offer its students by way of moral guidance, and what should it offer? What I can suggest here is only that moral education is a very important aspect of life politics. Facing consumerism we are feeling that we desperately need moral education to construct our cooperative public life and flourish our social well-being and to foster public spiritedness, citizenship, virtues and personal character. In this art, morality appeals man to have a moral commitment for others' well-being and public well-being as well as personal well-being in pursuit of which we become morally excellent person. To be a moral person means to live a life that has moral meaning which develops personal moral visions of what is illusory in life and what is authentic. In this sense moral education cannot teach or instill a certain single set of values because moral values are themselves plural. it must be emphasized that moral education cannot imposes some single moral views on youths today as the nature of moral judgement and moral responsibility is such that it rests ultimately within the relation between the individual and community. So the most important is that how moral education passes on moral responsibility to the students in the guidance of moral reasoning and judgement and to develop students' visions to be a virtuous person in leading a moral life in which integrate social well-being and personal well-being. In this perspective, it is the task of moral education to guide students to form the ability and character to commit moral vision, moral judgement and responsibility as active, free and equal citizens.

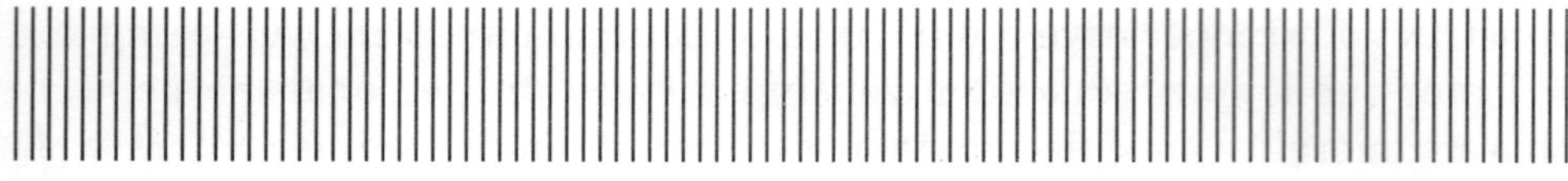

CHAPTER

42

Children as Consumers in the Global Scenario

—N. Veerapandian
—S. Abbas

Introduction

The market for children's products and food is enormous. Parents on the one hand have a hard time raising children the way they want to, while on the other hand, kids are being increasingly influenced by commercialism that often goes against what parents are trying to do.

Advertising to Children is Big Business

Consider the following:

1. Children are a captive audience: The average American child watches an estimate between 25,000 to 40,000 television commercials per year. In the UK, it is about 10,000;
2. \$15-17 billion is spent by companies advertising to children in the US. Over \$4 billion was spent in 2009 by the fast food industry alone;
3. The marketing seems to be worth it. For example,
   - —Teens in the US spend around \$160 billion a year
   - —Children (up to 11) spend around \$18 billion a year
   - —'Tweens' (8-12 year olds) 'heavily influence' more than \$30 billion in other spending by parents, and "80 per cent of all global brands now deploy a 'tween strategy.' "

— Children (under 12) and teens influence parental purchases totaling over $130-670 billion a year.

Encouraging and Increasing Childhood Consumerism

As mentioned above looking at the rise in consumption, larger houses were an example of the things promoted to increase consumption. So too was the encouragement to provide more toys and other items for children:

The [U.S.] federal government played a major role in defining childhood. In 1929, Herbert Hoover sponsored a White House Conference on Child Health and Protection. The conference report, *The Home and the Child*, concluded that children were independent beings with particular concerns of their own.... The report advised parents to give their children their own [furniture, toys, playrooms etc]. "Generally a sleeping room for each person is desirable", it noted.... Take them shopping for their own "things and let them pick them out for themselves."

Through such experiences personality develops... [These] experiences have the advantage of also creating in the child a sense of personal as well as family pride in ownership, and eventually *teaching him that his personality can be expressed through things*. Thus in the space of some 30 years, the role of children in American life changed dramatically; they became, and remain, pillars of the consumer economy, with economic power rivaling that of adults.

Children wield enormous purchasing power, both directly and indirectly (indirectly in the sense that they are able to persuade and influence parents on what to buy).

Observe a child and parent in a store. That high-pitched whining you'll hear coming from the cereal aisle is more than just the pleadings of single kid bent on getting a box of Fruit Loops into the shopping cart. It is the sound of thousands of hours of market research, of an immense coordination of people, ideas and resources, of decades of social and economic change all rolled into a single, 'Mommy, pleeease!'

"If it's within [kids'] reach, they will touch it, and if they touch it, there's at least a chance that Mom or Dad will relent and buy it," writes retail anthropologist, Paco Underhill. The ideal placement of popular books and videos, he continues, should be on the lower shelves "so the little ones can grab Barney or Tele-tubbies unimpeded by Mom or Dad, who possibly take a dim view of hyper-commercialized critters."

And advertising to children isn't just for purchasing children's items; they influence other items:

The minivan was created, for example, because children demanded more room. Then they decided the three-door behemoth was uncool, helping give rise to the SUV. "Every auto manufacturer has a strategy to target children," [James McNeal, a market researcher who specializes in the children's market] adds.

This has long been understood: The renowned behaviourist was also vice president of the J. Walter Thompson advertising agency and a spokesman for the idea, then novel, that marketing is not just about peddling products that people need; it's also about creating a society of consumers ever eager for more. Famous for claiming that any child, conditioned early enough, could be turned into anything—"a doctor, lawyer, artist, merchant-chief and, yes, even into beggar-man and thief"—he left a key vocation out. If shopper had been on his list, it would have been a prescient boast.

Heavy Advertising Targeted at Children

Marketers see children as a future—as well as current—market and hence brand loyalty at a young age helps in the quest of continued sales later.

The Journal of the American Medical Association has said that children between the ages of two and seventeen watch an annual average of 15,000 to 18,000 hours of television, compared with 12,000 hours spent per year in school. Children are also major targets for TV advertising, whose impact is greater than usual because there is an apparent lessening of influence by parents and others in the older generation...According to the [Committee on Communications of the American Academy of Paediatrics], children under the age of two should not watch television at all because at that age, brain development depends heavily on real human interactions.

In the European Union, revenues to television networks and producers have reached between $620 and $930 million.

Advertising to Children Considered Harmful

Sweden, since 1991 has banned all advertising during children's prime time due to findings that children under 10 are incapable of telling the difference between a commercial and a programme, and cannot understand the purpose of a commercial until the age of 12.

In the US, research from the American Psychological Association (APA) shows that children under the age of eight are unable to critically comprehend televised advertising messages and are prone to accept advertiser messages as truthful, accurate and unbiased. This can lead to unhealthy eating habits as evidenced by today's youth obesity epidemic. For these reasons, a task force of the American Psychological Association

(APA) is recommending that advertising targeting children under the age of eight be restricted.

The research on children's commercial recall and product preferences confirms that advertising does typically get young consumers to buy their products.... Findings show that children recall content from the ads to which they've been exposed and preference for a product has been shown to occur with as little as a single commercial exposure and strengthened with repeated exposures.

Furthermore, ... these product preferences can affect children's product purchase requests, which can put pressure on parents' purchasing decisions and instigate parent-child conflicts when parents deny their children's requests....

... there are concerns regarding certain commercial campaigns primarily targeting adults that pose risks for child-viewers. "For example, beer ads are commonly shown during sports events and seen by millions of children, creating both brand familiarity and more positive attitudes toward drinking in children as young as 9-10 years of age. Another area of sensitive advertising content involves commercials for violent media products such as motion pictures and video games. Such ads contribute to a violent media culture which increases the likelihood of youngsters' aggressive behaviour and desensitizes children to real-world violence," said Dr. Kunkel [senior author of the task force's scientific report].

Bans, Regulation, Self-regulation, Media-literacy

Advertising is in all areas of children's lives, from television commercials, to ad placement within programmes (and video games), to toys, the Internet, mobile telephones, and more. The concern of the impacts on children has led to many trying to control advertising in some way.

Banning Ads and the Fear or Unintended Consequences

Sweden, since 1991 has banned all advertising during children's prime time due to those concerns mentioned above regarding advertising to children being harmful.

The European Union is now considering issues related to advertising targeted at children and whether there should be a Europe-wide ban or regulation.

Since April 2007, the has UK banned junk food advertising during television programmes aimed at children aged 7 to 9. As of January 1, 2008, that ban has been extended to all children under 16.

Some argue that this industry provides jobs for people so banning advertising would be ill-advised.

Others question the effectiveness of outright bans in advertising. For example, a ban would mean lost revenues of media outlets, as many pour a large amount of advertising revenues back into programming.

The Responsible Advertising and Children Programme (RACP) is an industry organization representing advertisers, agencies and media worldwide. They argue that education and self-regulation is the way to go (as most companies in most sectors tend to argue), and also warn of job losses if there are outright bans:

We believe that educating children to understand the purpose and context of marketing communications helps them to develop the skills to critically interpret commercial communications in the context of their daily lives. This is crucial in preparing them for interaction with the reality of a media-filled world.

... advertising finances children's programming on free-to-air television.... 94 per cent of the net revenues coming from advertising aimed at children are reinvested in children's programmes. In the digital economy, there is no alternative method to ensure investment in original children's programming and in the acquisition of programme rights.

... Not only does marketing communications help to guarantee quality children's programming, it also aids competition in the wider economy, creates jobs and enhances consumer's choices of goods and services. In return, advertisers are active and enthusiastic supporters of strong self-regulation ensuring that we meet the expectations of parents, regulators, and society at large.

Education and self-regulation deliver effective and responsible marketing communications.

With less programming for children, they may end up watching more adult content, as Juliet Schor notes, also writing in the Nordicom publication mentioned earlier. However, she seems to disagree with the view above, that 'there is no alternative' to advertising for financing children's programming:

Bans also raise the possibility of negative unintended consequences. For example, if a ban on advertising to children were to be enacted, it would reduce the financing available for children's programming. If the quantity and quality of their programming declined, children would be likely to watch more adult media. This, in turn, would expose them to other types of inappropriate advertising and content. At the very least, government regulations on advertising need to be coupled with adequate financing mechanisms for quality children's programming.

Schor also notes that one exception to the above concerns would be in schools, where the additional concerns with bans (legal, logistical, pragmatic) are not as difficult in a controlled environment such as school.

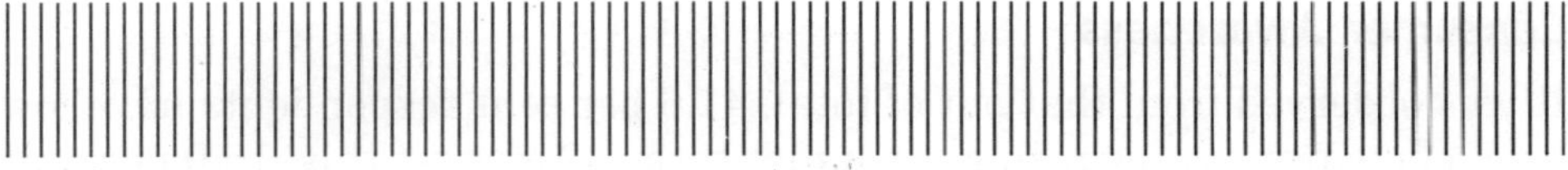

CHAPTER

43

Comparative Study of Consumer Awareness among Males and Females

— Mr. M. Mathialagan

Introduction

Majority of Indian Consumers are ignorant and do not know the role of Consumption *vis-à-vis* economic system. The entire marketing operation is aimed at profit maximization at the expense of consuming people. Mal practices like adulteration, short weights and measures, high prices, false and deceitful advertisement and packaging are pervading the market even when Government of India claim to have passed maximum legal laws protecting consumers than any other country in the world.

Earlier Studies

Indian consumers are cheated through defective weights and measures to the Rs. 1600 crores a year. Though government has passed several acts and laws to protect consumer and seek redressed of their grievances they are not in a position to utilize their knowledge or are simply ignorant of these (John 1974, Gupta and Ogale, 1988). Laws are not popular because they are framed in highly technical terminologies that it would not be possible to comprehend by a laymen (Anonymous 1976).

Few institutions such as J.J.M. Ahmedabad and sporadic researches at individual level have been conducted (John, 1974: Bhatia 1973; Bhatt 1977). The problem is multi-dimensional and multi-action is needed where incorporation of research institution and academician is required. Therefore the current investigation is undertaken with the objectives.

Consumer Awareness

It was observed from that out of total, 41.6 per cent respondents have low level of awareness regarding consumer terms. Amongst this, 15.0 per cent are males and 26.6 per cent females. Only 23.3 per cent respondents had partial awareness out of which 15 per cent are male and 8.3 per cent females. Out of total, 85 per cent respondents had high level of awareness with 20 per cent belonging to males and 15 per cent of females. Finding of John's study (1974) also confirmed that majority of respondents have partial consumer awareness.

Legal Awareness

Analysis of data regarding legal awareness showed that majority of males and female respondents were aware about the legal laws protecting the consumers against adulteration of fold stuffs (90% males, 86.6% females), adulteration of drugs (90% males, 86.6% females; short weighing (86.6% each of males and females); false weights and measures (86.6% males, 76.6% females); using stones for weights (80.6% males, 63.3% females); using hand made balance (76.6% males and 50% females) and using deceitful packaging (70% males and 43.3% females). It was concluded from the above findings that males were having letter awareness regarding legal laws than female respondents.

Awareness of Respondents Regarding Consumer Terminology

Level of awareness regarding various terminologies was observed. It was inferred from the table findings that more number of female respondents (66.6%) were aware of these specific terms than men. It may be attributed to the fact that it is related more to clothing which is frequently purchased by women than men.

Source of Information Regarding Consumer Technology

Majority of male and female respondents got some information of consumer interest through T.V. (86.6% males and 6.6% females) followed by radio, newspaper and magazines. Journals were least commonly used sources of information (33.3% males and 36.3% males) It can be concluded that mass-media can effectively be used to promote information and awareness especially to educated respondents.

Awareness Regarding Consumer Organizations

The data that 80 per cent males and 53.3 per cent females were aware about consumer organisations working in and around their area. On the contrary, only 40 per cent males and 26.6 per cent females had shown any interest in joining these organisations. The reason given by majority of them was lack of time and no interest in joining them, as it will yield no results. It was once analyzed that unless consumer awareness is created, the efforts of the government and voluntary organisations can't achieve the desired results.

H_O : Sex Postulated to be positive co-relates Level of Awareness of selected sample.

Level of awareness between males and females was tested by employing 't' test. The results indicated that awareness level of both male and female respondents showed significant difference. Male respondents were significant difference. Male respondents were significantly more aware than the female respondents' 't' value – 3.40.

Thus, overall the findings gave an insight into the extent of consumer lack of awareness of many facts that are of much relevance for their own welfare.

Recommendations

- Promote general awareness of the rights of the consumer by encouraging consumer education and supplying information.
- Bringing together the consumers, traders and policymakers to exchange information of mutual interest for better co-ordination.
- Enlighten the business community on its ethical and legal obligations to maintain quality of the products or services and to be transparent in dealing with consumers.
- Publish periodical and product specific booklets, pamphlets, cassettes, CDs, Slides, documentary films and other devices of mass communication for promoting awareness in English and regional languages, highlighting the problem in specified areas like real estate, public utilities, non-banking financial agencies etc.,

Conclusion

Industrial and consumer markets in India have been witnessing many changes driven by globalization and privatization. Consequently, production oriented market has been shifting towards customer oriented market. Consumers now have varied choices and they are more knowledgeable and demanding too. Hence, consumer awareness is very indispensable.

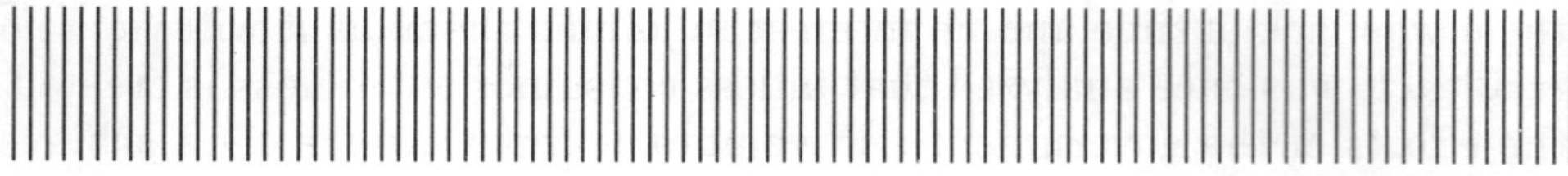

CHAPTER

44

Global Consumerism

Challenges and Prospectives

—Dr. P.K. Venkatachalam
Mr. A. Rathinam

Introduction

Consumerism is one of the most popular social issues and is becoming increasingly publicized as time passes. The scope of the movement is so extensive that it draws attention from a variety of disciplines.

The consumer of the future will be increasingly demanding, skeptical, and critical. Marketers who fail to understand the changes that are occurring in consume behavior in today's marketplace are doomed to be less successful than they otherwise might be. Thus, the topic of consumerism is of prime importance for the marketer because it holds an important key to present and future success. Understanding consumers and being able to adapt to their changing demands will reward the innovative marketer.

Definition of Consumerism

Consumerism encompasses the evolving set of activities of government, business and independent organizations that are designed to protect the rights of consumers. It is concerned with protecting consumers from all organizations with which there is an exchange relationship. There are consumer problems associated with hospitals, libraries, schools, police forces, and various government agencies, as well as with business firms.

Globalization

It is the process whereby national economies and business systems are becoming deeply interlinked with each other.

The world is moving away from relatively independent national economies toward a single global system.

Firms are selling their products worldwide for a variety of reasons:

(*a*) With the buildup of 'multinational fever' and the general attractiveness of multinational markets, consumers in other parts of the world are increasingly seeking products or services originating in one country out;

(*b*) Many firms have learned that overseas markets represent the single most important opportunity for their future growth when their home markets reach maturity. This realization is propelling them to expand their horizons and seek consumers scattered all over the world;

(*c*) Consumers all over the world are increasingly eager to try 'foreign' products that are popular in different and far-off places.

Consumerism

Fundamental rights of consumers

The rights of consumers are the foundation for the current interest in consumerism.

(*a*) The right to safety (consumer safety): Consumers regularly complain about shoddy or defective merchandise and poor services. It is one thing to be cheated or deceived by a product, but it is quite another to be physically injured by an unsafe product.

(*b*) The right to be informed (consumer information): Consumer rights with regard to information relate to the marketer's provision of adequate information which neither deceives nor misleads.

It includes:

(*i*) Deception of consumers;

(*ii*) Corrective Advertising;

(*iii*) Affirmative Disclosure;

(*iv*) Unit Pricing;

(*v*) Nutritional Labelling;

(*vi*) Open Dating;

(*vii*) Truth in Lending.

(*c*) The right to choose (consumer choice): Consumers actually have less choice than might be possible and desirable because of the economies of scale necessary in order to enter and compete effectively in certain industries. For example, in the cereal industry it is claimed that a small new producer of cereal would find it virtually impossible to enter and be successful. Therefore, some consumerists support expanded choice for the consumer through regulations designed to control corporate power in the marketplace.

(*d*) **The right to be heard (consumer redress):** The consumer has the right to be listened to in the marketplace. That is, consumer input as a means of setting government policies should be facilitated and, more importantly, responded to in an equitable way.

There are numerous weapons at the consumer's disposal which may be used to obtain redress. Such activities include complaint letters, boycotts, class action suits, and other means. The remedies sought by these means include restitution and punishment. But the best way that the marketer can be protected from consumer redress is to prevent problems before they happen. Listening to consumers, therefore, may warn of situations which can be remedied before they become problems.

(*e*) **The right to clean environment (Environmental Concerns):** The fifth consumer right, is the right to a clean environment – to be assured that the environment the consumer lives in is free from pollution. Widespread and large-scale pollution seems to be a by-product of an economically developed society, but it is also an area of great concern for many consumers.

(*f*) **The right to privacy (Consumer Privacy):** The sixth consumer right relates to privacy. Consumer information collected, merged and exchanged through computer and communication technologies has become the main resource that business and government use to facilitate the millions of daily transactions engaged in by consumers. Only relevant and socially-approved personal information should be collected and it should not be disclosed to others outside unless agreed to by the individual.

Legislative Responses to Consumerism

Consumerism has had an impact on legislative attempts to enhance consumer rights. Examples of this type of legislation include:

- Fair Packaging and Labelling Act;
- Consumer Product Safety Act;
- The National Environment Act;
- The Toxic Substances Control Act;

- Cigar Labelling Act;
- Consumer Credit Protection Act;
- The Clean Air Act.

Global Challenges and Prospectives

Prospectives

The Challenge of going global has been given meaning by the following prospective:

(*a*) The spread of market-based economic systems (More no. of privately owned business where price is fixed based on supply, demand and govt. regulations) *e.g.*, Efforts of European Union to form a single market; North American Free Trade Agreement; ASEAN Free Trade Area;

(*b*) The decline of barriers to international trade and foreign direct investment;

(*c*) The falling costs of communication and transportation;

(*d*) Rapidly expanding middle classes in Asian Countries.

Challenges

Today, almost all major corporations are actively marketing their products beyond their original homeland borders. In fact, the issue is generally not whether to market a brand in other countries but rather how to do it (as the same product with the same 'global' advertising campaign, or 'tailored' products and localized ads for each country.) Because of this emphasis on operating as a multinational entity, the vocabulary of marketing now includes terms such as glocal, which refers to companies that are both 'global' and 'local'; that is, they include in their marketing efforts a blend of standardized and local elements in order to secure the benefits of each strategy.

Hence the corporations have to face the following challenges:

(*a*) Gathering and interpreting correctly the information that organizations need to meet the sophisticated needs of organizations in this 21st century;

(*b*) Developing effective consumer research methods to keep abreast of the rapid changes in consumer trends and lifestyles (how lifestyles and needs are changing, how family structures and relationships are changing, how purchase behaviors and consumption pattern are changing);

(*c*) Understanding consumer behaviour from a broader perspective as an important part of life in its own right.

Questions to be answered while developing a global marketing strategy:

(*a*) Is the geographic area homogenous with respect to culture?

(*b*) What needs can this product fill in this culture?

(*c*) Can enough people afford the product?

(*d*) What values are relevant to the purchase and use of the product?

(*e*) What are the distribution, political and legal structure concerning this product?

(*f*) How can we communicate about the product?

(*g*) What are the ethical implications of marketing this product in this country?

Conclusion

With so much diversity present among the members of just one nation, it is easy to appreciate that numerous larger differences may exist between citizens of different nations having different cultures, values, beliefs, and languages. If international marketers are to satisfy the needs of consumers in potentially very distinct markets effectively, they must understand the relevant similarities and differences that exist between the peoples of the countries they decide to target.

When consumers make purchase decisions, they seem to take into consideration the countries of origin of the brands that they are assessing. Consumers frequently have specific attitudes or even preferences for products made in particular countries. These country-of-origin effects influence how consumers rate quality and sometimes, which brands they will ultimately select.

As increasing numbers of consumers from all over the world come in contact with the material goods and lifestyle of people living in other countries and as the number of middle-class consumers grows in developing countries, marketers are eager to locate these new customers and to offer them their products. The rapidly expanding middle classes in countries of Asia, South America, and Eastern Europe possess relatively substantial buying power because their incomes are largely discretionary (necessities like housing and medical care are often provided by the state for little or no cost).

For some international marketers, acculturation is a dual process: First, marketers must learn everything that is relevant to the product and product category in the society in which they plan to market, and then they must persuade the members of that society to break with their traditional ways of doing things to adopt the new product. The more similar a foreign target market is to a marketer's home market, the easier is the process of acculturation. Conversely, the more different a foreign target market, the more difficult the process of acculturation.

Some of the problems involved in global analysis include differences in language, consumption patterns, needs, product usage, economic and social conditions, marketing conditions, and market research opportunities. There is an urgent need for more systematic and conceptual global analyses of the psychological, social, and cultural characteristics concerning the consumption habits of foreign consumers. Such analyses would identify increased marketing opportunities that would benefit both international marketers and their targeted consumers.

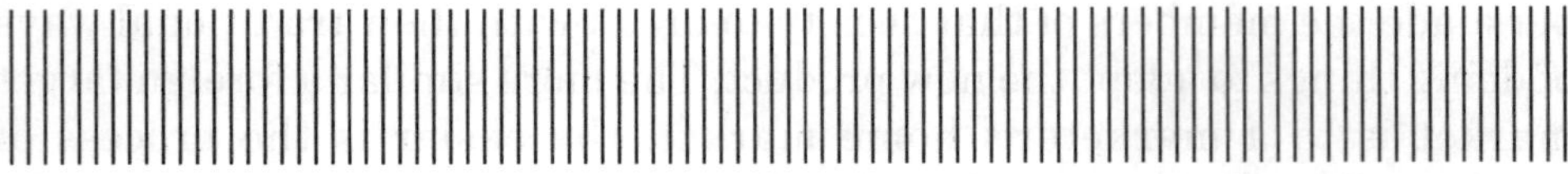

CHAPTER

45

Customers' Market and Total Quality Management

—M. Natharshah

Introduction

Over a period of time the Quality of life of our people has risen to greater heights. Thanks to advancement in technology and marketing which has given us access to many useful goods and services. The consumer goods market is flooded with lots of goods and the consumer selects what he wants. If only the marketer brings out a need based Quality product that satisfies the buyers, he will be able to survive. For this, the marketer has to adopt the concept of TQM which fulfil both organizational as well as individual needs.

Definition and Meaning of TQM

TQM means meeting the requirements of the internal / external customer consistently by continuous improvement in the quality of work of all employees.

Under TQM, Quality is emphasized from the customers' view point rather than the producers' view point.

TQM aims at meeting (or) exceeding the requirements and expectations of customers for a product/service.

TQM is a broad management approach. It focuses Quality and also productivity, flexibility, timeliness and customer responsiveness.

TQM Principles

(*i*) Customer Satisfaction
(*ii*) Customer Perception of Quality
(*iii*) Customer Complaints
(*iv*) Service Quality (or) Customer Service
(*v*) Customer Retention
(*vi*) Employee Involvement
  (*a*) Employee Motivation
  (*b*) Employee Empowerment
  (*c*) Terms and Teamwork
  (*d*) Recognition and Reward Schemes
  (*e*) Performance Appraisal
(*vii*) Continual Process Improvement
(*viii*) Supplier Partnership

(i) Customer Satisfaction

In today's buyers market 'the customer is the king'. Even the definition of Quality, 'Quality is what customer requirements'.

Customers favour the delivery with right Quality, in right Quantity, at the right time, at right cost and at the right place in addition to safely, ethical transaction of the organization.

(ii) Customer Perception of Quality

Quality is what customer perceives it to be. However, as the customers go on changing their needs, the quality level needs are to be improved continuously to meet the customers demand. That's why the basic concept of TQM philosophy is continuous process improvement.

(iii) Customer Complaints: (Customer Feedback)

A complaint is any response or opinion of a customer upon a product or service, which does not meet his expectations. It is collected through various tools such as comment card, customer Questionnaire, focus groups, Toll free telephone numbers, customer visits, report cards, the internet and computer.

(iv) Service Quality (or) Customer Service

Customer service is the set of activities an organization uses to win the customers and retain their satisfaction. This service is provided before, during or after the sales of the product.

(v) Customer Retention

Customer retention is the process of retaining the existing customers. It is obvious that customer retention is more powerful and effective than customer satisfaction.

Customer care can be defined as every activity which occurs with in an organization that ensures that a customer is not only satisfied but also retained.

Customer retention costs 5 times as much to attract a new customer as it costs to keep an old one.

(vi) Employee Involvement

Employee involvement is the back bore of a TQM movement. An effort TQM requires the total involvement from every person at all levels in the organization. Employee involvement leads to meet the organization goals and objectives. It also improves the Quality and Productivity at all levels of the organization. Some of the important aspects of employee Involvement are:

(*a*) Employee Motivation;

(*b*) Employee Empowerment;

(*c*) Terms and Teamwork;

(*d*) Recognition and Reward Schemes;

(*e*) Performance Appraisal.

(a) ***Employee Motivation:*** Scott defines, "Motivation means a process of stimulating people to accomplish desired goals". Motivation improves employee involvements which result in job satisfaction and thus reduces absent deism and turnover.

(b) ***Employee Empowerment:*** Empowerment in work setting involves giving people the means, ability and authority to do something they have not done before.

(c) ***Teams and Teamwork:*** A team consists of group of people working together to achieve common goals. Teamwork is the cumulative actions of the team.

TQM is based on the involvement of everyone in making improvements. So working in teams is an inseparable part of the TQM environment. Now a day, teamwork is adopted universally as the organizational mechanism for involving people in quality improvements.

(*d*) ***Recognition and Reward Schemes:*** Recognition is a process where by management shows acknowledgement of an employee's interest and to propel them towards continuous improvement, it is essential to recognize the people. This acknowledgement may be financial, psychological or both in nature.

Reward is a tangible one, such as increased salaries, commissions, cash bonus, gain sharing, etc, to promote desirable behaviour.

(*e*) ***Performance Appraisal:*** It is a systematic and objective assessment or evaluation of performance and contribution of an individual. It is used to identify employees for salary revision, promotion, transfer, demotion, and lay-off.

(vii) Continual Process Improvement

TQM has been defined as a philosophy based on quest for progress and continual improvement in the areas of cost, reliability, quality, innovation, efficiency and business effectiveness. TQM is a continuous learning process which never stops.

(viii) Supplier Partnership

In today's competitive environment to meet the growing demands for high Quality and zero-defeat products, many organizations have recognized the importance of suppliers. Also suppliers are regarded as partners in the organizations. According to the quality champions' view, a commitment to continuous quality improvement cannot be translated into reality with treating the suppliers as partners.

Since, supplier quality can substantially affect the quality of the product, one the organizations should work with suppliers in a partnering atmosphere. Thus organizations that intend to achieve world-class levels of manufacturing excellent, now to look at suppliers as a part of the total process of delivering the right kind of output to customers.

Quality Council

It is a team to provide over all direction for achieving the total quality culture (TQC):

The Quality Council is composed of:

(*i*) The chief executive officer (CEO);

(*ii*) The senior managers of the functional areas such as design, marketing, finance, production and Quality; and (*iii*) A coordinator or consultant.

Duties of the Quality Council

1. To establish the core values and Quality statements.
2. To establish the strategic long-term plan with goals and the annual Quality improvement program with objective.
3. To plan the training and education programmes.
4. To perform and monitor the performance measures for each functional areas of the organization.
5. To establish / revise the recognition and reward system periodically.

V. Quality Statements

1. Vision Statement.
2. Mission Statement.
3. Quality Policy Statement.

1. ***Vision Statement:*** It is a short declaration of what on organization aspires to be tomorrow. (*e.g.*) "To continuously enrich knowledge base of practioners in mobility industry and institutions in the service of humanity". —*Society of Automotive Engineers(SAE)*
2. ***Mission Statement:*** It is usually one paragraph, describes the function of the organization. It provides a clear statement of purpose for employees, customers, and suppliers. *(e.g)* To meet customers' transport and distribution needs and by being the best at moving their goods, on time, safely and damage free.

   —*A Railway company.*
3. ***Quality Policy Statement:*** It is a guide for every one in the organization as to now they provide products and service to the customers.

   It should be written by the CEO with feedback from the workforce and be approved by the Quality Council. (*e.g*) "Xerox is a quality company; Quality is the basic business principle for Xerox. Quality means providing our external and internal customers with innovative. Products and services that fully satisfy their requirements. Quality is the job of every employee." —*Xerox Corporation.*

VI. Conclusion

Doing things right entails efficiency. Doing right things entails effectiveness. TQM always emphasizes business effectiveness in terms of Quality, Cost, reliability and productivity. It also reduces mistake, waste, rework and cycle time. Every Excellency is possible under TQM Umbrella only if we establish a specific formalized system throughout the organization. As such, we have to adopt any International standards than adapt with particular standard requirements. If we are willing to adopt ISO standard requirements, we would adopt Quality management system (QMS) then can ensure TQM principles throughout the organization.

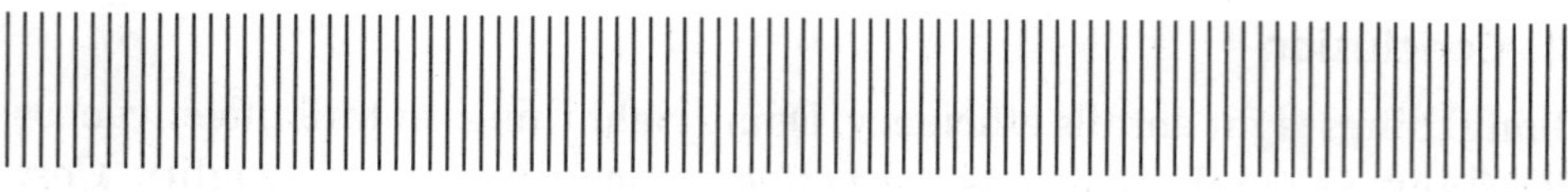

CHAPTER

46

Psychological Aspects of Consumerism

—R. Bhuvaneswari
—K. Sudha

Introduction

Business is not an end in itself but a means of human welfare. What is good for public is good for Business. 'Caveat Emptor' (let the buyer beware) is still the motto of many marketers. Therefore, need was felt to protect the interest of consumers.

Consumer movement is a universal phenomenon. Awareness of consumer is crucial to the present day existence in the market driven economy where the consumer is the hub of market dynamics. The consumer once regarded as a king has lost his pivotal position. He is taken for a ride by the advanced processing techniques coupled with persuasive powers of psychological advertising and is always subject to exploitation. If he is made to be aware of his rights as consumer and use the enforcement machinery available to establish his rights, he will be protected against exploitation ushered up his original position as the king. This perhaps may be the cause for the emergence of consumerism.

The main objective of consumerism is to create awareness and ensure the consumer's rights to product safety, adequate information, sufficient choice and clean environment. Consumer exhibits different buying problems by purchasing different brands. In order to satisfy the Consumer understanding psychological aspects are important for the marketer's survival.

Psychological Aspects of Consumerism

Psychological aspects of consumerism refer to the behaviour and mental process of consumers. Consumer's attitude comprises of three components:

1. Affective or feeling component

Emotions associated with given object.

2. Cognitive component

It refers to the beliefs of a consumer about a given object. It consists of perceptions, beliefs and ideas.

3. Overt component

It is concerned with the way of one intend to behave towards a particular environment.

Consumer's emotional response can be:

1. Conscious;
2. Semiconscious;
3. Unconscious.

Its response reflects the consumer's personalities. They vary according to their environment, income, education, Sophistication and personal exposure.

Example: Perception of different consumers in globe.

Consumers	Red	Blue	Green	Yellow	White
Americans	Danger	Masculinity	Safety	Cowardice	Purity
France	Aristocracy	Freedom	Criminality	Temporary	Neutrality
Egypt	Death	Faith	Strength	Happiness	Joy
Indians	Creativity	Truth	Prosperity	Success	Death
Japanese	Anger	Villainy	Energy	Grace	Death
Chinese	Happiness	Heaven	Ming Dynasty	Wealth	Purity

Evolution of Consumerism

The major causes of consumerism in India have been identified as rising prices, poor product performance and service qualities, product shortages and deceptive advertising. Government has been very responsive to the consumer needs through legislative action.

Consumer concern with mental and physical act including their motives and causes of individuals and groups regarding orientation, purchase, use, maintenance and disposal of goods and services from the market and public leading to functionality and the achievements of consumer goals and values.

PREMISES OF CONSUMERISM

1. Consumers are not strictly rational.
2. Consumers do not behave in random manner.
3. Consumer behaviour stems from innate and acquired needs and involves complex combinations.
4. Whether behaviour is impulsive of the result of ling deliberations, it is an expression of conscious.
5. Unconscious search for satisfaction of physiological, economic or socio-psychological needs.

Fundamental Rights of Consumerism

1. Right to safety.
2. Right to inform.
3. Right to choice.
4. Right to be heard.

Acts Empowered for Consumerism

1. The prevention of Food Adulteration Act 1954.

   —Designed to protect the health of the public by prohibiting adulteration of food.
2. The Essential Commodities Act 1955.

   —To control the interest of the general public in distribution of consumer goods.
3. Weights and Measures Act 1958.

   —Enacted to safeguard the consumer against the exploitation of weighing measures of commodities.
4. The Monopolies and Restrictive Trade Practices Act 1969.

   —To regulate the monopolistic and restrictive trade practices.
5. Drugs and Cosmetics Act1940.

   —To safeguard the quality of drugs manufactured and marketed
6. Packaged Commodities order 1975.

   —To regulate the packaging of different products.
7. Other Acts.

Dangerous Drug Act 1930.

The drugs and Magic Remedies Act 1954.

Household Electrical Appliances order 1976.

Factors Determining Consumerism

Consumer who is motivated by certain needs and goals. He gathers information from environment and responds to the information according to his influences of the physical, economic, psychological, social and cultural faction.

1. Society — Friends, relatives and club etc.
2. The family — Husband and wife.
3. Culture — Languages, morals, law, customs, tradition.
4. Social class — upper class, middle class and lower class.
5. Reference groups — Opinions, beliefs, aspiration and ethics.
6. Status symbols — Mannerisms, dress, ornaments, and possessions.

Expectations of Consumers

(1) Unadulterated goods.

(2) Correct weight and measures.

(3) Quality goods.

(4) Replacement provision.

(5) Uniform and reasonable price.

(6) Choice in selection.

(7) Service after sale, if necessary.

(8) Complete information of goods.

(9) Absence of fraud and misrepresentation.

(10) Availability of essential commodities.

Life Style of Consumerism

Social Class	Life Style	Purchasing Tendencies
1	2	3
Upper class	Good Taste Graceful living Interest in art and culture Individual expression	Quality merchandise expensive hobby and recreation, Art books, travel.

...(Contd.)

1	2	3
Middle Class	Respectability Conformity Propriety Social esteem	Items and fashion related to self presentation; Good clothing, neighbourhood
Working Class	Fun oriented parochial and sophisticated taste Focus on possession and not ideas	New appliances, Sporting events newest and biggest items
Lower Class	Close family relationship Neighbourhood oriented	Status symbol products enchasing self esteem;

Source: Adopted from Hawkins, best and Coney—Consumer behaviour, p. 173

Approaches to Consumerism

1. ***Normative approach***

   Consumers learn how to decide but not necessarily what to decide.

2. ***Prescriptive approach***

   What consumers should decide given their budget and objective.

3. ***Predictive approach***

   Predictions on what will happen if rational hypothesis are formulated would be derived.

4. ***Descriptive approach***

   Factors influencing consumer behavior are explored with a view to using them in above three approaches.

Effective Movement of Consumerism

(1) Attending the breach of guarantees or warranties by forming legal action committees.

(2) Conducting short term courses for the member.

(3) It must be conscious of establishing their right.

(4) More and more consumer organizations have to be opened.

(5) Consumerism may be taught even from elementary school level.

(6) United and organized actions by the consumers and essential.

(7) Introduction of more legislation in favour of consumer welfare.

(8) Consumer service centre should be opened.

(9) Government must take initiative to safeguard the interests of the public.

(10) Black marketeers, hoarders, profiteers must be convicted and their names must be published.

Consumer Privacy

Consumer information collected, merged and exchanged through computer and communication technologies has become the main resource that business and government use to facilitate the millions of daily transactions engaged in by consumers.

In 1970's *United States of America* formulate the six basic computer age *privacy rules* for consumer.

(1) Socially approved personal information should be collected by private or public organization.

(2) This information determined the consumer rights, benefits and opportunities.

(3) These provide guidelines to the consumer how it will be used.

(4) Individuals should have practical procedure for inspection to make evaluative decision.

(5) Sensitive personal information should be circulated for legitimate purpose.

(6) Organizations must crate and apply effective data security measures for consumers.

Challenges of Consumerism

1. Consumers are moving towards 'cultural universals' (male grooming, career oriented, women etc).
2. Consumers do not choose 'best' option but satisfying option.
3. They use entire range of subjective reaction.
4. Willing to be guided by impulsion and personal impression.
5. Makes it difficult to speak of true decision making.
6. Reasons include too many options.
7. Guilty feelings.
8. Information gathered during conversations may well suffice.
9. When decision is judged 'important' consumer attempts to be 'as rational as possible' to reduce cognitive dissonance.
10. They can be 'deviant'.
11. Unlike impulsive buyers do not buy in order to possess the desired object but to liberate themselves.

Conclusion

Thus the consumerism as social movement an organized effort of consumers, seeking redress, restitution and remedy for dissatisfaction that they have accumulated in the acquisition of at their standard of living. Marketing is the battle of perception not products. Understanding the psychology of consumer is indispensable to marketers for effective planning of business strategies. Hence it is essential to draw an account of the probable consumer behavioural patterns to face the challenges of 21st century.

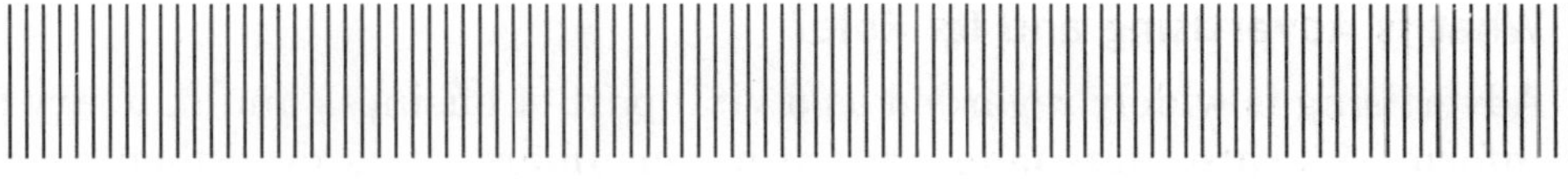

CHAPTER

47
Advertising and Its Impact on Consumerism

— V.S. Rajakrishnan
— R. Natarajan

Introduction

The Industrial Revolution in the 18th century was a turning point in the history of mankind. Man started talking about his political, economic and social rights. He also talked about his rights as a consumer. The Industrial Revolution resulted in mass production and paved the way for the market economy. Simultaneously it gave rise to the evolution of advertising techniques that became a vital component of marketing strategies. More production must necessarily lead to more consumption and if more consumption is to materialize, aggressive and even atrocious adoption of marketing strategies are to be attempted. More production does not simply refer to essential goods but rather to non-essential and luxurious ones. Presently the mass production of goods is not need-based but 'need creating'. That sumps up the crux of the problem faced by consumers who are forced to consume for the sake of consumption. Now thanks to be IT revolution, the production has further gained momentum and aggravated the situation to a considerable extent. Modern technologies have no doubt made a great impact on the quality, availability and safety of goods and services. But the fact of life is that consumers are still victims of unscrupulous and explosive practices adopted by the sellers and manufacturers.

At the juncture it is relevant to make a mention of the role played by the advertisements in the mass media. In recent years, the quantity of false, misleading and offensive advertising is on the increase and has contributed to the acceleration of consumerism substantially.

What is Advertising and Its Role?

Advertising is widely regarded as a vital part of business and industry to inform, educate, persuade and gain consumers. It is described as an immensely powerful instrument for the elimination of ignorance and in today's wired world it works rather quickly. There has always been an intense competition among the manufacturers to sell their wares. The size of the Indian advertising industry is estimated at Rs.10,000 crores p.a. and is responsible for selling products and services worth Rs.3,00,000 crores p.a. In the absence of a set of guidelines to ensure truth, decency and fairplay in the advertising, consumers will have an increasing disbelief in it and false advertising will also contribute to unfair competitions. This menace has been checked by the Government which has strengthened the 'Powers' of the consumers through various acts: CPA, Bureau of Standards Act, Magic Remedies Act, Drugs and Pharmaceuticals act, etc. However no judicial system nor statutory regulator can cope with all the issues that can arise in the manner of administering and regulating advertising content.

Self-regulations in Advertising

It is the recognition of the advertising industry that all adverting should be legal, decent, honest and truthful with a sense of social responsibility to the consumer and to the society as a whole with due respect to the rules of their fair competitions. The result is the establishment of Advertising Standards Council of India (ASCI), to ensure truthfulness and honesty of representations and claims made by advertisements.

- to safeguard against misleading advertisements; and
- to ensure that ads. are not offensive to generally accepted public decency.

Conceptual Considerations

The term 'Consumerism' needs explanation. It originally referred to man's way of using things/services *i.e.* 'the pattern of consumption necessary for living ' We cannot deny the basic rights to life the realization of which gets changed owing to scientific and technological advancement over the years. The term also refers to the activities of government, business and independent organizations that are designed to protect individuals from policies that infringe upon their rights. Now the term has gained negative connotation and it is the 'preoccupation of society with buying goods'. (Compact Oxford Dictionary Thesaurus, 2005 p.183). The New Shorter Oxford Dictionary, 1993, p490 tells us that consumerism means 'preoccupation with consumer goods and their acquisition', How did this change in the social behaviour happen? The march towards the culture of consumerism was a bit slow even in 1960s and 1970s. Still the ideal of simple living and high thinking' pervaded the Indian masses. But since 1980s the culture of consumerism started galloping thanks to the surplus production of non-essential and luxurious goods which is a hidden threat to humanity as competition and profit making become the sole motives of the manufacturers and sellers. The tremendous and mind-boggling techniques in advertising have made people inebriated and brain washed and lured into buying and pilling of things.

A passion for goods has status symbol and more and more middle and lower middle class people have fallen a prey to the culture of consumerism. It is interesting to know that the growth rate in the production of consumer goods is easily between 20-30 per cent whereas it is less than 5 per cent in agriculture and basic industries. Consumerism has ultimately become a social cancer eating into the vitals of the society and the advertisements appearing in the media have aided and abetted it. It has been said that fertility rate has come down from 2.82 children per woman at the turn of this century to 2.15 children one of the main reasons being the impact of Consumerism! Above all it has widened the gulf between the rich and the poor more.

Advertising Gimmicks

As mentioned earlier, when men's needs were a few and confined to bare necessities as in the primitive societies, there was no scope for advertisement of products. The vendor crying his wares along the street is also, in a sense, advertising his or her product, but when the number of items and brands in the market increases steadily, advertising becomes an important means of disseminating information to prospective buyers. Advertisements, thus, have an educative role to play. When the market becomes more and more competitive, however, it becomes imperative to actively promote one's product to attract customers away from competing sellers or brands. The greater the competition, the greater the importance that advertising assumes. Advertisers, thus, try to come up with various means of attracting and wooing buyers. The more the sophistication of ideas, the more money it costs Advertisements can thus account for a large size of a manufacturer's budget. and who bears the cost of advertising? It is the consumer. Obviously one of the well-known soft drinks promoted by an MNC costs about Rs. 10 and the actual production cost is said to be around a rupee or two but about six rupees is spent on advertisement! Therefore in the present-day context, advertisements no more play the educative role but they resort to brainwashing the poor consumer. Examples are available in legions. Only a few, however, will suffice for our consideration.

Almost all the vernacular and a few English dailies carry full and or half a page ads of a local textile shop throughout the year letting the people know that prices have not been reduced but slashed. Crores and crores of rupees are spent on advertisements to entice the consumers, who are to bear the cost of ads, too. The advertiser very often employs the 'repeat' technique to catch the attention of consumers.

While umpteen number of gimmicks are resorted to by advertiser, the most offensive and unsavoury advertisements tactics is that of using the female form to promote all kinds of goods from tyres to men's briefs. The wordings are 'suitably' phrased to titillate and lure male attention. Of late, vulgarization of women in ads has become very common emotions.

The ads that appear in the visual media have far-reaching consequences and the consumer is subjected to various types of pressure. Not long ago, many children on seeing *Satkhiman* attempted to imitate him and in the process they lost their precious lives. Dabur India Ltd for its '*Dabur Lal Dant Manjan* (DD sports Oct-Nov.2004) showed a cricket personality opening a butted drink cap with his teeth to show that he uses '*Dabour Lal Dant Manjan*' and that his teeth are strong. Here again children in particular are prone to imitate such activities of their role models (who are usually cricketers) and in turn may damage their undeveloped teeth.

Since the sole aim of advertisers is to earn money, this has damaged the social fabric seriously. Materialism sans moral values of life has become the order of the day. It has seriously affected the familial structure: frequent quarrels between the husband and wife, indiscriminate buying of goods resulting in debts, dowry problem psychological problems, etc. As mentioned earlier, the gap between the rich and the poor alone has not widened but the gap between old and the young (the generation gap) has also become distinct and sharp.

Have to Overcome Consumerism?

Unless and until the impact and the influence of consumerism is overcome the society will be in moral and ethical bankruptcy. Anwar Fazal, a leading Malaysian consumer activist of 1980s proposed five principles to combat the menace of consumerism, which is unscrupulously promoted by advertisements.

Reduce : Let us try to reduce our requirements as much as possible

Reject : Let us give up that which is not needed or essential

Reuse : Let us use things which can be used again and again and avoid the *use and throw* culture

Recycle : Let us try to recycle things that can be subjected to recycling process and avoid wastage.

Rethink : Let us think again and again before we take decisions on buying

If we follow these five principles we can overcome the evil influence of consumerism and whatever may be the charm of an advertisement, nothing can influence us to take wrong decision.

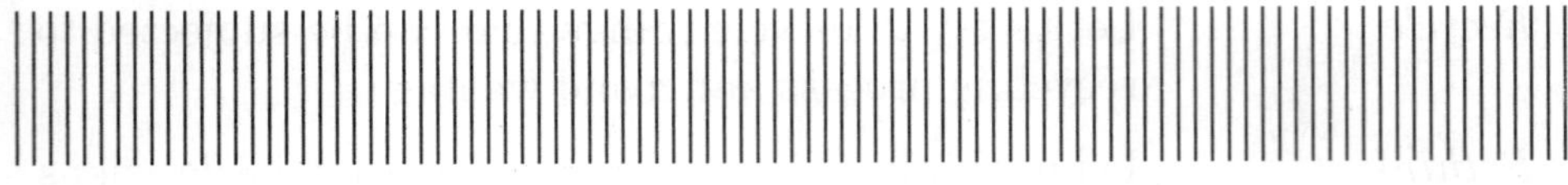

CHAPTER

48

Implementation of Total Quality Management (TQM)

—R. Senthil Kumar
—P. Arivalagan
—E. Prabhu

INTRODUCTION AND IMPLEMENTATION OF TOTAL QUALITY MANAGEMENT (TQM)

Introduction

Total Quality Management is a management approach that originated in the 1950's and has steadily become more popular since the early 1980's. Total Quality is a description of the culture, attitude and organization of a company that strives to provide customers with products and services that satisfy their needs. The culture requires quality in all aspects of the company's operations, with processes being done right the first time and defects and waste eradicated from operations.

Total Quality Management, TQM, is a method by which management and employees can become involved in the continuous improvement of the production of goods and services. It is a combination of quality and management tools aimed at increasing business and reducing losses due to wasteful practices.

Some of the companies who have implemented TQM include Ford Motor Company, Phillips Semi-conductor, SGL Carbon, Motorola and Toyota Motor Comp.

Definition

TQM is a management philosophy that seeks to integrate all organizational functions (marketing, finance, design, engineering, and production, customer service, etc.) to focus on meeting customer needs and organizational objectives.

TQM views an organization as a collection of processes. It maintains that organizations must strive to continuously improve these processes by incorporating the knowledge and experiences of workers. The simple objective of TQM is "Do the right things, right the first time, every time". TQM is infinitely variable and adaptable. Although originally applied to manufacturing operations, and for a number of years only used in that area, TQM is now becoming recognized as a generic management tool, just as applicable in service and public sector organizations. There are a number of evolutionary strands, with different sectors creating their own versions from the common ancestor. TQM is the foundation for activities, which include:

- Commitment by senior management and all employees
- Meeting customer requirements
- Reducing development cycle times
- Just in Time/Demand Flow Manufacturing
- Improvement teams
- Reducing product and service costs
- Systems to facilitate improvement
- Line Management ownership
- Employee involvement and empowerment
- Recognition and celebration
- Challenging quantified goals and benchmarking
- Focus on processes / improvement plans
- Specific incorporation in strategic planning

This shows that TQM must be practiced in all activities, by all personnel, in Manufacturing, Marketing, Engineering, R&D, Sales, Purchasing, HR, etc.

Principles of TQM

The key principles of TQM are as following:

- Management Commitment
  - —Plan (drive, direct)
  - —Do (deploy, support, participate)
  - —Check (review)

— Act (recognize, communicate, revise)

- Employee Empowerment
  — Training
  — Suggestion scheme
  — Measurement and recognition
  — Excellence teams
- Fact Based Decision Making
  — SPC (statistical process control)
  — DOE, FMEA
  — The 7 statistical tools
  — TOPS (FORD 8D - Team Oriented Problem Solving)
- Continuous Improvement
  — Systematic measurement and focus on CONQ
  — Excellence teams
  — Cross-functional process management
  — Attain, maintain, improve standards
- Customer Focus
  — Supplier partnership
  — Service relationship with internal customers
  — Never compromise quality
  — Customer driven standards

The Concept of Continuous Improvement by TQM

TQM is mainly concerned with continuous improvement in all work, from high level strategic planning and decision-making, to detailed execution of work elements on the shop floor. It stems from the belief that mistakes can be avoided and defects can be prevented. It leads to continuously improving results, in all aspects of work, as a result of continuously improving capabilities, people, processes, and technology and machine capabilities.

Continuous improvement must deal not only with improving results, but more importantly with improving capabilities to produce better results in the future. The five major areas of focus for capability improvement are demand generation, supply generation, technology, operations and people capability.

A central principle of TQM is that mistakes may be made by people, but most of them are caused, or at least permitted, by faulty systems and processes. This means that the root cause of such mistakes can be identified and eliminated, and repetition can be prevented by changing the process.

There are three major mechanisms of prevention:

1. Preventing mistakes (defects) from occurring (Mistake - proofing or Polka-Yoke).
2. Where mistakes can't be absolutely prevented, detecting them early to prevent them being passed down the value added chain (Inspection at source or by the next operation).
3. Where mistakes recur, stopping production until the process can be corrected, to prevent the production of more defects. (Stop in time).

Implementation Principles and Processes

A preliminary step in TQM implementation is to assess the organization's current reality. Relevant preconditions have to do with the organization's history, its current needs, precipitating events leading to TQM, and the existing employee quality of working life. If the current reality does not include important preconditions, TQM implementation should be delayed until the organization is in a state in which TQM is likely to succeed. If an organization has a track record of effective responsiveness to the environment, and if it has been able to successfully change the way it operates when needed, TQM will be easier to implement. If an organization has been historically reactive and has no skill at improving its operating systems, there will be both employee skepticism and a lack of skilled change agents. If this condition prevails, a comprehensive programme of management and leadership development may be instituted. A management audit is a good assessment tool to identify current levels of organizational functioning and areas in need of change. An organization should be basically healthy before beginning TQM. If it has significant problems such as a very unstable funding base, weak administrative systems, lack of managerial skill, or poor employee morale, TQM would not be appropriate.

However, a certain level of stress is probably desirable to initiate TQM. People need to feel a need for a change. Kantar (1983) addresses this phenomenon be describing building blocks which are present in effective organizational change. These forces include departures from tradition, a crisis or galvanizing event, strategic decisions, individual 'prime movers,' and action vehicles. Departures from tradition are activities, usually at lower levels of the organization, which occur when entrepreneurs move outside the normal ways of operating to solve a problem. A crisis, if it is not too disabling, can also help create a sense of urgency which can mobilize people to act. In the case of TQM, this may be a funding cut or threat, or demands from consumers or other stakeholders for improved quality of service. After a crisis, a leader may intervene strategically by articulating a new vision of the future to help the organization deal with it. A plan to implement TQM may be such a strategic decision. Such a leader may then become a prime mover, who takes charge in championing the new idea and showing others how it will help them get where they want to go. Finally, action vehicles are needed and mechanisms or structures to enable the change to occur and become institutionalized.

Steps in Managing the Transition

Beck hard and Pritchard (1992) have outlined the basic steps in managing a transition to a new system such as TQM: identifying tasks to be done, creating necessary management structures, developing strategies for building commitment, designing mechanisms to communicate the change, and assigning resources.

Task identification would include a study of present conditions (assessing current reality, as described above); assessing readiness, such as through a force field analysis; creating a model of the desired state, in this case, implementation of TQM; announcing the change goals to the organization; and assigning responsibilities and resources. This final step would include securing outside consultation and training and assigning someone within the organization to oversee the effort. This should be a responsibility of top management. In fact, the next step, designing transition management structures, is also a responsibility of top management. In fact, Cohen and Brand (1993) and Hyde (1992) assert that management must be heavily involved as leaders rather than relying on a separate staff person or function to shepherd the effort. An organization wide steering committee to oversee the effort may be appropriate. Developing commitment strategies was discussed above in the sections on resistance and on visionary leadership.

Management of resources for the change effort is important with TQM because outside consultants will almost always be required. Choose consultants based on their prior relevant experience and their commitment to adapting the process to fit unique organizational needs. While consultants will be invaluable with initial training of staff and TQM system design, employees (management and others) should be actively involved in TQM implementation, perhaps after receiving training in change management which they can then pass on to other employees. A collaborative relationship with consultants and clear role definitions and specification of activities must be established.

In summary, first assess preconditions and the current state of the organization to make sure the need for change is clear and that TQM is an appropriate strategy. Leadership styles and organizational culture must be congruent with TQM. If they are not, this should be worked on or TQM implementation should be avoided or delayed until favourable conditions exist.

Remember that this will be a difficult, comprehensive, and long-term process. Leaders will need to maintain their commitment, keep the process visible, provide necessary support, and hold people accountable for results. Use input from stakeholder (clients, referring agencies, funding sources, etc.) as possible; and, of course, maximize employee involvement in design of the system.

Always keep in mind that TQM should be purpose driven. Be clear on the organization's vision for the future and stay focused on it. TQM can be a powerful technique for unleashing employee creativity and potential, reducing bureaucracy and costs, and improving service to clients and the community.

Conclusion

TQM encourages participation amongst shop floor workers and managers. There is no single theoretical formalization of total quality, but Deming, Juran and Ishikawa provide the core assumptions, as a "...discipline and philosophy of management which institutionalizes planned and continuous... improvement ... and assumes that quality is the outcome of all activities that take place within an organization; that all functions and all employees have to participate in the improvement process; that organizations need both quality systems and a quality culture.".

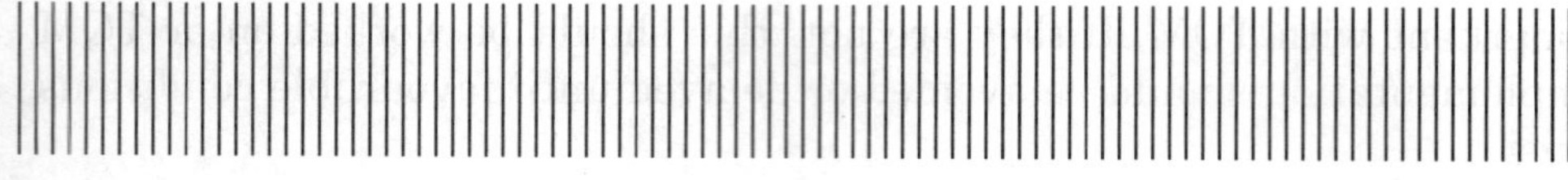

CHAPTER

49

A New Era in Consumerism

— S. Pradesh Kumar

'Consumerism' is likely to dominate the Indian market in the next Millennium, thanks to the economic reforms ushered in and the several agreements signed under the World Trade Organisation. The transition will be from a predominantly 'sellers market' to a 'buyers market' where the choice exercised by the consumer will be influenced by the level of consumer awareness achieved. By 'consumerism' we mean the process of realizing the rights of the consumer as envisaged in the Consumer Protection Act (1986) and ensuring right standards for the goods and services for which one makes a payment. This objective can be achieved in a reasonable time frame only when all concerned act together and play their role. The players are the consumers represented by different voluntary non-government consumer organisations, the government, the regulatory authorities for goods and services in a competitive economy, the consumer courts, organisations representing trade, industry and service providers, the law-makers and those in charge of implementation of the laws and rules.

Consumer Protection Act

The issues relating to consumer welfare affects the entire 986 million people since everyone is a consumer in one way or the other. Ensuring consumer welfare is the responsibility of the government. Accepting this, policies have been framed and the Consumer Protection Act, 1986, was introduced. A separate Department of Consumer Affairs was also created in the Central and State Governments to exclusively focus on ensuring the rights of consumers as enshrined in the Act. This Act has been regarded as the most progressive, comprehensive and unique piece of legislation. In the last international conference on consumer protection held in Malaysia in 1997, the Indian Consumer Protection Act was described as one "which has set in motion a revolution in the fields of consumer rights, the parallel of which has not been seen anywhere else in the world."

The special feature of this Act is to provide speedy and inexpensive redressal to the grievance of the consumer and provide him relief of a specific nature and award compensation wherever appropriate. The aim of the Act is also to ensure the rights of the consumer, *viz.* the right of choice, safety, information, redressal, public hearing and consumer education.

The Act defines the consumer as one who purchases goods and services for his/her use. The user of such goods and service with the permission of the buyer is also a consumer. However, a person is not a consumer if he purchases goods and services for resale purpose.

The most important feature of the Act is the provision for setting up a three-tier quasi-judicial machinery popularly known as 'consumer courts' at national, state and district levels. The apex court, National Commission functions in Delhi. Every State Government has a State Commission. The third tier is in each district and is called district forum. As on January 1999, there are 543 district forums. All these courts have handled nearly 13 lakh cases of which about 10 lakhs cases have been disposed of. The disposal of 77 per cent of the cases is not a mean achievement. However, it should be noted that only 27 per cent of the total cases have been disposed of within the prescribed period of 90 days or 150 days (where testing is required). This fact really causes concern for the Government and the consumers in general. The National Commission has identified the reasons for the slow disposal and has come out with suggestions for amending the Act with a view to improving the disposal rate within the time limit prescribed in the Act. The Government has been contemplating a number of amendments to the Act and these amendments will be brought out in the next session of Parliament.

The consumer movement in India is as old as trade and commerce. In Kautilya's *Arthashastra*, there are references to the concept of consumer protection against exploitation by the trade and industry, short weighment and measures, adulteration and punishment for these offences. However, there was no organised and systematic movement actually safeguarding the interests of the consumers. Prior to independence, the main laws under which the consumer interests were considered were the Indian Penal Code,

Agricultural Production, Grading and Marketing Act, 1937, Drugs and Cosmetics Act, 1940. Even though different parts of India exhibited different levels of awareness, in general, the level of awareness was pretty low.

An average Indian consumer is noted for his patience and tolerance. Perhaps because of these two traditional traits and due to the influence of the *Mahabharata*, the *Ramayana* and the *Bhagavad Gita*, he considers the receipt of defective goods and services as an act of fate or unfavourable planetary position in his horoscope. When a new television or refrigerator purchased by him turns out to be defective from day one, he takes it reticently, blaming it on his fate or as the consequence of the wrongs committed by him in his previous birth. Very often he is exploited, put to avoidable inconveniences and suffers financial loss. It is rather paradoxical that the customer is advertised as the 'king' by the seller and service provider; but in actual practice treated as a slave or servant. Goods are purchased by him along with the label "Items once sold by us will never be received back under any circumstances whatsoever."

This unethical, illegal and unilateral declaration has to be viewed in the light of the practice in developed countries where the seller declares, "In case you are not fully satisfied with our product, you can bring the same to us within a month for either replacement or return of your money." This will clearly indicate the level of consumer consciousness. However, things are changing—slowly but steadily—and the momentum has increased considerably since the establishment of consumer courts and due to the efforts of a number of consumer organisations and the media. The next millennium will witness a high degree of consumer awareness and the concepts of 'comparative costs', 'consumer preference/ resistance/ abstinence' and 'consumer choice' will become vital aspects of the economy.

An analysis of the data from the consumer courts in different States shows that there is a direct relationship between literacy and consumer awareness. Statistics relating to Kerala and Bihar will justify this. The question to be considered is what can the Government do to improve the position?

The Government wears three hats to deal with cases of three different categories. The first one is dealing with the ministries and departments of government. Recently, the Standing Committee of Parliament on Health said Government hospitals should be brought under the purview of the Consumer Court. To this, we had pointed out the latest ruling of the Supreme Court which lays down that the Consumer Protection Act will apply only when the consumer pays for the goods and services and on this count the government hospital, where the services are not charged on the consumer, will not come under the Act. For such cases the government has developed the concept of 'Citizen's Charter'. All government departments dealing with the public are to publish a 'Citizen's Charter' clearly indicating the services offered and the procedure to be followed. All the information has to be made available in a single window. This programme is in its incipient stage and has a long way to go to achieve the desired levels of consumer satisfaction. The general reaction of the consumer to this is: what happens if what is stated in the Citizen Charter is not adhered to? Unless and until this is clarified, the responsibility fixed and those held accountable are dealt with, the purpose will not be achieved.

The second area is where the services/ utilities are provided and charged either by the government department or the agencies under its control. At present, a number of regulatory authorities have been constituted and the country is entering a new regime of 'regulatory economies' in the services sector. It is heartening to note that the regulatory bodies like the Telecom Regulatory Authority of India (TRAI) have given importance to the interests of consumers and this has been publicly declared as one of the main objectives. In the field of telecom, power, transport and water supply, the consumers today are going through a number of problems not knowing how to get their grievances redressed. The numbers of cases relating to these sectors are increasing in the consumer courts. It must be possible for the government to take steps to see that the areas of grievances are identified and remedial steps taken through proper systematization of procedure and working style.

There are a number of areas where the procedure has to be made simple and consumer-friendly. For example, when it was felt that the quality of bottled water purchased by the consumer has to be ensured by fixing standards, it came out that even though it is necessary and desirable, under the existing laws it cannot be done. The Ministry of Law pointed out and rightly so, that water is not 'food' as per the provisions in the Food Adulteration Act. The process of getting statutory notification in the interest of the consumer in this case, where all concerned are agreeable, is likely to take 12 to 18 months. In such a situation the only answer is to prevail upon the manufacturers to go for voluntary ISI (Indian Standards Institution) certification. This method is working in the case of bottled water, thanks to the cooperation of producers and the clear preference expressed by the active consumer groups.

Similarly in the area of 'investor protection' in spite of several steps taken by the regulatory authorities such as the Reserve Bank of India and the Securities and Exchange Board of India, the case of exploitation of consumers is increasing. This is an area of grave concern and requires concerted action by the regulators, government and the consumer organisations. We must find a way out to save the consumers from the unscrupulous functioning of non-banking finance companies.

The third category is the protection of consumers from the private sector dealing with goods and services. It is not to be construed that the entire business sector is keen on exploiting the consumers. These are established business firms which really care for consumer satisfaction, their own reputation and goodwill. Voluntary bodies like the Fair Business Practices Forum are functioning effectively and are quick in removing the grievances of the consumers. These can go a long way in reducing the number of cases in the consumer courts.

If the Government is to take a pro-active role in increasing consumer awareness, encourage consumer education, training and research and administer the infrastructural need of the consumer courts—then it should have enough funds. It is not easy to get adequate budget allocations for obvious reasons. The best way appears to be to work out methods by which the Central Consumer Welfare Fund is augmented and a similar fund is set up at State level also. It is gratifying to note that action has been initiated in this direction and there is every reason to hope that the future will be better.

The consumer has to be aware of his rights and play a key role. The success of "consumerism" is a strong function of consumer awareness and the assistance the movement gets from the government. The consumer movement got a boost and moral support from the late U.S. President John F. Kennedy in the historic declaration in Congress on March 15, 1962, declaring four basic consumer rights (choice, information, safety and the right to be heard). Subsequently, March 15 every year is celebrated as World Consumer Rights Day. However this annual ritual observation does not appear to have produced the desired results. A sub-continent like India with regional imbalances and diversity of languages requires not one but several Ralph Nadars. A recent survey has revealed that a number of consumers in the urban as well as rural areas are not very much aware of the consumer movement and the rights of the consumers. It is in this context that it is considered relevant to quote the objectives adopted by the General Assembly of United Nations in 1985.

Conclusion

We believe the more guidelines are required because there are always two sides of a coin, each instance of Consumer affairs could be easily termed as another 'Consumer mistreatment'. By the time market forces have time to operate, far too many consumers are dead, maimed, or impoverished. Within a nation-state, national laws may prevent some of this harm, but once national boundaries are crossed, their effectiveness is limited, and consumers can hope for very limited protection, If online trade proliferates and consumer fraud becomes a major problem, nation-states and commercial interests that provide online access are fairly restricted in the action they may take to curb unacceptable and deleterious practices. Certainly if consumers perceive online commerce as a hazardous place to make purchases, they will not choose this alternative, and a major opportunity for electronic commerce may be forfeited. Consequently, there is strong motivation for reputable business to observe high commercial standards of behaviour.

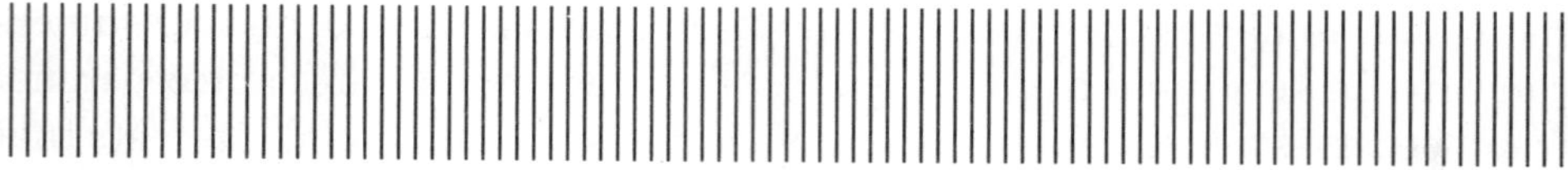

CHAPTER

50

Consumerism in India

— Dr. M. Mohamed Mohideen
— R. Prushothaman

Consumerism

Consumerism is an organised movement of citizens and government to strengthen the rights and power of buyers in relation to sellers. It is the ideology and a concept which has come to stay in business literature. The consumer is exposed to many hazardous-physical, environmental and exploitation due to unfair trade practices. He needs protection, for instance, against products which are unsafe for consumption such as drugs and adulterated food products and products which may cause badly injury such as defective electrical appliances. He needs protection against mal-practices and deceit by sellers. He should have adequate rights and right of recourse to redressal measures against defaulting businessmen. He needs protected against environmental pollution of air, water and noise and effective measures should be devised to keep the surroundings neat and clean.

Today, consumer is called the king of the market. He is at the centre stage of all market activities. It is constant endeavour of producers that the production of product must conform to the needs of consumer. In addition to the satisfaction of consumer, it also the endeavour of producer that their sale should be maximum. They, therefore try to increase their sales by all possible means. Some of the means adopted to increase sale are such as to serve both the producers and the consumers. On the other hand, some of the methods adopted to increase the sale are such as to sub serve the interest of producers but the same against the interest of consumer. In other words the consumers are exploited.

The last two decades have witnessed an over expanding interest in *consumerism* and which is in a very critic condition. The word *consumerism* has to be fully understood in its historical retrospect with reference to the consumer's position in common law, main areas of regulations, controls on advertising, labelling standards, etc. The word consumer means a person who uses goods and services.

And in our Indian system the consumer has six rights given for his protection from exploitation from the shopkeepers or sellers. Consumer exploitation means mistreatment or cheating with consumer by adulteration or in any other unfair form. To prevent consumer from exploitation our governments have passed many Acts from time to time. Some of them are as follows:

1. Drug and Cosmetics Act, 1940
2. Prevention of Food Adulteration Act, 1954
3. Essential Commodity (supply) Act, 1955
4. Monopolies and Restrictive Trade Practices Act, 1969
5. Standard of Weights and Measures Act, 1976
6. Consumer Protection Act, 1986

Need and Reasons

The need of strong consumerism in our country is on account of the following reasons:

1. In vast country like India, it is very difficult to organise the consumers. The people besides being the backward have linguistic, cultural and religious difference which makes the problems quiet intricate or complex.
2. Majority of our population is illiterate, uneducated, ignorant and ill-informed.
3. Poverty, lack of social awareness, accepting life as it is and passive outlook are some of the factors which make consumer movement difficult to increase.
4. There may not be a positive common objective for the consumers except their desire for safe quality products, for reasonable price and a feeling of strong negative reactions against the products. In wake of large scale production and the variety and choice conferred on the consumers, a consumer needs guidance which can only be appropriately provided by a consumer organisation.
5. The advertisement bombarded on the consumers make them quite confused and hence again a need for consumer guidance.

CONSUMER'S RIGHTS AND RESPONSIBILITIES

Consumer's Rights

Consumer rights are now an integral part of our lives like a consumerist way of life. They have been well documented and much talked about. We have all made use of them at some point in our daily lives. Market resources and influences are growing by the day and so is the awareness of one's consumer rights. These rights are well-defined and there are agencies like the government, consumer courts and voluntary organisations that work towards safeguarding them. While we all like to know about our rights and make full use of them, consumer responsibility is an area which is still not demarcated. In this chapter, I will give an overview of the 8 consumer rights, their implications and significance for a developing country like India, and also define the various aspects of consumer responsibility.

In the 20th century, the presence and influence of the market grew dramatically in consumer life. We began to purchase things from the market for a price. Soon, mass production and industrial production came into being, giving the consumer world an entirely new dimension. Have you ever wondered how much urban consumers depend on the market for fulfillment of even their basic needs? This over-dependence on the market and the inherent profit motive in mass production and sales has given manufacturers and dealers a good reason to exploit consumers. As a consumer, every one should know how market products are constantly under-weight, of inferior quality and do not prescribe to quality standards specified by quality-control agencies. Consumers not only do not get value for their money but also often have to suffer losses and inconvenience due to market manipulations.

In addition to six rights of consumer given by Government of India, The United Nations organisation also given two rights:

1. *Right to Basic Needs:* The Basic need means those goods and services which are necessary for the dignified living of people. It includes adequate food, clothing, shelter, energy, sanitation, health, care, education and transportation. All consumers have the right fulfill these basic needs.
2. *Right to Healthy Environment:* This right provides consumers the protection against environment pollution so that the quality of life enhanced. Not only this, it also gives stress that the need to protect the environment is for future generations as well.

Consumer's Responsibilities

The consumers have a number of rights regarding the purchase of things, but at the same time they have some responsibilities too. It means that the consumer should keep a few things in mind while purchasing them. They are as follows:

1. *Consumer should exercise his right:* Consumers have many rights with regard to the goods and services. They must be aware of their rights while buying. These rights are: Right to safety, Right to be informed, Right to representation, Right to seek redressal, Right to consumer education, etc.
2. *Cautious consumer / Do not buy blindly:* The consumers should make full use of their reason while buying things. They should not take the seller's word as final truth. In other words, while buying consumer must get information regarding the quality, quantity, price, utility etc. of goods and services.
3. *Filing complaint for the redressal of genuine grievances:* It is the responsibility of a consumer to approach the officer concerned there is some complaint about the goods purchased. A late complaint may find that the period of guarantee/warrantee has lapsed. Sometimes, consumers ignore the deception of businessmen. This tendency encourages corrupt business practices.
4. *Consumer must be quality conscious / Do not compromise on quality:* The consumers should never compromise on the quality of goods. Therefore, they should not buy inferior stuff out of greed for less prices. If the consumers behave like this, there cannot be any protection for them from any quarter. It is also the responsibility of the consumers only to buy goods with the ISI, Agmark, Woolmark, FPO etc. printed on them. All these symbols indicative of the good quality of the goods.
5. *Advertisements often exaggerate / Beware of false advertisement:* The seller informs the consumer about their things through the medium of advertisement. The sellers exaggerate the quality of their goods. Therefore, it is the responsibility of the consumers to recognise the truth of advertisement.
6. *Do not forget to get Receipt and Guarantee / warrantee card:* One should always get a receipt or bill for the things purchased. In case a guarantee/warrantee card is also offered by seller, it should also be taken. In case the goods purchased are of inferior quality or some defects appears and bothers the customers, these documents will be of great help in settling all kinds of dispute with the seller.
7. *Do not buy in hurry:* The first important responsibility of consumers is that they should not buy in hurry. It means that the consumers should make an estimate of the things they want to buy their along

with their quantity required by them. They should also take in consideration the place from where to buy the things.

ROLE OF DIFFERENT ORGANIZATIONS

Role of Judiciary

In our country judiciary plays a very vital role. On recommendation of the amendment of consumer protection Act in 2000 the consumer protection councils or forums are created at district, state and national level. Under the Act there is a provision of Three-tier Judiciary to redress the grievances of consumers in a simple, speedy and inexpensive way; namely

1. District Forum at District level
2. State Commission at State level
3. National Commission at National level

1. *District Forum:* According to consumer protection Act, state governments can set up one or more district forums in each District. There are three members including the presiding officer. Out of this one member must be a lady. They must have a qualification of District Judge and must be appointed by state government. Its main feature is that it can hear cases up to Rs.20 Lacs. Any appeal may go to state commission within 30 days.
2. *State Commission:* One state commission is appointed by the state government in each state. It also has three members out of which one is a lady member but they must have qualification of High Court Judge and should be appointed by state government. It can hear cases involving sum exceeds Rs.20 Lacs and upto Rs.1 Crore. Any appeal may go to national commission within 30 days.
3. *National Commission:* It is appointed by Central Government. It consists of five members out of which one must be a lady member. They must have qualification equivalent to Supreme Court Judge. It has a Jurisdiction to hear complaints amounting more than Rs.1 Crore. Any appeal may go to Supreme Court within 30 days.

Role of Non-Governmental Organizations

In addition to government many about 500 non-governmental organizations (N.G.Os) are making efforts in order to safeguard the interest of consumer. These organizations perform the following functions:

1. *Accelerating consumer awareness/Educating consumers:* The first priority of consumer organization is to accelerate consumer's awareness towards their rights. To accomplish this task which they

have to perform are:

(*a*) To publish Brochures, Journals;

(*b*) To arrange seminars, conferences and workshops;

(*c*) To educate consumers to help themselves;

(*d*) To provide special education to women about consumerism;

(*e*) To encourage to follow desirable consumption standards.

3. *Filing suit on behalf of consumer:* Whenever a consumer fails to raise his voice of protect regarding his complaints, these organisations come to his rescue and file a case in the court. By rendering services to consumers, the consumers get a feeling that they are not alone in their fight. They also run voluntary complaints for the guidance of consumers.
4. *Helping educational institutions:* These organisations tell the educational institutions the way to prepare courses of study keeping in view the interest of consumers.
5. *Promoting network of consumer association:* Consumer organisations are trying to grow their numbers. They want to cover all regions so that consumers of all regions get benefited by their services.
6. *Extending support to government:* Consumer organisations by informing government agencies about adulteration, artificiality, inferior quality products etc. This helps government to conduct proceedings in time.

Role of Consumer Coordinating Council

The name of the highest body of consumer Association is consumer coordinating council. This body has started many programmes for consumer protection. The main objectives of this council are:

(*a*) To establish coordination among consumers for their welfare;

(*b*) To educate and train activists working for consumer protection.

Role of Press/Media

Whenever there is any revolution or a campaign is run for Public Awareness, News papers and journals play a very significant role. Indian Express is the first for this noble cause . Press takes following steps to make consumer protection campaign a success.

(*a*) To publish articles

(*b*) To make available columns

(*c*) To show live telecasts.

(*d*) To publish consumer complaints

Role of Education Institutions

The importance of consumer protection is being realised at various levels of education *viz.* School, College, University. At school level institutions like C.B.S.E. had prepared syllabus in which central guiding points of consumer protection have been highlighted. Similarly at University level Indira Gandhi National Open University (IGNOU) has prepared a special course for under graduate and post-graduate students.

Role of Consumer Protection Council

The consumer protection council provides the establishment of a Central Consumer Protection Council by the central government and state Consumer Protection Council by state governments. The main objectives of the councils are:

1. To protect the rights of consumer;
2. To promote the rights of consumer

Conclusion

Consumer protection laws are federal and state statutes governing sales and credit practices involving consumer goods. Such statutes prohibit and regulate deceptive or unconscionable advertising and sales practices, product quality, credit financing and reporting, debt collection, leases, and other aspects of consumer transactions.

The goal of consumer protection laws is to place consumers, who are average citizens engaging in business deals such as buying goods or borrowing money, on an even par with companies or citizens who regularly engage in business. Historically, consumer transactions—purchases of goods or services for personal, family, or household use—were presumed fair because it was assumed that buyers and sellers bargained from equal positions. Starting in the 1960s, legislatures began to respond to complaints by consumer advocates that consumers were inherently disadvantaged, particularly when bargaining with large corporations and industries. Several types of agencies and statutes, both state and federal, now work to protect consumers.

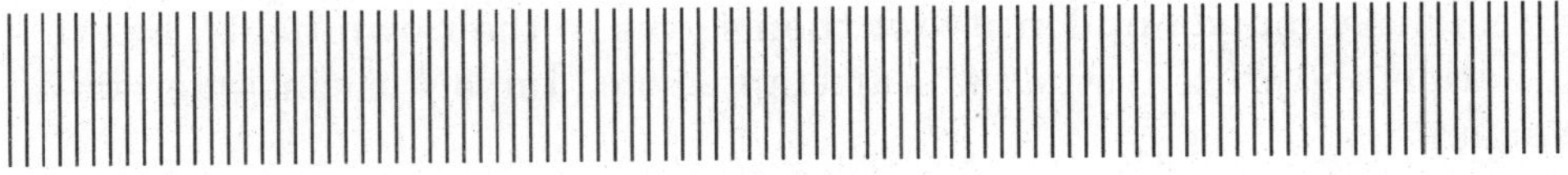

CHAPTER

51

Impact of Consumerism on Women

— P. Radhakrishnan
— K. Parimala Kanthi

Introduction

'Consumerism' is a phenomenon that has managed to stay in the limelight in many industrialized nations that recently went through an economic crisis. Although Consumerism has been on the scene for many decades in one form or another. The term Consumerism appears to be uniquely associated with the past decade. Today's consumption is undermining the environmental resource base. It is exacerbating inequalities. And the dynamics of the consumption-poverty-inequality-environment nexus are accelerating. By 'consumerism' we mean the process of realizing the rights of the consumer as envisaged in the Consumer Protection Act (1986) and ensuring right standards for the goods and services for which one makes a payment. This objective can be achieved in a reasonable time frame only when all concerned act together and play their role.

The players are the consumers represented by different voluntary non-government consumer organizations, the government, the regulatory authorities for goods and services in a competitive economy, the consumer courts, organizations representing trade, industry and service providers, the law-makers and those in charge of implementation of the laws and rules. The consumer has to be aware of his rights and play a key role. The success of 'consumerism' is a strong function of consumer awareness and the assistance the movement gets from the government. Woman are no longer weaker section, they have stepped into all the fields and have successfully found an identity for themselves in their own fields. For this situation, the present study was attempted, i.e., Impact of consumerism on woman.

Origin of Consumerism

Consumerism as the dedication of those activities of both public and private organizations, which are designed to protect individuals from practices, that impinges upon their rights as consumers. Consumerism is the discovery of the twentieth century. Two nations namely USA and UK have made pioneering efforts for protection of consumers' rights. Consumerism first began in USA in the early 1900s, when the American Government introduced two acts name'. The Food and Drug Act (1906). The Meat Inspection Act (1906) and creation of the Federal Trade Commission (1914) for protection of consumer interest. Ever since then, more and more consumer Acts and Laws have been passed in USA, UK, and many other countries. The movement received further impetus when the American President John F Kennedy (1962) sent an exclusive message on the protection of consumer interest to the Congress, in his address. The Presidential concern highlighted the primary rights—right to safety, right to be informed, right to choose, and the right to be heard. The term was not put to wider use until 1963 or 1964 when a variety of commentators identified it with the very visible concerns triggered indirectly by Rachel Carson and directly by Ralph Nadar's auto safety investigations and President Kennedy's efforts.

Objectives of the study: The study within its framework tried to bring out:

(*a*) To know the awareness among the women consumers about consumerism;

(*b*) To find out the women consumers awareness about Consumer Association;

(*c*) To know the knowledge of the women consumers about the Consumer Protection Act, 1986;

(*d*) To find out the woman consumers understanding about the malpractices and cheating in the market; and

(*e*) To suggest measures to enlighten about their rights.

Sample Selection and Data Collection

The consumer respondent of each category are divided into four *i.e.,* Students, Teachers in Colleges and schools, Businessmen and Housewives. Respondent from each category have been selected by applying Simple Random Sampling method. Thus, the total number of consumers selected for the study have come to 30. For the present study both primary and secondary data were used. Primary data was collected by administering a Questionnaire while the secondary data was pooled from the publisher's books, journals, dailies, and research publications.

Profile of the Respondents

Majority of the consumers (*i.e.*, 53.33 per cent fall in the age group between 35 to 45, more than 50 per cent have college level education, nearly 70 per cent of the respondents are from the nuclear family background and most of the consumers in the study and their income are ranging Rs. 5,000 to Rs. 10,000 per month.

Research Methodology

The said study was undertaken in a scientific way. The information and data required were collected by using structured Questionnaire with female respondents only. The research were restricted to Coimbatore City only. The respondents category were as follows:

Respondents Category

Sl.No.	Category	No. of Respondents	Percentage
1.	Students	9	30.00
2.	Teachers in colleges and schools	11	36.67
3.	Businessmen	3	10.00
4.	Housewives	7	23.33
	Total	**30**	**100.00**

While selecting sample, it was assumed that first three categories mentioned above are quite aware about consumerism, consumer movement and Government's role in this regard. Category two includes, teachers concern with curriculum having legislative measures protecting consumer interest and restricted unfair trade practices, but category four are not too aware about consumerism.

The findings of the study as follows:

Table 51.1 : Table showing Age of the Respondents

Sl.No.	Age	No. of Respondents	Percentage
1.	Below 25	3	10.00
2.	25 to 35	7	23.33
3.	35 to 45	16	53.33
4.	45 and above	4	13.33
	Total	**30**	**100.00**

Table 51.2 : Table showing Marital status of the Respondents

Sl.No.	Marital Status	No. of Respondents	Percentage
1.	Married	18	60.00
2.	Unmarried	12	40.00
	Total	**30**	**100.00**

Table 51.3 : Table showing Educational Qualification of the Respondents

Sl.No.	Educational Qualification	No. of Respondents	Percentage
1.	School level	8	26.67
2.	College level	15	50.00
3.	Professional	7	23.33
4.	Others—Please Specify	0	0.00
	Total	**30**	**100.00**

Table 51.4 : Table showing Occupational status of the Respondents

Sl.No.	Occupation Status	No. of Respondents	Percentage
1.	Students	9	30.00
2.	Teachers in Colleges & Schols	11	36.67
3.	Businessmen	3	10.00
4.	Housewives	7	23.33
	Total	**30**	**100.00**

Table 51.5 : Table showing Type of family of the Respondents

Sl.No.	Type of Family	No. of Respondents	Percentage
1.	Nuclear Family	21	70.0
2.	Joint Family	9	30.00
	Total	**30**	**100.00**

Table 51.6 : Table showing Monthly income of the Respondents family

Sl.No.	Monthly Income	No. of Respondents	Percentage
1.	Below Rs.5,000	2	6.67
2.	Rs. 5,000 to 10,000	20	66.67
3.	Rs.10,000 to 15,000	7	23.33
4.	Rs.15,000 and above	1	3.33
	Total	**30**	**100.00**

Table 51.7 : Table showing Respondents satisfaction of their purchase of household items

Sl.No.	Category	No. of Respondents	Percentage
1.	Yes	9	30.00
2.	No	21	70.0
	Total	**30**	**100.00**

Table 51.8 : Table showing Respondents awareness of consumerism

Sl.No.	Category	No. of Respondents	Percentage
1.	Yes	24	80.0
2.	No	6	20.0
	Total	**30**	**100.00**

Table 51.9 : Table showing Respondents Level of awareness about consumer associations

Sl.No.	Category	No. of Respondents	Percentage
1.	Outstanding	2	6.67
2.	Very Good	11	36.67
3.	Good	13	43.33
4.	Satisfactory	2	6.67
5.	Poor	1	3.33
6.	Very Poor	1	3.33
	Total	**30**	**100.00**

Table 51.10 : Table showing Status of the Respondent as purchaser

Sl.No.	Category	No. of Respondents	Percentage
1.	Regular purchaser of the household	23	76.67
2.	Occasional purchaser of the household	6	20.00
3.	Irregular purchaser of the household but influences purchase decision	1	3.33
4.	Mostly indifferent consumer	—	—
	Total	**30**	**100.00**

Table 51.11 : Table showing Respondents place of purchase of the house hold items

Sl.No.	Particulars	No. of Respondents	Percentage
1.	Departmental stores	10	33.33
2.	Grocery stores	15	50.00
3.	Retail stores	5	16.67
4.	Others—Please Specify	—	0.00
	Total	**30**	**100.00**

Table 51.12 : Table showing Respondents aware of some of the Malpractices indulged in the consumer household goods

Sl.No.	Particulars	No. of Respondents	Percentage
1.	Aware	26	86.67
2.	Not aware	4	13.33
	Total	**30**	**100.00**

Table 51.13 : Table showing Respondents face any of the Malpractices prescribed below

Sl.No.	Particulars	No. of Respondents	Percentage
1.	Underweighment	15	50.00
2.	Adulteration	11	36.67
3.	Pilfering	2	6.67
4.	Non-delivery of goods	1	3.33
5.	Proliferation of bogus cards	1	3.33
6.	Others—Please Specify	—	—
	Total	**30**	**100.00**

Table 51.14 : Table showing Respondents attend the meetings regularly in consumer protection associations

Sl.No.	Particulars	No. of Respondents	Percentage
1.	Regularly	1	3.33
2.	Sometimes	14	46.67
3.	Very rarely	15	50.00
	Total	**30**	**100.00**

Table 51.15 : Table showing Respondents know any one of the legislative responses to consumerism

Sl.No.	Particulars	No. of Respondents	Percentage
1.	Fair Packaging and Labeling Act	11	36.67
2.	Consumer Protection Act, 1986	13	43.33
3.	Consumer Product Safety Act	2	6.67
4.	The National Environmental Act	0	0
5.	The Toxic Substances control Act	1	3.33
6.	Cigar Labelling Act	—	0
7.	Consumer Credit Protection Act	2	6.67
8.	The Clean Air Act	1	3.33
	Total	**30**	**100.00**

Table 51.16 : Table showing Respondents Media of awareness towards consumer protection

Sl.No.	Particulars	No. of Respondents	Percentage
1.	Newspaper	14	46.67
2.	Television	3	10.00
3.	Friends	7	23.33
4.	Relatives	6	20.00
	Total	**30**	**100.00**

Table 51.17 : Table showing Respondents asking receipt for their purchases or not

Sl.No.	Particulars	No. of Respondents	Percentage
1.	Yes	23	76.67
2.	No	7	23.33
	Total	**30**	**100.00**

Table 51.18 : Table showing Respondents observe the Expired/ Manufacturing date of the household items

Sl.No.	Particulars	No. of Respondents	Percentage
1.	Yes	17	56.67
2.	No	13	43.33
	Total	**30**	**100.00**

Table 51.19 : Table showing Respondents response in joining the consumer associations

Sl.No.	Particulars	No. of Respondents	Percentage
1.	Very Good	2	6.67
2.	Good	12	40.00
3.	Fair	11	36.67
4.	Satisfactory	4	13.33
5.	Poor	1	3.33
	Total	**30**	**100.00**

Table 51.20 : Table showing Respondents know approaches to consumerism

Sl.No.	Particulars	No. of Respondents	Percentage
1.	Self regulation	5	16.67
2.	Consumer Associations	14	46.67
3.	Alert consumer	10	33.33
4.	State support	1	3.33
	Total	**30**	**100.00**

The *findings* of the study were as follows:

It is found that, the majority of the respondents are in the age group between 35 to 45. On the whole about 60 per cent of the respondents are married. The maximum percent *i.e.,* 50 per cent respondents educational qualification is college level. Majority of the respondents in the present study were fall under the category of teachers in colleges and schools. Majority of the respondents in the present study influencing educated unfortunately are unaware of the consumer movement and various consumer forums, cells, and Government agencies working for the protection of consumers right. Even among the respondents who have a little knowledge have not all coming forward and filed the cases with any consumer forums. However very small number of respondents have stated that they complained and booked cases against malpractices practiced by the traders but unfortunately they expressed dissatisfaction about the functioning of such forums. The majority of the respondents monthly income is Rs. 5,000 to 10,000 category and they are in the nuclear family. 70 per cent of the respondents are not satisfied their purchase, and most of the respondents *i.e.,* 80 per cent of the are aware of consumerism. Consumer associations were working in the interest of consumer with respect to safeguarding their rights and protecting them from unfair trade practices, about 13.33 per cent consumers were unaware (*i.e.,* satisfactory to very poor) of this. The role and importance of consumer association were found well known (i.e., outstanding and very good) in only 43.34 per cent respondents, shown in table no. 51.9. The housewives, students and people in service class were more unaware about the role of consumer associations.

Majority of the respondents status is respondent as the regular purchaser of the household items among the selected consumers in the study more than 50 per cent are buying household items in Grocery stores. 86.67 per cent aware of some of the malpractices indulged in the consumer household goods. The maximum percentage *i.e.,* 50 per cent of the respondents face underweighment in their purchases and majority of the respondents are very rarely to attend the meetings in consumer protection association. The most of the *i.e.,* 43.33 per cent respondents know the consumer protection Act, 1986. Those who aware of the consumer protection Acts most of them could know through newspapers, friends, relatives and Television alone. The majority of the respondents are asking receipt for their purchases and majority of them are not observing the expired date of the products. This, indeed, gives more scope for the traders to deceive the customers. It is also noticed that majority of the consumers through they are educated and consumers lack desire, interest and courage in joining consumer associations. Table No. 51.19 refers to responses in joining consumer associations.

About 83.34 per cent respondents were found really interested in joining consumer associations and most of them are already associated with consumer associations. It is unfortunate that 16.66 per cent respondents were found disinterested in joining consumer associations *i.e.,* these response was satisfactory and poor. It was also found that the majority of the respondents *i.e.,* 46.67 per cent of the respondents know approaches to consumerism in consumer associations.

Impact of Consumerism on Woman Consumers

There is no doubt that consumer is a backbone of all economic activities; therefore his interest should receive first priority. But today Indian consumer is one of the most neglected sections of the society. He faces a plethora of problems affecting his rights and interests. He is very often cheated in a number of ways such as adulteration, over pricing, underweighment and measures, fraudulent advertisement, deceptive packaging, black marketing, poor sales services etc., In this situation Consumer Guidance Society of India (CGSI) which was started in April 1966, by nine housewives and social workers, has a regular programme for testing the food items and consumer durables. According to the CGSI, quality has not yet become a heritage in India upon which national reputation can be built. The Government agencies, which have been formed to protect consumers, have realized that the consumer is a victim of many types of unfair and unethical tactics adopted in the market place. Prof.L.C.Thanu reported in his study that Indian consumers are cheated of about Rs.1, 000 crores a year through deceptive weight and measures. Further, he added that about 50 per cent of the food sold is adultered, 53 per cent Garam masala, 50 per cent Spices and 15 per cent Sugar are also adulterated in India.

Fortunately, consumer protection is now a widely accepted phenomenon in the country. A number of legal and institutional arrangements developed over the years directly or indirectly aim at safeguarding the interest of consumers. Further, the Government has brought into effect a progressive and comprehensive legislation in the form of Consumer Protection Act, 1986. This Act covers the goods and services produced by private, public, joint and co-operatives sector. To protect and promote consumers' rights, the Act envisages the formation of consumer protection councils at the central and state levels. The Act also envisages setting up of a Directorate of consumer protection to receive consumer complaints and consumer disputes redressal forum to deal with consumers' disputes.

The Government is also making effects with the help of certain departments voluntary organizations and media, to educate the general consumers regarding their rights as a consumer. The Government departments and organizations usually hold talks, exhibitions, seminars, workshops and open discussion with the consumers giving them useful recommendations to increase their awareness for accurate buying policies. The printed media *viz.,* newspapers, academics journals, magazines etc., often carry information which is properly noted could increase the consumer awareness.

In the present study there is the positive impact of consumerism on women consumers in Coimbatore City, because of the awareness among the consumer rights, existence of consumer forums, consumerism, consumer associations etc.

Conclusion

As a matter of good business practice a business must accept that consumers are essential constituents of business activities. In order to remain in the market place, business houses should accept consumers and consumer associations as equal partners in business and economic activities.

Business firms, traders should accept fair trade practice as the way of life. For this dedicated Government functionaries and affected consumers should come forward to file the case and seek the advice of the consumer forums. Then only slogan that *'Consumer is the king'* can become the real. For all these, the Government should frame necessary guidelines, rules and regulations and the same must be executed by its machinery, traders and businessmen should also realize their social responsibility and strive for the better society. Thus the trader, consumer and Government as a whole with single voice and mind can translate this slogan into reality for achieving healthy business environment for the prosperity of the nation as a whole.

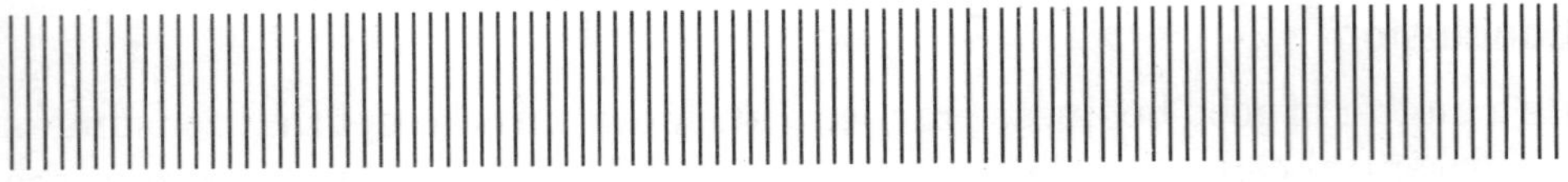

CHAPTER

52

The Consumer Protection Act in India

Past, Present, and the Future

—S. Anthony Raj

Introduction

Consumer protection in India dates back to 3200 B.C ancient India, human values were cherished and ethical practices were considered of great importance. This chapter examines the historical perspective of consumer protection in India from Vedic age to the future period.

CONSUMER'S RIGHTS AND RESPONSIBILITIES

Consumer's Rights

Consumer rights are now an integral part of our lives like a consumerist way of life. They have been well documented and much talked about. We have all made use of them at some point in our daily lives. Market resources and influences are growing by the day and so is the awareness of one's consumer rights. These rights are well-defined and there are agencies like the government, consumer courts and voluntary organisations that work towards safeguarding them. While we all like to know about our rights and make full use of them, consumer responsibility is an area which is still not demarcated. In this chapter, I will give an overview of the 8 consumer rights, their implications and significance for a developing country like India, and also define the various aspects of consumer responsibility.

In the 20th century, the presence and influence of the market grew dramatically in consumer life. We began to purchase things from the market for a price. Soon, mass production and industrial production came into being, giving the consumer world an entirely new dimension. Have you ever wondered how much urban consumers depend on the market for fulfillment of even their basic needs? This over-dependence on the market and the inherent profit motive in mass production and sales has given manufacturers and dealers a good reason to exploit consumers. As a consumer, every one should know how market products are constantly under-weight, of inferior quality and do not prescribe to quality standards specified by quality-control agencies. Consumers not only do not get value for their money but also often have to suffer losses and inconvenience due to market manipulations.

Consumer's Responsibilities

The consumers have a number of rights regarding the purchase of things, but at the same time they have some responsibilities too. It means that the consumer should keep a few things in mind while purchasing them. They are as follows:

1. *Consumer should exercise his right:* Consumers have many rights with regard to the goods and services. They must be aware of their rights while buying. These rights are: Right to safety, Right to be informed, Right to representation, Right to seek redressal, Right to consumer education, etc.
2. *Cautious consumer/ Do not buy blindly:* The consumers should make full use of their reason while buying things. They should not take the seller's word as final truth. In other words, while buying consumer must get information regarding the quality, quantity, price, utility etc. of goods and services.
3. *Filing complaint for the redressal of genuine grievances:* It is the responsibility of a consumer to approach the officer concerned there is some complaint about the goods purchased. A late complaint may find that the period of guarantee/warrantee has lapsed. Sometimes, consumers ignore the deception of businessmen. This tendency encourages corrupt business practices.
4. *Consumer must be quality conscious/Do not compromise on quality:* The consumers should never compromise on the quality of goods. Therefore, they should not buy inferior stuff out of greed for less prices. If the consumers behave like this, there cannot be any protection for them from any quarter. It is also the responsibility of the consumers only to buy goods with the ISI, Agmark, Woolmark, FPO etc. printed on them. All these symbols indicative of the good quality of the goods.

5. *Advertisements often exaggerate/Beware of false advertisement:* The seller informs the consumer about their things through the medium of advertisement. The sellers exaggerate the quality of their goods. Therefore, it is the responsibility of the consumers to recognise the truth of advertisement.
6. *Do not forget to get Receipt and Guarantee/warrantee card:* One should always get a receipt or bill for the things purchased. In case a guarantee/warrantee card is also offered by seller, it should also be taken. In case the goods purchased are of inferior quality or some defects appears and bothers the customers, these documents will be of great help in settling all kinds of dispute with the seller.
7. *Do not buy in hurry:* The first important responsibility of consumers is that they should not buy in hurry. It means that the consumers should make an estimate of the things they want to buy their along with their quantity required by them. They should also take in consideration the place from where to buy the things.

Consumer Protection Act in the Past

Vedas were the primary sources of law in India. *Manu Smriti* describes the social, political and economic conditions of ancient society. The punishment for adulteration unadulterated commodities and for breaking gems or for improperly bring (them) was the least harsh. Severe punishment was prescribed for fraud in selling seed corn. The king had the power to confiscate the entire property of a trader in two instances: (*i*) when the king had a monopoly over the exported; and (*ii*) when the export of the goods was forbidden. Kautilya's *Arthasastra* is considered to be a treatise and a prominent source, describing various theories of statecraft and the rights and duties of subjects in ancient society. Kautilya observed the superintendent of standardization should cause factories to be established for the manufacture of standard weights and measures. Trade guilds were prohibited from taking recourse to black marketing and unfair trade practice. Severe punishments were prescribed for different types of cheating.

Consumer Protection Act in the Mediaeval and Modern Age

Now consumer protection continued to be of prime concern of the rulers. During Sultanate period, the prices used were determined by local conditions. During the rule of Alauddin Khilji, strict controls were established in market place. Shopkeepers were punished for under weighing their goods. The essential Commodities Act of 1955, the Prevention of Food Adulteration Act 1954 and the Standard of Weights and Measures Act of 1976 are all used in the modern age.

Consumer Protection Act in the Future

In India, all the acts and laws are closely linked with our culture. Consumer protection has been vulnerable in the growing awaked community. Government is also reacting to the people of India in incepting new laws such as Right to Information Act. India, home to the majority of the world's consumers, is committed for working, for the welfare of consumers through new legal innovations.

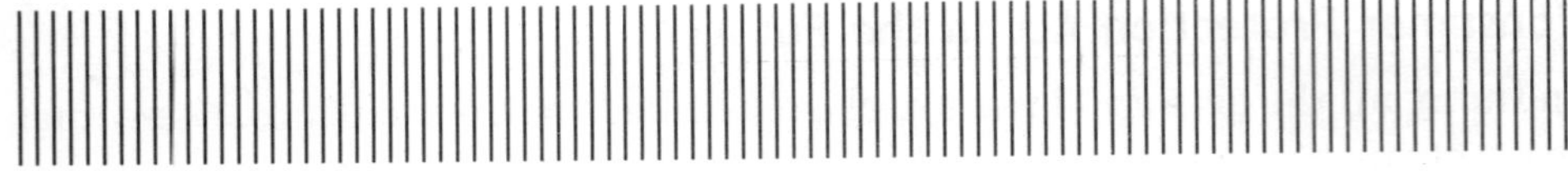

CHAPTER

53
Impact of Consumer Culture and Environment

—V. Pothigaimalai
—S. Meenakshi

Introduction

The impact of culture is natural and automatic that its influence on behaviour is usually taken for granted.

Culture is the complex whole includes knowledge, belief, art, morals, law, custom and any other capabilities and habits acquired by man as a member of society.

According to Philip Kotler, "culture is the most fundamental determinant of a person's wants and behaviour, whereas tower creatures are largely governed by-instinct, human behaviour is largely learned."

The Nature of Culture

1. Culture is an acquired quality, culture is not innate. Traits learned through socialization habits and thoughts are what is called culture man acquires the cultural behaviour because he has the capability of symbolic communication.
2. Culture is communicative in this way culture is communicated from one generation to the next generation as a result of this culture is constantly accumulating. The new generation benefits by the experience of the older generation through the communicability of culture.
3. Culture is social not individual. Every individual takes some part in

the transmission and communication of culture but culture social rather than individual.

4. Culture is idealistic in culture are included those ideal norms of behaviour according to which the members of society attempt to conduct themselves.
5. Culture fulfills some needs: culture fulfils those ethical and social needs which are ends in themselves. Social habits are included in culture.

Characteristics of Culture

The scope and complexity of culture more fully, it is useful to examine a number of its underlying characteristics:

(i) Natural impact

The impact of culture is natural and automatic, It is influence on behaviour is usually when consumer researches ask people why they do certain things, they frequently answer, 'Because it's the right thing to do'. This is natural impact of culture. This superficial response resettles ingrained influence of culture on behaviour.

(ii) Culture satisfies needs

Culture satisfies the needs of the people within a society. Culture offers order, direction and guidance in all human problem solving. However when a specific standard no longer, satisfies the members of a society it is modified or replaced, so that the resulting from gradually and continually evolves to meet the needs of society.

(iii) Culture is learned

Culture is learned. It may be following acquire, from his forms of culture learning:

1. *Formal learning:* It is the adults and older sibling teaches a young family member: How to behave.

2. *Informal learning:* It is the child learns primarily by imitating the behavior of selected others: Family, friends, TV heroes etc.,

3. *Technical learning:* The teachers instruct the child in an educational environment about what should we done, how it should be done, and why it to be done.

4. *Culture is shared:* Cultural characteristic, a particular belief, value or practice must be shared by a significant portion of the society thus the culture frequently as a group customs that link together the member of the society.

5. Culture is dynamic: The member must carefully monitor the socio – culture environment in order to market an exceeding product more effetely or to develop promising new product.

Elements of Culture

1. Enculturation and acculturation

The acquisition of culture anthropologists distinguish between the learning of one's own or native culture and the learning of some other culture. The former is known as enculturation.

2. Language and symbols

The member of the society must be Abel to communicate with each other through the common language in order to acquire a common culture. The symbol can be divided in to Verbal and Non-verbal.

3. Rituals

A ritual is a type symbolic active conceits of a series of steps called multiple behaviors in a fixed sequence and repeated over time.

Rituals extend over the human life cycle from birth to death including a host of intermediate events such as confirmation, graduation, marriage etc.

4. Culture in shared

Belief, value of practice must be shared by a significant portion of the society. So that the group customs that link together the members of a society.

Culture includes both abstract and material elements, which allow us to describe, evaluate, and differentiate cultures.

Abstract elements include values, attitudes, ideas, personality, types, such as religion or politics.

1. Values: Cultural of social values are those shared broadly across groups of people, whereas personal values etc.

2. Norms: Norms are rules of behavior held by a majority or at least a consensus of a group about how individuals should behave.

3. Rituals: A rituals is a type symbolic active conceits of a series of steps called multiple behaviours in a fixed sequence and repeated over time.

4. Symbol: The member of the society must be Abel to communicate with each other through the common language in order to acquire a common culture.

The symbol can be divided in to Verbal and Non-verbal.

Verbal symbols: These may includes a television announcement or an advertisement in a magazine;

Non verbal symbols: as blue figures, color, shapes, trademark etc.

Material Components

Cultural artifacts: It includes such things as books, computers tools, building, and specific products.

Other Material Components

- Technology
- Infrastructure

Sub-culture

A sub-culture is a distinct cultural group that exists as an identifiable segment within a larger, more complex society.

Sub- culture polls belief values customs that said them part from other members of the same society.

Characteristics of Sub-cultures

1. *Sub cultural distinctiveness:* The more a sub-culture seeks to maintain a separate identity the greater is it potential influence
2. *Sub cultural homogeneity:* A subculture with homogeneous values is more likely to exert influence on its members Hispanic Americans appear to be a diverse sub-culture composed of Mexican, Cubans.
3. *Sub cultural exclusion:* Sub cultural have sought exclusion from or have been excluded by the society.

Types of sub-culture: subcultures is classified by:

- Age
- Geography
- Religion
- Life style

Age : These group have sufficiently homogeneous and distinctive values of constitute a subculture.

Geography: Marketers can identity specific areas with homogeneous needs and values.

Religion: It can also be regarded as sub culture as a result of traditions and custom tied to the beliefs and passed on from one generation to the next.

Examples of Various Sub-cultural System

1. Asian American Sub-culture

Asian American are the third largest minority group with 10 million people representing about 3.5 per cent of the U.S. population and accounting for 120 billion in yearly purchasing power the reason for identifying Asian Americans as a sub-culture is the same as that for Africans Americans and Hispanic Americans strong ethnic identity.

2. Black or African-American Culture

It refer to a common heritage rather than to a skin colour, in the United States, the black heritage is conditioned by a shared history beginning with slavery, discrimination and suffering and segregation from the majority culture.

3. Multiethnic Micro Culture

Increased ethnic diversity within a nation often leads to interracial relationships and marriages, resulting in children belonging to multiple ethnic subculture. When it occurs it is difficult to determine which of the influences will affect behaviour and values.

4. Native American Culture

In a sense the truly 'American' culture is that of Native Americans although marketers view Native Americans as minority ethnic groups in today majority culture after nearly a century of assimilation into white society, there is a resurgence of identification with Native American culture both by Indian and white.

5. Hispanic or Latin Culture

Language and identity, rather than national origin, are the key elements in Hispanic culture, which may include any colour or race.

Latin is often preferred and increasingly, country of origin, such as Mexican Puerto Rican, or Cuban-American is preferred.

6. French-Canadian Culture

In North America is the French Canadian area of Canada, mostly in Quebec. The province of Quebec accounts for more than 27 per cent of the Canadian population and about 25 per cent of income and retail sales. The French culture was somewhat ignored by English oriented advertisers, thereby creating a social problem and limiting the effectiveness of communications to the French market.

Meaning of Culture Intelligence

- *Cultural intelligence:* as a system of interacting knowledge and skills, linked by cultural.
- *Meta-cognition:* that allows people to adapt to, select, and shape the cultural aspects of their environment.
- *Cultural knowledge:* Culture knowledge because it refers to content knowledge in a specific domain–here the culture domain.
- *Knowledge of culture:* identities, value, attitudes and practices makes for greeter predictability in social interaction, more accurate attributions, and ultimately more effective inter-cultural behaviour.
- *Cultural knowledge:* refers not only to a declarative or content component, but also to stored processes.

Cultural Skills

We have focussed on those individual differences that can be developed and used as a lever for improvement.

The term skill is the limiting ourselves to this them, there is still no shortage of contenders for skill elements that might contribute to cultural intelligence.

Cultural Metacognition

Metacognition is defined as knowledge of and control over one's thinking and learning activities.

Cross-culture

Cross-culture means whether and how to enter a foreign market, marketers need to conduct some form of cross cultural consumer analysis.

- Cross- cultural analysis is defined as the effort to determine to what extent the consumers of two or more nations are similar or different.

Cross-cultural Influences

- Marketing abroad has become an increasingly important part of American business. Today, three out of four manufacturing jobs are linked to products sold abroad, directly or indirectly. American companies such as Proctor and Gamble, Colgate-Palmolive, Johnson & Johnson earn more of their revenue abroad than in the United States.
- American firms are finding opportunities in Eastern Europe and Russia with the development of free-market systems. *e.g.* Procter

and Gamble has spent millions of dollars researching the Russian consumer's mind and airwaves with commercials that offer almost contrast to the dismal hardships of everyday life.

Cross-cultural Variations Influencing Consumer Behaviour

International marketers subscribing to an acculturated view of foreign markets have been affected by two-cross currents:

1. They recognize differences in customs and values between countries and a need to adapt marketing strategies to these differences;
2. They also recognize a greater commonality between countries in cultural values as the result of global communications through TV and more frequent travel.

Factors Influencing Cross-cultural

1. Consumer Customs and Values: American business people taken an ethnocentric view by assuming the values of American consumers are universal

Differences in cultural values among countries are likely to result in differences in product preferences and product usage.

A. Product Preferences

Example the five brands with the strongest image in the U.S. are Coco-cola, Campbell's, Disney, Pepsi and Katak.

B. Product usage

Are Likely to differ sharply across countries.

2. Language: It provides the mean of communicating the customs and beliefs of a culture .marketers must be aware of the meaning of languages and dialects when selling in foreign markets.

3. Symbols: Symbols in a culture also influences purchasing behaviour. Companies must be particularly sensitive to the use of color in advertising.

4. Economic environment: a country's economic environment influences consumer behaviour.

Applications of Cross-cultural and Global Influences

1. Localized strategies: substantial differences between countries in tastes, customs and product usage

Limits of localized strategies: it is the inability of management to recognize the need to adapt to local tastes and customs.

Example of Localized Strategies

Kellogg managed to attract Indians to its cereals, despite the fact that barely 3 per cent of the country reported eating cereal in surveys, by advertising the benefits of a lighter and more nutritious morning meal one tactic it used was to introduce rice flakes made of basmati a premium aromatic rice.

2. *Global strategies*: the cross-cultural differences cited suggest that companies should vary their strategy for a product from country to country.

Limits of global influences: The focus on global influences suggest that a company can market one standardized product with a uniform, worldwide advertising campaign.

3. *Flexible globalization*: it requires the company to establish an overall marketing strategy but to leave implementation to local executives who are aware of national traits and custom.

Cultural Values and Consumer Behaviour

Cultural Values as beliefs that a general state of existence is personally and socially worth striving for.

Cultural Values influencing consumer behaviour has been described two types:

1. Means-end chain
2. Laddering

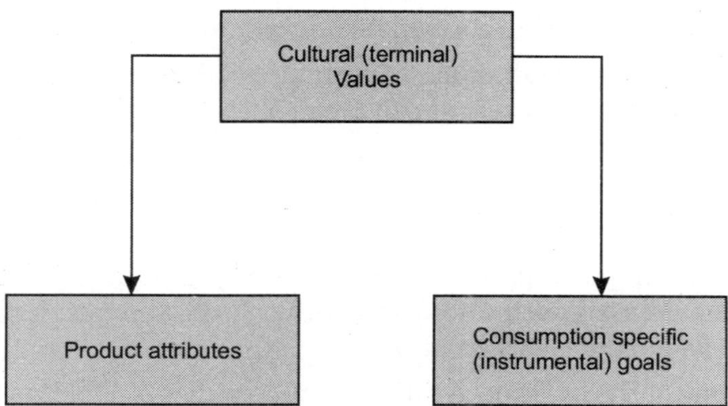

Conclusion

Findings of the study indicate that some societal implications of cross-cultural and sub-cultural influences namely the need to protect consumer rights abroad. Marketing is entering a challenging globalization affecting cultural and linguistic dimension of the market post. Liberalization scenario made the world markets a universal homogeneous group across countries the youth is the culturally more to the western culture of individualization achievement orientation.

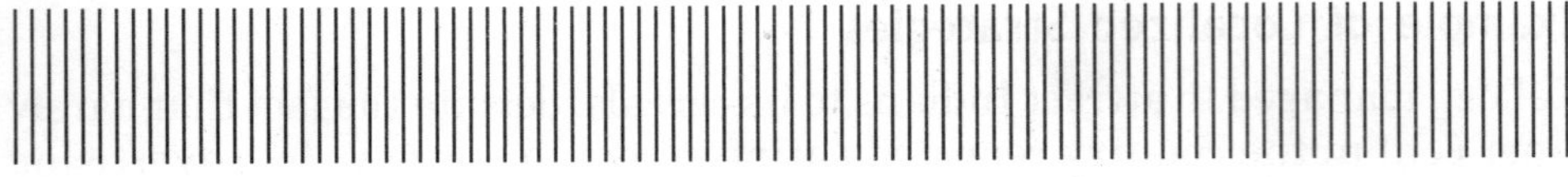

CHAPTER

54 Food-related Laws with Special Reference to Consumer

—Dr. A. Asick Iqubal
—Dr. A. Ziaudeen

Importance of Food

Food is an important part of religious observance and spiritual ritual for many faiths including Christianity, Judaism, Islam, Hinduism and Buddhism. The role of food in cultural practices and religious beliefs is complex and varies among individuals and communities.

The Holy Prophet Muhammad recommended even for pious man the quantity of food "*which is just sufficient to keep his back-bone erect*".

There is milk, honey, grapes, lamb, olives ... in fact, since Christians believe that all good things are a gift of God, every food has deep religious significance.

Eating is an important activity, which is required in order to live. It is God, who has created each and every thing. Food, hunger, living beings, all of them the part of God's creation.

Food is one of the basic necessities for sustenance of life. It is no wonder to say that community health is national wealth. Over the centuries of human existence on planet Earth, food, clothing and shelter have emerged as the three basic necessities. While clothing and shelter have emerged as basic needs in the due course of human evolution, right from the beginning of life, food has been the major source of energy and existence.

Every human being is a consumer in day today life availing goods and services for his necessity and fittest survival. A comparative approach to the visualization of food related laws with special reference to consumer is always valuable and advantageous.

There are number of pre-constitutional and post-constitutional laws, orders, rules that aim at the protection of the consumer interests with special reference to food aspect whether directly or indirectly. Some of these enactments are the Agricultural Produce (Grading and Marking) Act, 1937, the Prevention of Food Adulteration Act, 1954, the Monopolies and Restrictive Trade Practices Act, 1969, the Standard of Weights and Measures Act, 1976, Bureau of India Standards Act, 1986, the Prevention of Food Adulteration Act, 1954, the Fruit Products Order, 1955, the Meat Food Products Order, 1973, the Vegetable Oil Products (Control) Order, 1947, the Edible Oils Packaging (Regulation) Order, 1998, the Solvent Extracted Oil, De oiled Meal, and Edible Flour (Control) Order, 1967, the Milk and Milk Products Order, 1992. The Constitution of India which is the fundamental law of the land also contains a number of provisions which go a long way in protecting the rights of the consumers. These provisions include Article 21 which deals with the right to life and personal liberty, Article 47 which guarantees the right to health and Article 48-A which aims at a pollution free environment for all citizens etc. The Supreme Court has held that the right to life under Article 21 includes the right to a healthy and safe environment. Several Acts and orders prevailed in India to safeguard food safety and the health of the consumer. They were introduced to complement and supplement each other in achieving total food safety and quality. The Central Government declared the year of 2008-09 as 'Food Safety and Quality year'.

However due to variation in the specifications/standards in different Acts/Orders, and administration by different Departments and Ministries, there were implementation problems and a lack of importance given to safety standards over a period of time. The food industries were facing problems as different products were governed by different orders and ministries and the rules and regulations in the country needed consolidation. The following are the certain acts which focuses the right of consumer to approach the proper authority or adjudication for his grievance to be settled or sorted out.

The Agricultural Produce (Grading and Marking) Act, 1937

This Act provides for the grading and marking of agricultural and other allied commodities with the objective of making available only the quality agricultural produce including horticulture and livestock produce to the consumers. Under the provisions of this Act, the Central Government is authorized to make rules fixing grade designation to indicate the quality of any scheduled article, specifying grade designation, authorizing interested parties to grade, specifying conditions regarding manner of marking packaging etc and providing for the confiscation and disposal of produce marked otherwise than in accordance with the provisions of this Act etc.

It is a mark given under Agricultural Produce (Grading and Marking) Act popularly known as AGMARK Act. Affixing or printing AGMARK on a food product means that the particular food item satisfies the standard prescribed under the Act. It provides assurance of quality to the consumers. The AGMARK are given to agricultural, horticultural, forest and livestock products. The Act and the rules stipulate conditions governing use of the standards and lays down procedures for marking, packing and sealing etc. AGMARK is not mandatory; but to apply AGMARK to a product that does not conform to the standards prescribed is an offence. Approved laboratories undertake analysis and testing the purity of products and prescribe conditions for use of the label, packing and marking also. The complaints and grievances of the consumers in respect of AGMARK grade products can be made to Agricultural marketing advisor who is empowered to order free replacement of the product. A consumer can also approach consumer redressal agencies also *i.e.,* District Forum, State Commission and National Commission etc.

The Prevention of Food Adulteration Act, 1954

It is an Act to make provision for the prevention of adulteration of food. The Prevention of Food Adulteration Act is a welfare legislation to prevent health hazards by consuming adulterated food. The mensrea is not an essential ingredient. It is a social evil and the Act prohibits commission of the offences under the Act. The essential ingredient is sale to the purchaser by the vendor. It is not material to establish the capacity of the person vis-à-vis the owner of the shop to prove his authority to sell the adulterated food exposed for sale in the shop. It is enough for prosecution to establish that the person who sold the adulterated article had sold it to the purchaser including the Food Inspector and that Food Inspector purchased the same in strict compliance with the provisions of the Act [5]. The main objective of the Act is to protect the public from poisonous and harmful foods, to prevent the sale of substandard foods and to protect the interests of the consumers by eliminating fraudulent practices.

Definition of Food: any article used as food or drink for human consumption other than drugs and water and includes:

(*a*) Any article which ordinarily enters into or is used in the composition or preparation of human food;

(*b*) Any flavouring matter or condiments; and

(*c*) Any other article which the Central Government may having regard to its use, nature, substance or quality, declare, by notification in the official gazette as food for the purpose of this Act.

Initiative and Remedy to Consumer under this Act

The word 'Consumer' has not defined under the Prevention of Food Adulteration Act, 1954. But the provision provides that the Central Committee for Food Standards Consist of five representatives nominated by the Central Government to represent the consumers interests, one of whom shall be from the hotel industry.

The Purchaser or Consumer or recognized Consumer association can send any article of food to Public Analyst for analysis report after informing the vendor at the time of purchase his or its intention to have such article so analyzed.

The public analyst shall deliver a report to the Local (Health) Authority of the result of the analysis of any article of food submitted to him for analysis.

On receipt of the report of the analysis to the effect that the article of food is adulterated, the local (Health) authority shall, after the institution of prosecution against the persons from whom the sample of the article of food was taken. The person or persons who sent for analysis or public analyst, either or both of them may make an application to the Court within a period of ten days from the date of receipt of the copy of the report to get the sample of the article of food kept by the local (Health) Authority analyzed by the Central Food Laboratory. A Complaint under section 20 of the Act could be instituted not only apart from Central or State Government by a person authorized in that behalf.

Essential Commodities Act, 1955

The EC Act, 1955 gives powers to control production, supply, distribution etc. of essential commodities for maintaining or increasing supplies and for securing their equitable distribution and availability at fair prices. Using the powers under the Act, various Ministries/Departments of the Central Government have issued Control Orders for regulating production/ distribution/quality aspects/movement etc. pertaining to the commodities which are essential and administered by them.

The Essential Commodities Act is being implemented by the State Governments/UT Administrations by availing of the delegated powers under the Act. The State Governments/UT Administrations have issued various Control Orders to regulate various aspects of trading in Essential Commodities such as foodgrains, edible oils, pulses kerosene, sugar etc. The Central Government regularly monitors the action taken by State Governments/UT Administrations to implement the provisions of the Essential Commodities Act, 1955.

Powers to control production, supply, distribution, etc., of essential commodities—(1) If the Central Government is of opinion that it is necessary or expedient so to do for maintaining or increasing supplies of any essential commodity or for securing their equitable distribution and availability at fair prices, or for securing any essential commodity for the defence of India or the efficient conduct of military operations, it may, by order, provide for regulating, or prohibiting the production supply and distribution thereof and trade and commerce therein.

(2) Without prejudice to the generality of the powers conferred by subsection (1), an order made thereunder may provide:

(*a*) for regulating by licences, permits or otherwise the production or manufacture of any essential commodity;

(*b*) for bringing under cultivation any waste or arable land;

(*c*) for controlling the price at which essential commodity may be bought or sold;

(*d*) for regulating by licences, permits or otherwise the storage, transport, distribution, disposal, acquisition use or consumption of, any essential commodity;

(*e*) for prohibiting the withholding from sale of any essential commodity ordinarily kept for sale;

(*f*) for requiring any person holding in stock, or engaged in the production, or in the business of buying or selling, of any essential commodity;

(*g*) for regulating or prohibiting any class of commercial or financial transactions relating to foodstuffs or cotton textiles which, in the opinion of the authority making the order, are, or, if unregulated, are likely to be, detrimental to the public interest;

(*h*) For collecting any information or statistics with a view to regulating or prohibiting any of the aforesaid matters.

Fruit Products Order (FPO), 1955

Fruit Products Order—1955, promulgated under Section 3 of the Essential Commodities Act—1955, aims at regulating sanitary and hygienic conditions in manufacture of fruit, vegetable products. It is mandatory for all manufacturers of fruit, vegetable products to obtain a licence under this Order. To ensure good quality products, manufactured under hygienic conditions, the Fruit Product Order lays down the minimum requirements for:

1. Sanitary and hygienic conditions of premises, surrounding and personnel;

2. Water to be used for processing;
3. Machinery and equipment;
4. Product standards.

Besides this, maximum limits of preservatives, additives and contaminants have also been specified for various products.

The Solvent Extracted Oil, De-oiled Meal and Edible Flour (Control) Order, 1967

This Order is basically a quality control order to ensure that the solvent extracted oils in particular are not reached to the consumers for consumption before the same are refined and conformed to the quality standards specified in the Order for the purpose. Standards for the solvent (hexane), which is to be used for extraction of oil from the oil-bearing materials, have also been specified so as to eliminate possible contamination of oil from the solvent used.

Meat Food Products Order, 1973 (MFPO)

Meat Food Products Order, 1973 (MFPO) promulgated under the provisions of Essential Commodities Act, 1955 provides for sanitary and other requirements, limits of heavy metals, preservatives, insecticides, residue, etc., for meat food products.

Milk and Milk Products Order, 1992(MMPO)

Milk and Milk Products Order, 1992 administered by the Department of Animal Husbandry and Dairying under Ministry of Agriculture was promulgated on 9th June, 1992 under the provision of Section 3 of the Essential Commodities Act, 1955 with a view to maintain an increased supply of liquid milk of desired quality to the general public.

Vegetable Oil Products Order, 1998

The Vegetable Oil Products industry is regulated by this Order through the Directorate of Vanaspati, Vegetable Oils and Fats, Department of Food, Public Distribution, Ministry of Consumer Affairs, and Food and Public Distribution. The earlier two Orders—Vegetable Oil Products (Control) Order, 1947 and Vegetable Oil Products (Standards of Quality) Order, 1975 have been replaced by a single Order called "Vegetable Oil Products (Regulation) Order, 1998 for proper regulation of manufacture, distribution and sale of Vegetable Oil Products.

Edible Oils Packaging (Regulation) Order, 1998

In order to ensure availability of safe and quality edible oils in packed form at pre-determined prices to the consumers, the Central Government promulgated on 17th September, 1998, an Edible Oils Packaging (Regulation) Order, 1998 under the Essential Commodities Act, 1955 to make packaging of edible oils, sold in retail, compulsory unless specifically exempted by the concerned State Government.

Consumer Protection Act, 1986

The Consumer Protection Act, 1986 is a milestone in the history of socio-economic legislation in India. It aims at providing an informal, inexpensive and expeditious justice to the consumers aggrieved by defects in goods or deficiency in services.

An Act to provide for the better protection of the interest of consumers and for that purpose to make provision for the establishment of consumer councils and other authorities for the settlement of consumers' disputes and for matters connected therewith.

The word 'consumer' which means any person who:

(*i*) buys any goods for a consideration which has been paid or promised or partly paid and partly promised, or under any system of deferred payment and includes any user of such goods other than the person who buys such goods for consideration paid or promised or partly paid or partly promised, or under any system of deferred payment. When such use is made with the approval of such person, but does not include a person who obtains such goods for resale or for any commercial purpose; or

(*ii*) hires or avails of any services for a consideration which has been paid or promised or partly paid and partly promised, or under any system of deferred payment and includes any beneficiary of such services other than the person who hires 1[or avails of] the services for consideration paid or promised, or partly paid and partly promised, or under any system of deferred payment, when such services are availed of with the approval of the first mentioned person.

The word *'defect'* means any fault, imperfection or shortcoming in the quality, quantity, potency, purity or standard which is required to be maintained by or under any law for the time being in force or 1[under any contract, express or implied, or] as is claimed by the trader in any manner whatsoever in relation to any goods;

The word *'deficiency'* means any fault, imperfection, shortcoming or inadequacy in the quality, nature and manner of performance which is required to be maintained by or under any law for the time being in force or has been undertaken to be performed by a person in pursuance of a contract or otherwise in relation to any service.

Food Safety and Standards Act, 2006

It is an Act to consolidate the laws relating to food and to establish the Food Safety and Standards Authority of India for laying down science based standards for articles of food and to regulate their manufacture, storage, distribution, sale and import, to ensure availability of safe and wholesome food for human consumption and for matters connected therewith or incidental thereto. This Act is still in the infant stage and certain sections are not yet notified. This Act consists of 101 sections and 2 schedules. The Second Schedule gives the details of Food Act/Orders which will stand repealed on commencement of the section 97 of the Act. Those were:

1. The Prevention of Food Adulteration Act, 1954 (37 of 1954).
2. The Fruit Products Order, 1955.
3. The Meat Food Products Order, 1973.
4. The Vegetable Oil Products (Control) Order, 1947.
5. The Edible Oils Packaging (Regulation) Order, 1998.
6. The Solvent Extracted Oil, De oiled Meal, and Edible Flour (Control) Order, 1967.
7. The Milk and Milk Products Order, 1992.
8. Any other order issued under the Essential Commodities.

Act, 1955 (10 of 1955) relating to food

The Food Safety and Standards Act 2006 was introduced to overcome these shortcomings and to give more importance to safety standards. This Act consolidates the laws relating to food and establishes the Food Safety and Standards Authority of India (FSSA) for laying down science-based standards for articles of food and to regulate their manufacture, storage, distribution, sale and import, to ensure availability of safe and wholesome food for human consumption.

Suggestions

1. Need for creating awareness about food safety and services.
2. There should be emphasis on good manufacturing practices instead of detection of adulteration and prosecution.
3. More laboratories with sophisticated technology to meet the current scenario tests to be established.
4. The Food Safety and Standards Act, 2006 to be implemented soon to give efficacious results to the protection of Consumer.
5. The harmonization of multiple food laws is necessary to have a uniform and logical approach for regulating the quality of food.

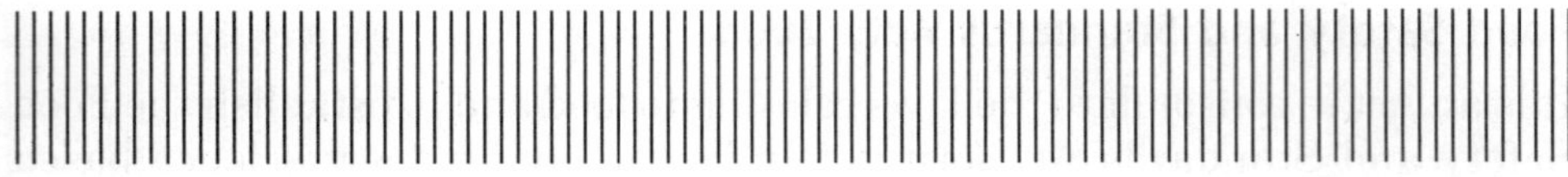

CHAPTER

55
Consumer Justice in India

—G. Jivek

In our day to day life we become consumer through buying goods or services. In the era of science and technology globalization, urbanization and modernization developed rapidly, which resulted into vast competition in market. The traditional view of buying goods and particular services changed and many products, services, and professions came under widened scope of consumer law. As a consumer we have much concern about the money, choice, health and safety of the life. Market is always dominated by the sellers and their attitude towards consumer as weaker section. In last few years' market is found to be influenced by the false, misleading advertisements or representations, bargaining, offering gifts, prizes, contests and hoardings attracting public for product or services.

Therefore, keeping view of consumer interest legislative and judicial contributions played a significant role in consumer justice. There is need to prevent exploitation of consumer from these sales, manufacturing or unfair trade practices. The scope of the Act extended to public services and utilities also.

To meet the goal of Welfare State, government also responsible to frame policies and implement properly. Government has responsibility to setup Consumer Forums to meet out the objectives of Consumer Protection Act, 1986. The Act is a General Law and if there is a Special Law on the disputed subject matter, then that Special Law will prevail.

The scope of the Act includes the possibility of forthcoming consumers who wants to join such consumer activity. It also includes the protection to consumers against the private and public body and the statutory bodies as well. The Act is to enable a consumer to ventilate his grievances before Forum where justice can be done without any procedural wrangles and hyper-technicalities.

The Act provides various rights to protect the interests of consumers; such rights are as follows:

- Right to safety
- Right to be informed
- Right to choose
- Right to be heard
- Right to seek Redressal
- Right to consumer education
- Other rights: Healthy environment; Trade codes etc.

When there is any defect, deficiency in service or unfair trade practice or price charged is excess then as a right complaint can be filed by the consumer before Consumer Redressal to get justice. Unfair trade practices are not only concerning the sale of goods but also cover the services, this view is laid down in Mukesh Jain *vs.* V. K. Gupta.

Therefore, provisions for Consumer Protection constructed in favour of consumers as held in the milestone case Lucknow Development Authority *vs.* M. K. Gupta.

Salient Features of Act

- To provides better protection of consumers
- To provides establishment of Consumer Dispute Redressal Agencies
- To provides setup of Consumer Councils
- To make awareness and provide consumer education
- No strict procedural rules
- No need of Lawyers to conduct case
- Provisions for appeal
- Doctrine of Caveat Emptor has been recognized and applied

This chapter highlights the some of the major areas in which consumer justice is done.

Housing Industry

In the era of urbanization the housing industry developed rapidly. The builders, contractors, promoters and developers, their agents deceiving peoples who contract with them by way of booking flats, developing lands. Therefore, Act provided protection to housing industries.

In the case of Lucknow Development Authority vs. M. K. Gupta the issues involved were:

(1) Whether a statutory authority like Lucknow Land Development Authority comes under Act?

(2) Whether housing as a service was covered under the Act?

Answering both issues in affirmatives Court held that, it is an authority and housing is a service, both covered under the Act. Recently, in Mukesh Kumar Verma *vs.* Krishna Builders, the amount was paid by the appellant for the construction of house and possession, which had not constructed properly amount to unfair trade practice and deficiency in service hence appellant entitled for relief.

Medical Profession

Doctor is considered to be God for patient.

The litigation of malpractices and medical negligence are increasing day by day. However there are technological innovations and sophisticated equipments that are put up for medical investigation and treatment of diseases. Though medical science has conferred great benefits to mankind these benefits at the same time are attended by risks. In Medical profession the matter of consultation, diagnosis and treatment is involved where a medical practitioner or hospital or nursing home renders service in consideration which falls within ambit of Sec. 2 (1) (o) of the Act, as held in Indian Medical Association *vs.* V. P. Shantha and Others.

The Supreme Court in Dr. Laxman Balkrishna Joshi *vs.* Dr. Trimbak Bapu Godbole laid down that a Doctor when consulted by a patient owes him certain duties, namely:

(*a*) a duty of care in deciding whether to undertake the case;

(*b*) a duty of care in deciding what treatment to give; and

(*c*) a duty of care in the administration of that treatment.

A breach of any of these duties gives a cause of action for medical negligence.

Mistaken diagnosis amount to deficiency in service. Similarly negligence of doctors in the operations, prescribing medicines, providing nutritious foods and facilities would amount to deficiency in service. In the case of Spring Meadows Hospital *vs.* Harjol Ahluwalia, Court awarded the damages to the parents of child who suffered irreparable brain damage due to negligence of doctors. Recently, in Kussum Sharma and Ors. *vs.* Batra Hospital and Research Centre, Court held that, there is no medical negligence on the part of doctors as long as they perform their duties and exercise ordinary degree of skills and competence. If it is not within well settled principles of medical negligence then appellant not entitled for relief.

Airlines Services

In the journey fare (ticket) cost of food was included which is the consideration for providing service of food. Any adulterate or low standard food provided by Airline Authority comes under deficiency in service and is liable for compensation.

Banking Services

As the development in the banking sector and technological revolution, the banker and customer relationship becomes matter of standard, prompt and quick service. The term 'customer' of a bank is not defined by law. Ordinarily, a person who has an account in a bank is considered as its customer, decided in Abdul Razak and Anr. *vs.* South Indian Bank Ltd. For the relationship of banker and customer there should be considerable duration of dealings, casual dealings does not constitute such relations, this view discarded by Kerala High Court and laid down that, person who has a bank account in his name and for whom the banker undertakes to provide the services as a banker considered to be a customer.

In Malti Bhat *vs.* State Bank of India, the consumer was a student preparing for the AMIE examination, for that purpose he remitted Rs. 200 as application fee and exam form, via a bank draft. The application was rejected as the Manager did not sign the draft. The student did not appeared for the examination, the National Commission awarded compensation of Rs. 35000 to the student. In Ganga Nagar Central Co-operative Bank Ltd. *vs.* Pupsha Rani and Anr, respondent opened an account with the bank and deposited money, but after some period his money was not in account and returned by the bank. The District Forum awarded compensation for deficiency in service, which was upheld by the Apex Court in the appeal.

Telephone Services

The telephone facility provided by the Telecom Department is a service under Act, as held in Union of India *vs.* Nilesh Agarwal.

In famous Three Coin Case where a person was in urgency to deliver message for delay in flight, he used the coin box to call but did not heard due to problem in working of phone. He lost three one rupee coins, Telecom Department refused to pay then he filed complaint before District Forum and awarded Rs. 3/- as refund, Rs. 750/- as damages and Rs. 250/- by way of costs.

Insurances Services

It is fundamental principle of the insurance that almost good faith must be observed by the contracting parties' *i.e.* insurer and assured. The obligation of good faith applies to both equally. If the contract is vague, the benefit should be given to the insured. In the advancement of insurance policy benefit should be given to consumer or his legal heirs. In Manjulaben Parmar *vs.* LIC, the assured had a life insurance policy under Jivan Mitra plan. He died within 10 months of taking policy. The LIC rejected claim of his widow. In appeal National Commission directed LIC to pay insured amount Rs. 40000 and further award of Rs. 20000 so as she was long time litigating claim, suffered harassment and mental agony.

Advertisement

An advertisement of any product and fault therein comes under preview of unfair trade practice. Therefore, medicine which guaranteed the birth of male child is unfair trade practice, as held in Consumer Education and Research Society *vs.* M/s Vasu Pharmaceuticals.

Advocacy

However, lawyers are rendering services to his client, but object of Act do not contain any provision which will bring the advocates within scope of Act. It was argued that the definition u/s – 2(1) (d) will not include a client, who has availed of the services of an advocate. It was challenged in Srimati and Others *vs.* Union of India and Others. This issue further made clear by the Supreme Court in Lucknow Development Authority *vs.* M. K. Gupta as follows:

"The term service has variety of meanings. It may mean any benefit or any act resulting in promoting interest or happiness. It may be contractual, professional, public, domestic, legal, statutory etc. The concept of service thus is very wide".

Educational Institutions

Though the education is not commercial activity in this country, treated as traditional and religious duty. Treated as charitable activity. Imparting education has been never treated as a trade or business in this country. But due to changing commercial purpose and injustice to students by the educational institutions Maharashtra State Commission, in Abel Pacheco Gracias *vs.* Principal, Bharati Vidyapeeth College of Engineering directed the College to refund the fees to complainant, who got admission in the Government College.

Again in case of Maharshi Dayanand University, Rohtak *vs.* Shakuntala Chaudhary, it was held that, result of the examination declared by the University was erroneous and incorrect. The University defaults from its primal duty. The examinees would clearly be entitled to compensation under the Act for deficiency in the services rendered.

Recently, in Banglore University *vs.* Dattatri S. the result declared by the University, in which mistake committed by the tabulator and candidate who secured sufficient marks for pass declared as fail. It was challenged and National Commission held that, imparting education, conduction examination, revaluation etc. not amount to service. Hence, complainant is not consumer and entitled to relief.

Financial Services

Financial services rendered by the Financial Corporation is a service for which borrower pays interest, and is within meaning of the Act.

Conclusion

While concluding this study, it is observed that present consumer movement has been developed tremendously. Constitutional object; justice, liberty and equality in the society sought to be achieved by this consumer movement. The commercialization in various sectors, particularly in degree or diploma from reputed education institutions is still awaited for justice.

The role of media also contributed lot in making awareness of public through advertisements like Jago Grahak Jago at the root level of the society. The philosophy of the justice as enshrined in the Constitution came to be true by this consumer movement in last 2-3 decades.

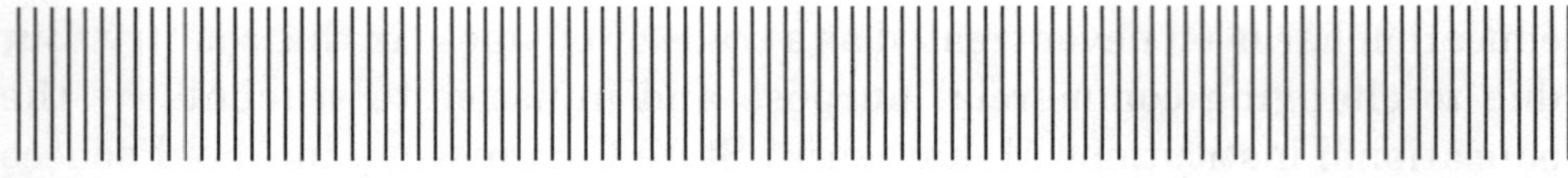

CHAPTER

56

The Phenomenon of Consumerism

—G. Balamurugan
—Dr. V. Nazarudeen

This chapter tries to elucidate the nuances involved in the consumerism and its effect on Indian society. It tries to throw some light on benefit gained by peoples in society. The Aim of this chapter is to enlighten the reader about the complications of this system without going into technicalities. In all it is an analysis of consumerism in India. A general attempt has been made to understand this system.

Today, consumer is called the king of the market. He is at the centre stage of all market activities. It is constant endeavour of producers that the production of product must conform to the needs of consumer. In addition to the satisfaction of consumer, it also the endeavour of producer that their sale should be maximum. They, therefore try to increase their sales by all possible means. Some of the means adopted to increase sale are such as to serve both the producers and the consumers. On the other hand, some of the methods adopted to increase the sale are such as to sub serve the interest of producers but the same against the interest of consumer. In other words the consumers are exploited

The last two decades have witnessed an over expanding interest in Consumerism and which is in a very critic condition. The word Consumerism has to be fully understood in its historical retrospect with reference to the consumer's position in common law, main areas of regulations, controls on advertising, labelling standards, etc. The word 'consumer' means a person who uses goods and services.

And in our Indian system the consumer has six rights given for his protection from exploitation from the shopkeepers or sellers. Consumer exploitation means mistreatment or cheating with consumer by adulteration, or in any other unfair form. To prevent consumer from exploitation our governments have passed many Acts from time to time.

Some of them are as follows:

1. Drug and Cosmetics Act, 1940
2. Prevention of Food Adulteration Act, 1954
3. Essential Commodity (Supply) Act, 1955
4. Monopolies and Restrictive Trade Practices Act, 1969
5. Standard of Weights and Measures Act, 1976
6. Consumer Protection Act, 1986

CONSUMER/CUSTOMER

Defining Consumer

According to Oxford Advanced Learner's Dictionary the word consumer means "A purchaser of goods or uses services'. And In Black's Law Dictionary, it is explained to mean 'one who consume individuals, who consume, individuals who purchase, use, maintain, and dispose of products and services'. A member of that broad class of people, who are affected by pricing politics, financing practices, quality of goods and services, credit reporting, debt collection and other trade practices for which state and federal consumer protection laws are enacted. But the definition of the term 'consumer' given in clause (d) of section 2(1) of the Act is comprehensive one so as to cover not only consumer of goods but also consumer of services. The definition is wide enough to include in consumer that only the person who buys any goods for consideration but also any uses of such goods with the approval of the buyer.

Similarly, it covers any person who hires or avails of any services for consideration and also includes any beneficiary of such services, when availed with the approval of the hirer. Thus, any user of goods or any beneficiary of services, other than the actual Buyer or hirer is a consumer for the purpose of the Act. And he is competent to make a complaint before the Consumer Disputes Redressal Forums under the Act. The Act aims to protect the economic interest of a consumer as understood in commercial sense as a purchaser of goods and in the larger sense of user and service. The important characteristic of 'goods' and 'service' under the Act is that such goods are supplied at a price to cover the costs, which consequently result in profit or income to the seller of goods or provider of service. It includes anyone who consumes goods or services at the end of the chain of production.

Consumer of Goods

Under sub-clause (i) of section 2 (i) (d) a consumer for the purpose of goods means any person, who:

(*a*) Buys any goods for consideration which has been paid or promised or partly paid and partly promised, or under any system of deferred payment; and

(*b*) Includes any user of such goods other than the person who buys them, when such use is made with the approval of the buyer; but

(*c*) Does not include a person who obtains such goods for resale or for any commercial purpose. Commercial purpose does not include use by a person of goods bought and used by him exclusively for the purpose of earning his livelihood by means of self-employment.

The above provision reveals that a person claiming himself as 'consumer' should satisfy that:

(1) There must be a sale transaction between the seller and the buyer;

(2) The sale must be of goods;

(3) The buying of goods must be for consideration;

(4) The consideration has been paid or promised or partly paid and partly promised or under any system of deferred payment;

(5) The user of the goods may also be a consumer when such use is made with the approval of the buyer.

However, the term 'consumer' does not include a person who obtains any goods for resale or for any commercial purpose. It is obvious that the parliament intended to restrict the benefits of the Act to ordinary consumers purchasing goods either for their own consumption or even for use in some small venture which may have embarked upon in order to make a living as distinct from large scale Manufacturing or processing activity carried on for profit. Persons buying goods either for resale or for use in a large-scale profit making activity will not be 'consumers' entitled under the Act.

Consumer of Services

The second category of consumer laid down under the Act is that of hirer or user of services. Under Sub-clause (ii) of section 2 (1) (d) of the Act, a consumer for the purpose of services means any Person, who:

(*a*) Hires or avails of any services for consideration which has been paid or promised or partly paid and partly promised or under any system of deferred payment;

(*b*) Includes any beneficiary of such services other than the person who hire or avails of them, when such services are availed of with the approval of the hirer; but

(*c*) Does not include a person who avails of such services for any commercial purpose. Commercial purpose does not include a person of services availed by him exclusively for the purpose of earning his livelihood by means of self-employment.

The Consumer Protection (Amendment) Act, 2002 has excluded from the definition of 'consumer' any person who avails of services for commercial purpose. The commercial undertakings which are already excluded from approaching the redressal agencies in respect of defective goods will thus be excluded from seeking relief from such agencies in respect of deficient services as well.

Need and Reasons

As Under section-6 of Consumer Protection Act, consumer has the following rights:

1. Right to safety: It is Right to safety against such goods and services as are hazards to health, life and property of the consumer. For example, spurious and sub-standard drugs ; appliances made of low quality of raw material, such as, electric press, pressure cooker, etc. and low quality food products like bread, milk, jam, butter etc. Consumers have the right to safety against loss caused by such products.

2. Right to be Informed/Right to Representation: Consumer has also the right that he should be provided all those information on the basis of which he decides to buy goods or services. This information relates to quality, purity, potency, standard, date of manufacture, method of use, etc. of the commodity. Thus, producer is required to provide all these information in a proper manner, so that consumer is not cheated.

3. Right to choose: Consumer has the full right to buy good or services of his choice from among the different goods or services available in the market. In other words, no seller can influence his choice in an unfair manner. If any seller does so, it will be deemed as interference in his right to choice.

4. Right to be Heard: Consumer has the right that his complaint be heard. Under this Right the consumer can file complaint against all those things which prejudicial to his interest. First there rights mentioned above (Right to Safety; Right to be Informed; Right to choose) have relevance only if the consumer has right to file his complaint against them.

5. Right to Seek redress: This provides compensation to consumer against unfair trade practice of the seller. For instance, if the quantity and the quality of the product do not confirm to the promise of the seller, the buyer has the right to claim compensation, such as free repair of the product, taking back of the products, changing of the product by the seller.

6. Right to consumer education: Consumer education refers to educate the consumer constantly with regards to their rights. In other words, consumers must be aware of the rights they enjoy against the loss they suffer on account of goods and services purchased by them. Government has taken several measures to educate the consumers. For instance, Ministry of civil supplies publishes a quarterly magazine under the title "Upbhokta Jagran". Doodarshan telecasts programme titles "Sanrakshan Upbhokta Ka".

In addition to this six rights of consumer given by Government of India, the United Nations Organisation also given two rights:

1. *Right to Basic Needs:* The Basic need means those goods and services which are necessary for the dignified living of people. It includes adequate food, clothing, shelter, energy, sanitation, healthcare, education and transportation. All consumers have the right to fulfil these basic needs;
2. *Right to Healthy Environment:* This right provides consumers the protection against environment pollution so that the quality of life enhanced. Not only this, it also gives stress that the need to protect the environment is for future generations as well.

ROLE OF DIFFERENT ORGANIZATIONS

Role of Judiciary

In our country judiciary plays a very vital role. On recommendation of the amendment of consumer protection Act in 2000 the consumer protection councils or forums are created at district, state and national level. Under the Act there is a provision of Three-tier Judiciary to redress the grievances of consumers in a simple, speedy and inexpensive way; namely:

1. District Forum at District level
2. State Commission at State level
3. National Commission at National level

1. District Forum: According to Consumer Protection Act, state governments can set up one or more district forums in each District. There are three members including the presiding officer. Out of this one member must be a lady. They must have a qualification of District Judge and must be appointed by state government. Its main feature is that it can hear cases up to Rs.20 Lacs. Any appeal may go to State Commission within 30 days.

2. State Commission: One State Commission is appointed by the state government in each state. It also has three members out of which one is a lady member but they must have qualification of High Court Judge and should be appointed by state government. It can hear cases involving sum exceeds Rs.20 Lacs and upto Rs.1 Crore. Any appeal may go to National Commission within 30 days.

3. National Commission: It is appointed by Central Government. It consists of five members out of which one must be a lady member. They must have qualification equivalent to Supreme Court Judge. It has a Jurisdiction to hear complaints amounting more than Rs.1 Crore. Any appeal may go to Supreme Court within 30 days.

Role of Non-Governmental Organizations

In addition to government many about 500 non-governmental organizations (N.G.Os) are making efforts in order to safeguard the interest of consumer. These organizations perform the following functions:

1. *Accelerating consumer awareness/Educating consumers:* The first priority of consumer organization is to accelerate consumer's awareness towards their rights. To accomplish this task which they have to perform are:

   (*a*) To publish Brochures, Journals;

   (*b*) To arrange seminars, conferences and workshops;

   (*c*) To educate consumers to help themselves;

   (*d*) To provide special education to women about consumerism;

   (*e*) To encourage to follow desirable consumption standards.

2. *Filing Suit on behalf of consumer:* Whenever a consumer fails to raise his voice of protect regarding his complaints, these organisations come to his rescue and file a case in the court. By rendering services to consumers, the consumers get a feeling that they are not alone in their fight. They also run voluntary complaints for the guidance of consumers.

3. *Helping educational institutions:* These organisations tell the educational institutions the way to prepare courses of study keeping in view the interest of consumers.

4. *Promoting network of consumer association:* Consumer organisations are trying to grow their numbers. They want to cover all regions so that consumers of all regions get benefited by their services.

5. *Extending support to government:* Consumer organisations by informing government agencies about adulteration, artificiality, inferior quality products etc. This helps government to conduct proceedings in time.

Role of Consumer Coordinating Council

The name of the highest body of consumer Association is consumer coordinating council. This body has started many programmes for consumer protection. The main objectives of this council are:

(*a*) To establish coordination among consumers for their welfare;

(*b*) To educate and train activists working for consumer protection.

Role of Press/Media

Whenever there is any revolution or a campaign is run for Public Awareness, Newspapers and journals play a very significant role. Indian Express is the first for this noble cause. Press takes following steps to make consumer protection campaign a success:

(*a*) To publish articles

(*b*) To make available columns

(*c*) To show live telecasts

(*d*) To publish consumer complaints

Role of Education Institutions

The importance of consumer protection is being realised at various levels of education *viz.* School, College, University. At school level institutions like C.B.S.E. had prepared syllabus in which central guiding points of consumer protection have been highlighted. Similarly at University level Indira Gandhi National Open University (IGNOU) has prepared a special course for under graduate and post- graduate students.

Role of Consumer Protection Council

The consumer protection council provides the establishment of a Central Consumer Protection Council by the Central Government and state Consumer Protection Council by state governments. The main objectives of the councils are:

1. To protect the rights of consumer
2. To promote the rights of consumer

Conclusion

Consumer protection laws are federal and state statutes governing sales and credit practices involving consumer goods. Such statutes prohibit and regulate deceptive or unconscionable advertising and sales practices, product quality, credit financing and reporting, debt collection, leases and other aspects of consumer transactions.

We believe the more guidelines are required because there are always two sides of a coin, each instance of Consumer affairs could be easily termed as another 'Consumer mistreatment'. By the time market forces have time to operate, far too many consumers are dead, maimed, or impoverished. Within a nation-state, national laws may prevent some of this harm, but once national boundaries are crossed, their effectiveness is limited, and consumers can hope for very limited protection, If online trade proliferates and consumer fraud becomes a major problem, nation-states and commercial interests that provide online access are fairly restricted in the action they may take to curb unacceptable and deleterious practices. Certainly if consumers perceive online commerce as a hazardous place to make purchases, they will not choose this alternative, and a major opportunity for electronic commerce may be forfeited. Consequently, there is strong motivation for reputable business to observe high commercial standards of behaviour.

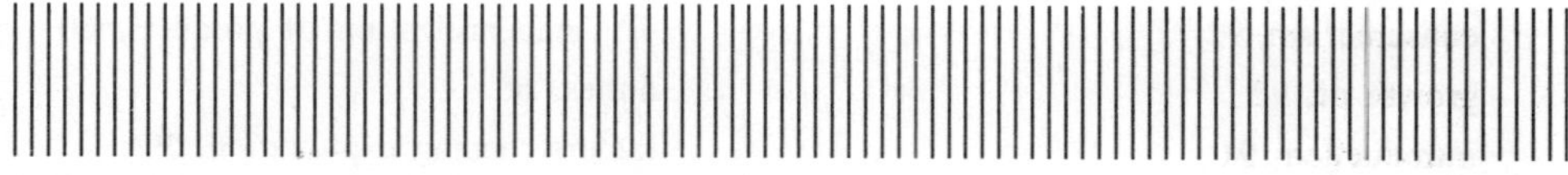

Index

U